The Life of the Senses

SENSORY STUDIES SERIES

General Editor: David Howes
ISSN: 2052–3092

As the leading publisher of works on the social life of the senses, Bloomsbury is pleased to announce this new series dedicated to exploring the varieties of sensory experience. By delving into the sights, sounds, scents, savours, textures and rhythms of diverse times and places, Sensory Studies provides many stimulating insights into how people make sense of the world through the senses. Incorporating approaches from across the humanities and social sciences, this series offers a fresh way to understand culture within a diversity of contexts. It will feature translations into English of key works in other languages, beginning with François Laplantine's *The Life of the Senses*. It will also present critical investigations of the sensory dimensions of politics and religion, food and architecture, art and commerce, affect and performance, among other topics.

Through positioning the senses as both object of study and means of inquiry, the Sensory Studies series will make for sensational reading and testify to the deep interpretive and explanatory power of sensuous scholarship. "The sensoriom is a fascinating focus for cultural studies" (www.sensorystudies. org).

The Life of
the Senses

Introduction to a Modal
Anthropology

François Laplantine

Translated by Jamie Furniss
With an Introduction by David Howes

Bloomsbury Academic
An imprint of Bloomsbury Publishing Plc

BLOOMSBURY
LONDON · NEW DELHI · NEW YORK · SYDNEY

Bloomsbury Academic

An imprint of Bloomsbury Publishing Plc

50 Bedford Square	1385 Broadway
London	New York
WC1B 3DP	NY 10018
UK	USA

www.bloomsbury.com

BLOOMSBURY and the Diana logo are trademarks of Bloomsbury Publishing Plc

First published 2015

Original Text © François Laplantine, 2005

This translation of *Le social et le sensible* is published by arrangement with Téraèdre Publishing.

English language translation © Jamie Furniss, 2014

British Library Cataloguing-in-Publication Data

A catalogue record for this book is available from the British Library.

ISBN: HB: 978-1-4725-2484-3
PB: 978-1-4725-3196-4
ePDF: 978-1-4725-3480-4
ePub: 978-1-4725-2238-2

Library of Congress Cataloging-in-Publication Data

A catalog record for this book is available from the Library of Congress.

Series: Sensory Studies, 2052–3092

Typeset by RefineCatch Limited, Bungay, Suffolk
Printed and bound in Great Britain

CONTENTS

The Extended Sensorium:
Introduction to the
Sensory and Social Thought
of François Laplantine

David Howes

François Laplantine is the paragon of a hybrid thinker. He studied philosophy under Paul Ricoeur in the Paris of the late 1960s, but an encounter with the great psychoanalytic anthropologist, George Devereux, drew him out of philosophy and into both psychoanalysis, which exposed him to the underside of conscious or "rational" thinking, and into anthropology, which immersed him in the study of modes of living and thinking undreamt of in Western philosophy, such as the Afro-Brazilian religion known as Candomblé.[1] Another important influence during his student days was the cinema, particularly the New Wave cinema of Godard and Truffaut. As Laplantine notes in conversation with Joseph J. Lévy, his training was philosophical by day and cinematographical by night, when he would go with his friends to see films (Lévy 2002: 14). Cinema-going became a lifelong passion, and he continuously references filmmakers and film scenes in his writing the way other scholars cite academic texts.

Laplantine defines cinema as made up of "permanently transforming sensations" (p. 116). He does not treat film as an object but rather as a "way of knowing". It is a way of knowing that exceeds language (the standard medium of philosophy) on account of the way it traffics in auditory and visual sensations—that is, in "sounds and images in motion" (in Lévy 2002: 132).[2] The ostensible aporia between words and images is not a barrier for Laplantine, as it was for the young Wittgenstein, who famously wrote: "The limits of my language are the limits of my world" (2004: 34). Rather, it is an invitation, an opportunity to think otherwise, which is to say to think *sensually*. Cinema does not seek to state "what is the case"; it shows. Cinema is the art of showing things in ways that words cannot, whence its appeal to Laplantine, and a growing number of English-speaking anthropologists attuned to the senses, such as Lucien Castaing-Taylor (1994), Anna Grimshaw (2001), David MacDougall (2005) and Sarah Pink (2006).[3]

Attending to the Sensible

Attending to "the sensible" (*le sensible*) is a key theme of Laplantine's approach to the social.[4] For him, "modes of living in society cannot be reduced to systems of signs" (contrary to Lévi-Strauss), and "the social does not exist except by way of the sensible" (contrary to Durkheim) (in Bragard 2007: 20). He criticizes Durkheim for saddling anthropology with the idea of "the social fact" as a purely objective construct, stripped of any temporality, subjectivity, or sense-ability. While this move may have been necessary to the establishment of sociology and anthropology as "social sciences" distinct from the "natural sciences" of psychology and biology, the fact remains that "social phenomena are sonorous, visual, tactile, gustatory and olfactory phenomena" (in Bragard 2007: 15). This leads directly into Laplantine's definition of anthropological fieldwork as a form of participant sensation in a given culture's mode of living:

> The experience of fieldwork is an experience of sharing in the sensible [*partage du sensible*]. We observe, we listen, we speak with others, we partake of their cuisine, we try to feel along with them what they experience (p. 2).

There is no finer definition of the methodology of sensory ethnography than this, and Laplantine is one its most consummate practitioners.

Laplantine's career as an ethnographer spans four different terrains (and continents): Ivory Coast, France, Brazil, and most recently the cities of Tokyo and Beijing.[5] His scholarly output is equally far-ranging. It consists of over two dozen books: in ethnopsychiatry, medical anthropology, the anthropology of religion, political anthropology, urban anthropology, ethnographic description, cinema, and other works that defy classification on account of their hybridity, such as *Le métissage* (with Alexis Nouss), *Transatlantique*, and *Le social et le sensible*. The last book, which is translated here under the title *The Life of the Senses*, will be the first of Laplantine's books to appear in English. This moment has been far too long in coming, as it was for Michel Serres' *The Five Senses: A Philosophy of Mingled Bodies* (1985/2008), another French text of key relevance to the expanding field of sensory studies.[6]

Before delving into the argument of this book, I would like to draw attention to a particularly formative experience which Laplantine underwent in the early 1980s, that he has not discussed much in his writing, but which Lévy managed to draw out of him in the interview. In 1983, Laplantine went to Brazil at the invitation of some former students. There he continued his exploration of alternative forms of consciousness and healing that had begun in France (e.g. Laplantine 1985) through studying Kardecian

Spiritism, Umbanda and Candomblé. He was initiated into the first grade of Candomblé, which he came to regard as a form of "sacred theatre". In his interview with Lévy, he relates how Candomblé initiation begins with the identification of one's *orixa*, the "master of the head" who then orients one's personality. This identification is achieved through a divinatory technique which involves throwing cowry shells (originally from Africa) on the ground; the disposition of the shells is then interpreted by one's master. In Laplantine's experience, Candomblé apprenticeship is

> absolutely not by the book, not intellectual, but tactile, olfactory, musical, chromatic and above all alimentary. It is based on a system of precise correspondences between the personality of each [apprentice] and the cosmos, in its various components: food, colors, perfumes and musical sounds. Living in ignorance of this harmony is to falsify one's life and to risk falling sick, according to the adepts of Candomblé. An accord is therefore sought between the singular personality of each one and the cosmos in community [with others] (in Lévy 2002: 76).

A complete initiation takes many years, and involves periods of complete isolation in a *tereiro*, spending hours quietly meditating. At other times, the apprenticeship is of "an extreme sensoriality". As Laplantine relates,

> It is an experience of sensory awakening [*l'éveil des cinq sens*] and also of symbolic filiation in a relation of dependence to the one who initiates you and guides you simultaneously to a heightened personalization and a heightened socialization (in Lévy 2002: 77).

Three things stand out about these observations: the emphasis on the communal, the emphasis on the sensual, and their interconnection. Laplantine was already attuned to the social due to his anthropological training, and attuned to the sensate due to his love of cinema. The experience of initiation sensitized him to the intricacy of their interrelationship. This nexus would constitute the fulcrum of his thinking going forward and issue, finally, in the extraordinary treatise you have before you.

Modal Thinking

The Life of the Senses is part philosophy, part anthropology, part film theory and part philology (both in the conventional sense of the "science of language" and the archaic sense of the "love of learning and literature").[7] A good place to pick up the multiple threads of Laplantine's argument is Chapter 5, where he takes aim at "categorical thought".[8] Categorical thought, which Western culture inherits from the Greeks, attributes properties to those things it isolates from the flux of existence and cleaves to the logic of the excluded middle. As such, it is inimical to life and living (*la vie et le vivant*), which are processes of continuous transformation. Life itself is rhythmical, and to model or categorize it (which is to say, to fix it) is false, for the model eliminates the temporal and processual in the name of the essential. For instance, is dawn night, or is it day? Categorical thought balks at this question because of its will to impose a (binary) logic of identity—the logic of this or that with no remainder.

Categorical thought is exemplified by a long string of Western thinkers, from Plato to Descartes, and from Kant to Durkheim. But there is also a counter-tradition, comprised of the pre-Socratics, Spinoza, Rousseau, and Bergson, among others, who encourage us to focus on duration, modulation, and rhythm instead of essence and identity. Laplantine rescues this counter-tradition from obscurity, and extolls its virtues. "Sensible thnking" (*la pensée sensible*), or "modal thinking" as he also calls it, is continuous with the world, sensitive to the slightest gradations and movements and affects. Laplantine holds that cinema affords an illuminating experience in this regard. Cinema is inherently temporal (compared to painting, for example, which is spatial); it traffics in images rather than ideas, and in emotions rather than reason. Cinema can thus serve as a lens for integrating life into thought by attuning us to the continuous flow and modulations of experience. In short, cinema is good to think with, and not only with but *through*.

It might be wondered whether Laplantine's love of cinema (or cinephilism) has perhaps blinded him to the fact that the movie camera does not treat the senses equally since it magnifies vision and augments listening while screening out all the other senses. In other words, cinema gives only limited access to the sensible. While this concern is real (Howes 2003: 57–58, 2008), it is mitigated in Laplantine's case first by the multisensory memories and sensibility that his Candomblé initiation instilled in him, and second by the fact that he takes Marcel Mauss's classic 1936 essay on the body as the starting point for his approach to anthropology. Laplantine credits Mauss (the nephew and inconstant disciple of Durkheim) with being the first to theorize social existence as modal existence. In the following passage, Mauss relates how he arrived at the idea of "techniques of the body":

> A kind of revelation came to me in hospital. I was ill in New York. I wondered where previously I had seen girls walking as my nurses walked. I had the time to think about it. At last I realized that it was at the cinema. Returning to France, I noticed how common this gait was especially in Paris; the girls were French and they too were walking in this way. In fact, American walking fashions had begun to arrive over here, thanks to the cinema (Mauss 2007: 52).

Mauss went on to propose that there are grounds for studying all the different modes of "disciplining" bodily movements including "especially those fundamental fashions that can be called the modes of life, the *model*, the *tonus*, the 'matter,' the 'manners,' the 'way'" (Mauss 2007: 59).

Taking his cue from Mauss, Laplantine dedicates the first chapter of this book to an analysis of *ginga*. *Ginga* refers to a swaying, sinuous way of walking, which is characteristically Brazilian. (Think of the swinging hips of the girl from Ipanema.) This kinaesthetic style also forms the basis of a number of dance styles including samba and the erotically-charged *umbigada* ("navel-to-navel"). It is above all manifest in the comportment of the *malandro*, who is a loiterer, a good-for-nothing, but at the same time one who is always on the make, and occasionally strikes it rich. Carnival is the element of the *malandros*. *Ginga* is also fundamental to the martial art/dance style known as *capoeira*, in which all parts of the body must be alert, responsive to the slightest feint or attack by one's opponent. *Ginga* then is an energized, rhythmic, swaying or curving/curvaceous style of movement.

"The undulating rhythmicity of *ginga* is a pulsation, a vibration of the body", writes Laplantine, which also informs a style of music—namely, *bossa nova*, which is a cross between samba and jazz. *Bossa nova* "caresses the ear with its words and its notes". It is the perfect medium for expressing that peculiarly Brazilian sentiment, *saudade*. *Saudade* has to do with reviving the past in the present and taking pleasure in the pain of loss.

In 2007, Laplantine went to Japan to take up an appointment as a visiting professor at Tokyo's Chuo University. He prepared for this trip by immersing himself in Japanese film, and then translated his lived impressions of Japanese culture generally and the city of Tokyo in particular into *Tokyo, ville flottante* (2010). The latter book is another fine example of Laplantine's modal approach to the study of the social, or what he calls the "anthropology of the sensible". According to Laplantine, the Japanese privilege form (not idea), percept (not concept), concrete (not abstract), and transformation (not essence). The culture oscillates between high-tech and tradition, the pragmatic and the frivolous, extravagance and asceticism, extreme flexibility and standing on ceremony, a strong sense of duty and a craving for distraction (e.g. karaoke, pachinko bars), self-effacement and national pride. Japan is a highly disciplined, hypercivilized society with an overwhelming emphasis on security, serenity, harmony and integration which is nevertheless pervaded by a profound consciousness of impermanence (e.g. the seasonal cycle, seismic activity, Tokyo itself is built on a marsh). In what other society does one find aesthetic appreciation of a few unpretentious objects, as in the tea ceremony, and expertise in seasonal representation, as in the art of flower arranging, so bound up with social distinction? Social distinction is normally about permanence, not fugacity (see further Daniels 2010: 108–112).

Laplantine evokes a lively sense of the apparent antinomies (or rather, alternate modes) of Japanese culture and how they nevertheless hang together. He is particularly astute in his observations regarding the discontinuance of tradition by contemporary Japanese youth, and the insights into this phenomenon which various Japanese filmmakers provide. Laplantine kindly accepted my invitation to write a synopsis of his experience of urban Japan as a supplement to this book, and it is included here under the title "Sensing Tokyo". His exposition of how the surfaces, rhythms and intensities of daily life in Tokyo contrast with the textures of urban experience in a European city such as Paris is a model example of the comparative method in sensory studies.

The Extended Sensorium

"Life" or "life itself" is a hot topic in contemporary anthropological theory (e.g. Ingold 2011), but nowhere is it treated with as much finesse or in as much philosophical depth as it is in this book (Lévy 2013). "The body" is another major focus of contemporary anthropology (Lock and Farquhar 2007) but few have gone so far as Laplantine does when he affirms "all anthropology is anthropology of the body" (in Bragard 2007: 14; see further Saillant 2013). What is more, Laplantine is not interested in simply papering over the divide between mind and body the way other thinkers do when they postulate such synthetic notions as the "mindful body" or "embodied cognition". In place of positing some totalizing "unity of body and mind", he digs deeper to uncover and highlight the *multiplicity* of the body's modalities of perception—the senses. In Laplantine's oeuvre, the accent is always on plurality and mixity (*métissage*) rather than unity or totality (see e.g. Laplantine and Nouss 1997).

Western culture has long been saddled with the opposition between "the life of the mind" and "the life of the senses". (Think of the opposition between the cerebral character of Narcissus, who becomes an abbot, and the lusty character of Goldmund the wanderer in the well-known novel by Hermann Hesse [1968].) "The life of the mind" is, furthermore, identified with "the examined life", which is the only life worth living, according to conventional Western notions. On further examination, however, the life of the mind—which is to say categorical thinking—misses the whole point of life and is (actually) hopelessly imprecise when confronted with the oscillations and infinitesimal gradations of life and living (*la vie et le vivant*). Moreover, categorical thinking kills by a thousand cuts, beginning with the separation between the intelligible and the sensible. But life can never be so cut and dried as categorical thought presents it to be, according to Laplantine. Over and over he draws our attention to the continuity of sensation and the ultimate indomitability of the life of the senses. Whence the title of this book. Contemplating its arguments will prove a life-changing experience for those who heed Laplantine's call for an awakening of the senses.

What Laplantine here proposes by way of an "anthropology of the sensible" or "modal anthropology" is known in the English-speaking world as the "anthropology of the senses" or "sensory anthropology" (Classen 1997; Howes and Pink 2010).[9] The anthropology of the senses is one of numerous approaches that emerged out of the sensory turn in the humanities and social sciences beginning in the 1990s. Other such approaches include the history of the senses (Classen 1993, 2000; Smith 2007), sociology of the senses (Synnott 1993; Vannini *et al.* 2012), philosophy of the senses (Rée 1999; Macpherson 2010), and sensuous geography (Rodaway 1994; Paterson

2009). All of these disciplinary diversions flow into the interdisciplinary field now known as "sensory studies" (Bull *et al.* 2006). The field of sensory studies may also be conceptualized along sensory lines, beginning with visual culture (Evans and Hall 1999; Heywood and Sandywell 2012), followed by auditory culture or sound studies (Bull and Back 2003; Pinch and Bijsterveld 2013), taste culture (Korsmeyer 2005), smell culture (Classen, Howes and Synnott 1994; Drobnick 2006), and the culture of touch (Classen 2005, 2012).

This quickening of the senses (and attention to the senses) within and across the various disciplines of the humanities and social sciences has led to the breakup of the hegemony which psychology formerly exercised over the study of the senses and perception. It has underscored the sociality of sensation and the extent to which the perceptual is political—not private and subjective the way psychology would have it. As Laplantine observes, "there exists a political and a historical dimension to sensory experience, which exceeds what individuals can consciously experience" (p. 83).

The growing recognition that the sensorium is a social formation has led to widespread questioning of the adequacy of the account of perception that comes out of psychology and the brain sciences generally. Laurence Kirmayer captures the gist of this critique in his description of the "hierarchical systems view of neural organization"—also known as the theory of the "extended mind" (Clark and Chalmers 1998; Clark 2008)—that has emerged within cognitive neuroscience in recent years:

> Contemporary cognitive neuroscience understands mind and experience as phenomena that emerge from neural networks at a certain level of complexity and organization. There is increasing recognition that this organization is not confined to the brain but also includes loops through the body and the environment, most crucially, through a social world that is culturally constructed. On this view, "mind" is located not in the brain but in the relationship of brain and body to the world (Kirmayer quoted in Howes 2011: 165–166).

Kirmayer goes on to state that, ideally, "we want to be able to trace the causal links up and down the hierarchy in a seamless way". Such an objective will remain out of reach, however, for as long as cognitive neuroscientists continue to privilege the brain and cognition over the mediatory role of the senses in the production of experience (see Howes 2011; Howes and Classen 2014: Chapter 6). By shifting the focus of inquiry from the intelligible to the sensible (that is, from cognition to sensation), Laplantine opens the way for reconceptualizing the theory of the extended mind as a theory of the extended sensorium. The theory the extended sensoruim holds that the senses, which are always already socially conditioned, mediate the relationship between mind and body, idea and object, self and environment (see Bull *et al.* 2006). The senses are the "loops through the environment" of which Kirmayer speaks, at once bearers and shapers of culture. By attending to the "ways of sensing" through which people make sense of the world, it becomes possible to arrive at a full-bodied, multimodal understanding of the richness and diversity of *being alive*.

Acknowledgments

I wish to thank the author, François Laplantine, for generously allowing this book to be translated into English and published as the first volume in the Sensory Studies series. I also wish to thank Jean Ferreux, whose publishing house, Téraèdre, has done so much to promote the sensory turn in French scholarship, for his authorization. We are all indebted to Jamie Furniss for producing a translation which is sensitive to the many nuances of Laplantine's ways of thinking and writing. Furniss brings the same philological sensibility—that is, the same "love of language, literature and learning"—to the translation of this book as Laplantine brought to writing it. Finally, I am indebted to the editorial staff at Bloomsbury for their encouragement and support of this endeavor.

D.H., 10 August 2014

Translator's Preface

Many words in French, like any language, combine multiple meanings that no single English term can express. For example—there are better examples of this, but perhaps none is as central to the present text—the word *sens*. In French, the word *sens* means both "sense" (as in the sense of smell, but also having "a sense" of something) and "meaning". This is also true, though in my view to a lesser extent, in English, since we also use "sense" both in relation to sensation and in phrases such as "to make sense"; and the two meanings converge in the term sensible, which if anything has a stronger connotation of "being reasonable" than of "related to sensation". Despite the possibility of this dual meaning in English, the term is not used, contextually, in the same way, such that I have had to choose to translate most occurrences of *sens* as either "meaning" or "sense". For instance does the phrase "saturation du sens" (which I propose to translate as "sense saturation", trying to retain some ambiguity) mean something closer to "sensory overload" or "the saturation of meaning"?

Having to often choose one or the other meaning seems especially ironic and unfortunate in the context of the translation of a work that criticizes (Chapter 5) precisely the way we are called upon to judge and subordinate the two sides inherent "in the polysemy of the word *sens*, which designates at once the sensible and the sensical, sensation and signification".

Since signification also means "meaning" in French and the author appears to have intended to use both terms differently, I have kept "signification" in English despite its infrequent use and more literal or mechanically semiotic definition (the process of signifying, as opposed to significance, sense, underlying truth).

A final remark on the challenges of translating the constellation of words around "sense". The central phrase the "life of the senses" in this translation in fact glosses several different occurrences in French, mainly *la vie du sensible* and *la vie des sensations*.

There are also a number of terms in the work that were difficult to translate because they evoke societal questions that, while not unknown in the English-speaking world, are not in the forefront of public debate, and to the extent that they are, tend to be posed in very different terms and on the basis of very different normative assumptions. For example, hardly a day goes by in contemporary France without articles in *Le Monde* or shows on *France Culture* debating the *question identitaire, les communautés,* and *le vivre-ensemble*. In English, as least the version of it that I use, identity is a reputable topic for research and, though not without risks of essentialization, not on the whole negatively connoted. Community is mildly, even outrightly positive in its connotations. But for many people in contemporary France, *communauté* is a dangerous concept, and an even more dangerous "thing". The in-group homogeneity, connotation of enclave, and overall mosaic or archipelago societal structure implied by the existence of "communities" are often regarded as anti-Republican and contrary to the notion of equal citizenship. Another example, discussed also in a footnote, concerns the question of the French "suburbs". In English the term evokes a uniform landscape of single-family dwellings with two-car garages, a kind of American Dream (some would say, nightmare) of WASPs pushing around lawnmowers as they try to keep up with the Jones'. Meanwhile, the "inner city" is the place of gang and ethnic violence. The Anglophone (and above all North American) spatial imaginary completely inverts the geography of most French cities, in which the *Centre Ville* is the place of broad boulevards whereas it is in the suburbs, *banlieues*, that immigrants and other ethnic and religious minorities (who live cramped in concrete high-rises) riot and light cars on fire. The debate around the "identitary question" is crystal clear for any French reader; it invokes integration, multiculturalism, immigration, whether France is a "Catholic" and "White" country, the rise of the Front National and the Le Pens. And while the debate over how it is to be achieved is very acrimonious, there is a consensus that the *le vivre-ensemble*, or "living-together" is somehow the key to resolving these problems, or is at least the kind of social harmony that they threaten. These political questions are very much in the background, and sometimes the foreground of Laplantine's work, and have been hard for me to properly convey in the translation. The problem is not just that English lacks a distinct adjectival form for the word identity, but that identity does not have the same political content for Anglophone readers as it is likely to have for Francophone ones.

I have tried to flag specific challenges and choices I faced at the places in the text where they arose, either through footnoting or by reproducing the original term directly in the text, generally in square brackets behind the English, but occasionally without giving an English term at all. This I hope will provide some of the information a reader who wishes to give close attention to the text will need to make up their own mind about a word's correct interpretation, rather than just having to "take my word for it". Every translation is an English rendering of what *one* reader got from the original. This is one reason I find it exciting to read both an original and its translation, but also frustrating when translators include no information about source terms that are ambiguous or lack precise English equivalents. I have tried to balance the desire to produce the sort of translation I would like to see as someone who knows French against the fact that many readers may not know the nuances of the original, or if they do may nevertheless have no desire to engage in close textual analysis of Laplantine's work, and would therefore find too much linguistic detail tedious (how I would feel if this were a translation from a language I do not speak, say, German).

There is one instance of use of French terms in the text that is perhaps significant enough to merit a brief remark here. It concerns the well-known problem of how to render in English three classic linguistic terms of analytic and methodological importance for French authors—*langage, langue* and *parole*. My approach to this has varied depending on the context. In cases where the term in the French original appeared to be used by the author in an explicit effort to distinguish it from the other terms, I either give the original in square brackets following the English term chosen, or simply give the French directly, in italics. In some instances, where the usage appears to be generic, and to avoid weighing down the translation, I preferred the English term best suited to the context, without specifying the French original. In choosing an English term for *langage* I generally opted for language *simpliciter*, to attempt to convey the generality of the category. For *langue* I generally preferred referring to *a* language, in the sense of *la langue française*, the French language. *Parole* corresponds fairly directly to the English term speech, so poses somewhat less of a problem.

Finally, a remark on my general approach to this translation. Former Supreme Court of Canada Justice Morris Fish told me once that in his youth there was an active Yiddish theater scene in New York City that put on Shakespeare plays which were advertised as having been "translated . . . *and improved!*". The line between translating and rewriting is a fine one: how much of an author's syntax, for example, can be broken on the grounds that in English, "one wouldn't write it that way"? The rules of contemporary English we are taught require that every sentence have a verb and a noun, otherwise it is a fragment. Stylistically, we are told to prefer short sentences and open punctuation. Those are not rules, either of grammar or style, in French, a language in which one has to push "Shift" on the keyboard to access the full stop, the default being the semi-colon. So, if a sentence is a "run-on", a "fragment", or simply seems unclear in the original, is the translation the chance to "improve" it, or should that style be deliberately reproduced? My approach has been to do as little "translation and improvement" as possible: I have tried to stay as close to the original word choice, sentence structure, and punctuation as I felt the English language could bear. But of course that is a subjective judgment, and some readers will surely feel that the text has too many Gallicisms—while others will say I have allowed myself too much licence.

J.F., 11 June 2014

Prologue

The theme—more than the object—of this book is something that has been mistreated, repressed, forgotten over five centuries of rationalocentrism yet which, since the 1970s, has been resurfacing: the sensible, the life of the emotions, the body, and the physical character of thought as it takes shape.

The model of knowledge that was largely dominant in the 1960s left things as they were: with social phenomena being considered as a system of relations between previously cut-up terms, in other words as like a language, a particular language [*langue*]—constituted of a lexical stock and grammatical laws—which is but a minute part of language in general [*langage*]. This model does not enable us to question the division on which only those societies we imprecisely call "Western"—since today the "West" exists equally in Seoul, Singapore, São Paulo—are founded. This divide, most often taken for granted despite there being absolutely nothing universal about it, separates the intelligible and the sensible, cognition and emotion. It aims not only to distinguish, but to hierarchize. Everything that is situated on the side of sensations and emotions is placed "below" and is deemed dangerous because it is incontrollable, the expression of a loss of self-control that lies just beneath the surface of the seemingly trifling expressions we hear every day: "I'm sorry, I spoke without thinking", "I let myself get carried away", "I was angry", "I was beside myself"; while, with an implacable logic that responds tit for tat, everything that had previously been situated on the side of the intelligible and intelligence is placed "above": the order of reason and civilization.

Whereas an emotion is not something we think, but rather are subject to, "letting ourselves go", it is through reason that we "pull ourselves together" again. It is in this movement, so prone to giving rise to semantic slippages, that the following antithetical but in no way symmetrical pairs are constituted: intelligible/sensible, reason/emotion, active/passive, and sometimes even nature/culture, which can go as far as to subdivide itself into masculine/feminine.

Obviously this model, as such, is rarely affirmed today. It is often either tempered and, so to speak, softened, or else jettisoned by those seeking to restore dignity to that which had been devalued. What I will show is that it is not sufficient to reassert the value of the body (against the mind), emotion (against reason), orality (against writing) in order to change modes of knowledge. Our way of knowing remains precisely the same if all we do is convert minus signs into plus signs.

Despite so much work having been done over the past years (particularly in cinema, theater, music, dance, literary criticism, theory of translation, and psychoanalysis), the social sciences still rest on a certain number of unquestioned—or at least insufficiently questioned—assumptions, which lead them essentially to either reproduce or try to rework the old paradigm.

One of anthropology's principal tasks—indeed its vocation—is to carry out a radical critique of these assumptions. A large part of its work is aimed at showing that associating thought with abstraction, or affirming correlatively that experiencing sensations or emotions is not thinking but being subject to, is the result of a current of thought and a history that are specific to Europe. In most societies and in particular in the Amazonian societies among which I spent time in Brazil and Peru, this distinction between knowing and sensing (*sentir*) has no relevance.

The true object-subject of anthropology, which is to say above all ethnography, has always been the emotions. The experience of fieldwork is an experience of sharing in the sensible. We observe, we listen, we speak with others, we partake in their cuisine, we try to feel what they experience along with them. Only a conception of the field warped by the defensive anti-psychologism of the social sciences at the time of their constitution could give rise to the belief that a "new object"—the sensible—has appeared.

This book proposes to examine the assumptions that have begun to be exposed here, and to do so on the basis of my experience of Brazilian society and a reexamination of a certain number of texts, but also films (since, we will see, cinema, which is made up of image fragments and snippets of sound, forces us to be attentive to the concrete singularity of the sensible). Along the way we will orient ourselves toward a horizon of knowledge that is no longer that of the anthropology of signs or structure, but rhythm. This is the horizon of an anthropology that I propose to call *modal anthropology.*

1

The Brazilian Art of the *Ginga*: Walking, Dancing, Singing

It is in the continuity of rhythm and not the discontinuity of sign that
it is possible to understand the characteristic way in which so many
Brazilians walk. This is called *ginga* or also *gingado*, and it inspires
many forms of conduct that I have observed over more than twenty years
in Brazil.

The *ginga* (originally the name of an African tribe from the Congo) is a
movement of the body. It is a way of moving around while making all the
parts of the body undulate, in particular the legs, hips, shoulders, and head.
People speak of the *gingado* of young girls or young women, paying
particular attention to the *balança* (swaying) movement of their hips, or of
the *gingado* of homosexual men. It is also possible to refer to the gait of
people from Rio de Janeiro as *ginga carioca*, distinguishing it from the *ginga*
of people from Salvador-da-Bahia.

Gingar and *Dansar*

This undulating way of walking is above all a way of dancing. We encounter
it in a long-standing style of dance, the *umbigada* (literally "navel-to-navel"),
which very oddly contributed to the birth of the Portuguese *fado*, itself not
a dance but a form of singing, and one that is extremely prudish. In
the *umbigada*, which is one of the very first forms of samba, as in the *forró*
of the Nordeste or the Amazonian *lambada*, the hips curve and the thighs
touch. It is a highly sexualized *ginga* that is an unambiguous invitation to
love-making.

While the art of samba dancing (which is the rhythm of the Rio Carnival)
displays a less ostensibly erotic meaning, it is no less animated by the same
gingado movement. *Sambar* (to dance the samba) is a manner of *gingar*, a
walk-dance of extreme sensuality that is learned from early childhood in the
morros that overlook the city of Rio.

Another form of *ginga* (which can be closely linked to the preceding
one in the *samba de roda*) is the choreography of Candomblé. The gods

evoked in these forms of worship arrive dancing. They cross the Atlantic. They return from Africa by "possessing" their followers through dance steps that are those of the rhythm of the tide. And to speak of the different manners of "dancing the *orixa*", of "incorporating the *orixa*", that is to say of entering into trance, one says of the body that it is *transfigurado* (transfigured), *virado* (turned), *gingado* (animated by a swaying movement).

The same term is therefore used to designate a way of walking and way of dancing. Since in both cases (dancing while walking, moving laterally while dancing), we are in the presence of a sort of "dancing walk", as Noh theater actors say. It is nevertheless necessary to distinguish what Eugenio Barba (2004) calls "pre-expressive behaviour" and "behaviour in an organized performance situation".

Ginga as a form of undulating walk is a "pre-expressive behavior", that is, part of everyday life, which of course was acquired, learned, repeated, and has become a reflex. But in this individual bodily memory there is, formally speaking, no rituality. *Ginga* as a way of dancing with others belongs to what Eugenio Barba describes as "extra-daily techniques", and Jean-Marie Pradier (1996) as "spectacularly[1] organized human behaviours". They are, as in the Candomblé religions and Umbanda, as in Carnival or *capoeira*, which will be discussed subsequently, ritually codified "on-stage" and performative behaviors, in which the stage may be the space of the *casa* (in Candomblé and Umbanda dances) or of the *rua* (in Carnival and *capoeira*). We can of course consider, with Goffman, that in all these situations of daily life we are always actors playing roles on a stage. That being said, samba dancing, be it in the setting of the *casa* (in the nightclubs called *gafeiras* in Rio) or the *rua* (Carnival), and *a fortiori* the choreography of Candomblé, entail a much more explicit scripting.

Finally, in these different cases, the *mise en scène* of the social (as minimal as it may be), takes place through sensation [*le sensible*]. All of the senses are mobilized in the bodily behaviors of Candomblé, which are ceremonies with simultaneously visual (chromatic, in particular), auditory, tactile, gustatory, and olfactive dimensions. As for *ginga* as a way of moving in the street, it only invokes sight (looking and being looked at) and touch (in particular of the ground). But it is a sinuous way of walking of extreme sensuality.

In *ginga*, the walk appears as though it is slowed by a movement of horizontal oscillation of the body. It is this movement (in particular of the hips and the shoulders) that from the beginning of the Conquest the Portuguese restrained among their black household servants. Still today, in the eyes of part of the middle class, and even more so to bourgeoisie, it does not fail to appear to be a somewhat suspect, even immoral, way of behaving with one's body. It is perceived as a loosening, as much physically as psychologically, and provokes a reaction of simultaneous hypercorrectness in dress and bodily rectitude on the part of followers of Brazil's increasingly numerous evangelical movements.

Gingado and *Jeitinho*

It is here that we realize that the *gingado* is liable to encounter the *jeito* and even more the *jeitinho* (literally, a "little trick", not exactly the French "*système D*"[2]), that art of getting by and scheming that is characteristic of behaviors described as *malandros*.

A character of murky etymology and personality, whom we can equally consider a creation of literary fiction and urban popular culture, in particular of the city of Rio de Janeiro, the *malandro* escapes definition. He is not outrightly dishonest, but he is not honest either. He does not radically reject the established order but, rather, constantly ridicules it.

What in Brazil is called the *malandragem*, which is not without echoes of Ulysses' *mètis*, is the art of getting by, of scheming and of improvising in novel situations. It is the skill of the *jeitinho*, which consists of turning the world to one's advantage. It is not easy to understand and therefore to translate in the framework of a categorizing and classificatory thought process that the *malandro* himself couldn't care less about. Three notions may nevertheless assist us: *cordialidade* (cordiality), theorized by the historian Sergio Buarque de Holanda, the *casa*, and the *rua*, both analyzed by the anthropologist Roberto Da Matta.

Cordialidade is that capacity to react through sentiment, the heart, and perhaps more still through the body, rather than the head and the intellectual elaboration of emotions. It implies extremely personalized relations. The *casa* is one of the preeminent settings for this cordiality and warmth. As for the *rua*, it is practically the opposite of the *casa*. It is the anonymous and rigid world of the decree, or more exactly of conformity to the abstract impersonality of the law that must be obeyed. The *rua* is most often experienced in Brazil—and to a certain extent in the Latin societies of Europe and the Americas—as a negative principle. Or to put it differently, Brazil, through its *malandro* component, pushes to its extreme one of the tendencies of societies in which obedience to the State, payment of taxes or respect for the traffic code are regarded by many as veritable calamities. These are societies in which one always gladly prefers the firefighters to the police and in which part of the population is constantly searching for tricks for getting around the law.

The *malandro*, it will have been understood, cannot stand formal rules, regulations, uniforms, punctuality, hierarchy. He never arrives on time, misses appointments (or at least those from which he has nothing to gain) and is absolutely refractory to the very idea of work. But, in spite of ridiculing the values of the *rua*, he is not a man (sometimes a woman) of the *casa* either. He is a nomad, a vagabond who goes from one house (for him, a love-story) to another. He cannot establish or stabilize himself in marriage any more than he can in language. The spaces he most often only passes through in an oscillating movement of the hips and shoulders tend to be shady spots where one meets barflies, cheats, and prostitutes. He also happily hangs out in the places where *macumba* is practiced (called, it should be noted, *casas*), where he recognizes himself in the fantastical divinities called *Exus*, ambivalent and resolutely urban entities that Christianity has rushed to demonize. The *Exus* are mediators that are invoked, like Hermes, to "open difficult paths", surmount delicate situations, figure out a scheme (the Brazilian *jeitinho*), win the lottery, do business, or conquer the heart and body of the woman or man one covets. Without the *Exus*, who maintain themselves as far as possible from bourgeois respectability, nothing is possible for the *malandro*.

He therefore often lives in the *rua*, but with personalized *casa* values. He brings two universes into contact and enjoys moving through interstices and border zones. He brings poor and rich into contact, may himself become rich then find himself broke the next day. He is a tightrope walker. Individualistic and even egotistical to the extreme, he is not, however, antisocial: he gladly plays the role of a righter of wrongs who brings help to widows and orphans. Lies do not bother him in the least, he who practices the art of getting the most out of every situation, and yet he is totally sincere. He is a scoundrel if you wish, and sometimes even an outlaw, but a likeable outlaw, an outlaw with a big heart, who rarely goes as far as full-blown criminality or robbery. You can say that he is a marginal, an adversary in any case of policed language and good manners, but he takes it upon himself to correct injustices by ridiculing established authority. Yet he does not aim to change the world, does not get involved in politics, does not believe, or if so very little, in God, especially in the singular. He is forever elevating misconduct into a model, but many consider that this "pattern of misconduct" (Linton 1956) is not, when it comes down to it, all that unacceptable.

Inconstant, inconsistent, short-sighted, without any depth, living in the present for the sake of pleasure, not remaining in one place, never being where people thought they would find him, the *malandro*, or rather the character of the *malandro*, profoundly transformed Brazilian literature. *Macunaíma, o herói sem nenhum caráter* (*Macunaima, the hero without any character*) by Mario de Andrade (1979), is the very embodiment of the *malandro*. In this burlesque, erotic and libertarian anti-epic, which is not without echoes of *Pantagruel*, but also Joyce's *Finnegan's Wake*, the anti-hero Macunaima, a black Indian with blue eyes, the composite symbol of a "nation without a character", after a lazy childhood, roams the virgin forest where he meets his mother whom he kills by mistake. He seduces the queen of the Amazons who entrusts him with a talisman, which he loses. It falls by chance into the hands of a resident of São Paulo. Accompanied by his brothers, Macunaima leaves in search of it, finds it again, and transforms himself into a constellation.

Finally, the *malandro* (who roams undulatingly across the large Bahian frescoes of Jorge Amado before continuing his career on the silver screen, notably with Chico Buarque and Ruy Guerra's 1988 *Opera do malandro*) is a Carnival character or, more precisely, there cannot be a successful Carnival without a *malandro*. The carnivalesque ritualities do not work without ambiguity, incongruity, nonconformity, ruse, farce, tricks. Respectful conduct is substituted, but only temporarily, with transgressive conduct, the dull uniformity of daily life with the creation of multiplicities, played, sung and danced to a point of drunkenness.

Ginga and Rhythmics of Curvature

The *malandro*'s inseparably physical and psychological conduct, on the borderline of legality, by no means exhaust the *ginga*'s full range of possibilities. The movement involved in *capoeira* (which is at once a game, a dance, and a martial art) is also called *ginga*. It is an alternatively offensive and defensive movement that consists of moving inside a circular space (*la roda*), swaying and rocking the body back and forth, with the goal of surprising and fooling the adversary.

In the *ginga* of *capoeira*, every part of the body is alert and may be moved: the hands, the elbows, the head, the shoulders, but more still the lower body. The feet (necessarily bare, like in Camdomblé rituals, and firmly planted on the ground) are, as Grotowski (2002/1978) puts it, "the centres of expression and communicate their reactions to the rest of the body". The position of the knees, slightly bent (like in tennis, boxing and fencing), allows for both propelling and relaxing the body which can, depending on the the the move of the adversary, jump, squat, or take a step forward, backward, to the side. The hips ensure the coordination of the continual flow of movement, which never slows or rests. Thus, as *capoeiristas* say, "*capoeira parada não da*", literally "*capoeira* without movement is not possible".

The *ginga* of *capoeira*, which is given its tempo by a musical bow called *berimbau*, is precisely this constant back-and-forth rocking movement in which one must be ready to react (and thus to move) at every instant in response to the move of the adversary in front of you, who is also a partner. This play of attack and counter-attack, but also of dodging, is a dance step of extreme complexity that demands a great deal of liveliness on the part of the actor-dancers, a whole series of feints and tricks designated in the language of Brazil by the not strictly equivalent terms of *malicia, manha, mandiga* and *malandragem*.

What drives this intricate overlap of successive micro-movements involving the whole body, or rather, according to Eugenio Barba's expression (2004), the "body-mind", is sight. The art of *capoeira*, which advances and retreats in an oscillation between simulation and dissimulation, requires looking into one another's eyes, observing the gaze, the expressions, the face, the smile of the other. To decode the other's intentions, one must never lose focus, while the goal is precisely to distract, however minimally, the person facing you.

Finally, it is necessary to emphasize the fact that *capoeira* is a stage art, a performance art that uses the street as its scenographic space. From *ginga* as a way of walking to *ginga* as a way of dancing (as in samba) or praying (as in Candomblé), we observe, in the same sinuous movement of the body, a transition from pre-expressivity to performance, as Eugenio Barba writes (2004: 11), specifying that organized representation transforms "the performer's daily body-mind into a scenic body-mind" (2004: 109).

One last notion must also be introduced. It concerns what Afro-Brazilian culture, which is a religious culture, refers to as *axé*. *Axé* is nothing other than life, strength, and energy, an energy which in *capoeira* is at times suspended, at times expanding but quick to implode. The notion of *axé* is fairly close to what the Japanese call *koshi*, another polysemic term that designates the life force, but also a precise part of the body: the hips.

Ginga as a movement of lateral undulation of the body that draws its inseparably physical and psychic energy from the power of the *axé* (which is personalized in the extreme for each individual), may thus be more or less socialized or ritualized, and more or less scripted.[3] What in Rio is called *o jogo de cintura* is a less scripted movement. Its goal is to avoid obstacles by slipping and weaving amidst the crowd. It is bodily movement consisting of a particularly clever (*maliciosa*) adaptive capacity, which we encounter both in the behavior of *malandros* and in Brazilian football, from Pelé to Romario.

We understand nothing about Brazilian society without this art of slipping, dribbling, swinging, also of advancing through a conversation oscillating between *yes* and *no*. Brazil moves according to the rhythmicity of curvature, which defies the straight line and all that is orthogonal.

Ginga is therefore a body language of flexibility and plasticity, but also of determination. While it is located—or rather moves and unfolds—at antipodes with the behaviors of physical rigidity belonging to many Europeans and North Americans, it is not, as such, indolence or slovenliness. There is a fast *ginga* (as in some *capoeira* movements) and a slower *ginga*, but which is no less precise and determined. The fluidity of *ginga*—which is not unreminiscent of surfing—may give rise to great inventiveness and even extreme artistic virtuosity, such as in the choreography of Rodrigo Pederneiras and the Grupo Corpo company. *Gingar* consists of undertaking something with vigor, intelligence and skill. It is a movement, an energetic but also playful and sensual rhythm. It is a *way of being Brazilian* (which is far from being shared by all Brazilians), a sinuous, lateral and never frontal way of moving undulatingly, of entering into relations with others, of experiencing pleasure, not of having a body but being a body capable of constantly transforming itself.

Ginga, which obeys a rhythmicity of difference (relative to the policed physical behaviors and the good manners of the *gente fina*) and not one of harmony's simultaneity, entails an affirmation of the value of the curved line. It was the painter Di Cavalcanti who first suggested that *O Brasil é uma mulher* (Brazil is a woman) and that its lines are curves. Curves there are, everywhere, even where one wouldn't expect. In the very heart of the eminently vertical metropolis of São Paulo snake long, rounded buildings. In Brasilia itself, Niemeyer and Lucio Costa's architecture imposes the curved line. One would also have to mention the "environmental art" of Helio

O iticica

Oiticica, an art that is marked by its impregnation with the architectural
fluidity of Rio's favelas and bodily flexibility training in the Mangueira
Samba school. This aesthetic has been referred to as the "*ginga* aesthetic".[4]

It would be senseless to draw up a catalogue of Brazilian curves since one
would have to inventory everything that exists or is done in this country with
the extraordinary art of moving from one point to another while turning and
zigzagging. The language itself is no longer Portuguese, but Brazilian. It is
not swishing like the former, but is not for that reason uneven like the Spanish
language either. Thus, to pronounce *casa* in Spanish, you must bring out the
slightly coarse nature of the *s*: *casssa*. Whereas in Brazilian, ascend, but very
slowly and singingly, on the first *a*, soften the *s*, then descend very slowly on
the last *a*, which must be only murmured: *a caasa*.

This art of speaking in a manner that explores novel modalities not
just of the language but of *voice* runs through the whole field of Brazilian
culture, in which feelings and emotions are constituted of oblique forms.
The emphasis of the Brazilian language on the paroxytone (stress on the
penultimate syllable) allows, more easily than with French's stressed syllable
or even Portuguese pronunciation, for the sentence's oscillating movement,
which begins in Brazil with oscillation in the words.

Ginga and Bossa Nova

The remarks just made invite us to take into consideration the intensity of
ginga body language in all its dimensions or rather potentialities. The
undulating rhythmicity of *ginga* is a pulse, a vibration of the body. A way of
walking and dancing, it is also way of speaking and singing.

There exists in Brazil a style of song and music particularly characteristic
of this oscillation: bossa nova. This style evolved from *samba-canção* (sung
samba) as a result of the latter experiencing a certain fatigue at end of the
1940s, and, more still, its encounter with jazz. Beginning in the 1950s,
Brazilian musicians moved to the United States (guitarist Laurindo Almeida
recorded *Brasilliance* with Bud Shank in 1956), while North American jazz
composers—Dizzy Gillespie, Stan Gretz, Quincy Jones—came to play in
Brazil. They brought jazz with them, but also soaked up samba rhythms.

Bossa nova is a Brazilian style of music. It is even the most tender of all
Brazilian music. It was formed in the crucible of Rio de Janeiro around João
Gilberto, Baden Powell, Vinícius de Moraes and Tom Jobim. But it is not
only Brazilian. Very soon its melodies, hummed the world over (*Garota de
Ipanema, Desafinado Chega de Saudade* . . .), made this "export" (in the
sense of the modernist movement of São Paulo) something international. In
1961, Dorham composed *Blue Bossa* and *Hot Stuff From Brazil*. In 1962,
Charlie Byrd and Stan Getz recorded *Jazz Samba*, while Tom Jobim organized
a concert at Carnegie Hall in New York. This was the same period when
Miles Davis recorded Jobim's *Corcovado*, Getz interpreted *Girl from
Ipanema* with Astrud Gilberto, Herbie Mann played with Baden Powell,

Laurindo Almeida with the Modern Jazz Quartet, Luís Eça with Art Blakey, Jobim with Frank Sinatra. It would also be necessary to evoke the contributions of Paul Desmond, Duke Ellington, and Ella Fitzgerald to the interpretation of bossa nova and, in France, of Georges Moustaki, Claude Nougaro and Pierre Narouh, who sings the French version of *Samba da Benção* in Calude Lelouch's *Un homme et une femme* (1966).

What characterizes bossa nova above all is its rhythm. It consists, after the encounter with jazz bands, of introducing chord inversions, rhythmic suspensions, and slight syncopations into samba, initially earned it the nickname *violão gago* ("stuttering guitar"). It creates undulating sonorities reminiscent of ocean swell (*bossa nova* can be translated as "new wave"). Another characteristic of bossa nova is that its undulation, which is totally different from extraverted samba (the strong *batucada* of Afro-Brazilian rhythms), from jazz—described in Brazil as *quente* (hot)—and from the romantic seduction of popular singers on the radio, partakes in an aesthetic of scarcity. "I composed with a sparingness of elements" Tom Jobim said. "Play less, make myself more heard by rarifying the notes to increase the tension . . . I had taken apart the samba rhythm in order to play it on the piano with a single finger". This resulted in *Samba de uma nota só* (One Note Samba).

Bossa nova is a softened samba that has acquired a sense of reserve. Its rhythm is indeed that of the samba. In the beginning, it was called *uma sambinha* (little samba). It's a samba that is out of step, stretched in time and which has given up any effect. But it is not, or rather is not only samba, but a hesitation, an oscillation *between* the rhythms of samba and the tempo of jazz. It's a samba that has been metamorphosed by jazz's *swing*.

Finally, bossa nova is not, contrary to samba, a music for dancing, but rather a music for singing and listening to. It is an intimate form of singing (*o canto falando*, spoken song) that consists of whispering. At the opposite of that art of profusion that is samba, bossa nova is never lyric. It is a slight pulsing of the body, a breath that is always waiting, so flowing and indefinite that it cannot be stopped, contained, completed. Although relaxed, bossa nova is not outrightly joyous but instead slightly sad. It is a music of infinite discretion, absolutely not radiant, that accompanies, or better still suggests, the imperceptible transitions of nightfall. It strips samba of its brilliance and shine. It inflects it through its low intonations towards the subdued notes and half-tones of waning luminous and auditory intensity.

One of bossa nova's key themes is singing minute sways of feeling, particularly the feeling of *saudade*, which is not exactly melancholy (a feeling of time passing) and even less nostalgia (missing a time past), but presence and absence, pleasure and suffering lovingly interlaced, the presence of the past in the present, which does so much harm, so much good, and which consists of suffering from past pleasure and taking pleasure in the suffering of today. Thus, bossa nova does not exactly sing of love but rather, like in the Portuguese *fado*, of loving lost love. And it does so, as Tom Jobim, who is, with João Gilberto and Vinicius de Moraes, one of its creators, once put it, a "deconstruction of the samba rhythm" through jazz.

This soft and delicate rhythm, which is not one of brutal syncopations yet also rejects the straight line in favor of the curved one, and advances slowly, slightly out of tune, caressing the ear with words and notes, is one of the modulations of what in Brazil is called *ginga*, which consists of advancing with a horizontal, oscillating movement of the body. It implicitly and sometimes even explicitly evokes the way of walking while undulating the hips of a large number of women in Brazil and in particular young girls from Ipanema. It suffices, in order to realize this, to listen to the words of the bossa nova by that same name, *Garota de Ipanema*, composed by Tom Jobim and Vinicius de Moraes: *Com seu gingado cheio de graça/com seu balança que é mais do que um poema* . . . (With her gracious *gingado*/with her way of swaying that is more beautiful than a poem . . .).

2

The Choreographic Model

We cannot say of the body, even outside of Brazil, that it is this or that, but rather that it continually transforms itself and is already not, at the moment when I speak of it, what it was a few seconds ago. Attempting to describe, recount, sing or even to film and dance the movement of the body in perpetual becoming is to adopt a horizon of knowledge that cannot but be one of a "negative anthropology", in Adorno's sense. It is to have recourse to a writing of time and of the multiple, or rather to invent it. Of the multiple understood in the meaning that Gilles Deleuze gave it (1993: 3): "the multiple is not only what has many parts but also what is folded in many ways".

Folds

The notion of multiplicity thus understood (and not simply plurality, even less pluralism) appears to me to be particularly fertile for orienting us toward what today is called an anthropology of the body. We begin to realize this by examining the different meanings of the *fold*, a word from the Latin *plicare*[1] which means literally to pull a soft material back over itself, and which gave birth to the two verbs *plier* [to fold] and *ployer* [to bend, bow, buckle]. To *plier* (which we find in the words *repli* [withdrawal], reply, and accomplice) is a physical activity. Being subject to a *supplice* [torture] consists of bending the knees like in the act of sup*pli*cation, which consists of inclining and prostrating oneself before someone. As for the term *ployer* (which we encounter in deploy and employ), which etymologically signifies to open something that was previously folded by stretching it out, it was initially used to designate the movements of the body.

Plier and *ployer* involve a bending. They require flexibility or at least potential elasticity. Only that which is flexible can be folded or bent. They are activities that consist of bending, inflecting, reflecting, curving, even of twisting. They are accomplished through a movement of torsion, sometimes even contortion of the body, or of thought in movement. There is indeed a close relationship between movement and thought: thinking, Nietzsche believed, happens while walking.

There exists a difference between the *plural* and the *multiple*. The *plural* (from the Latin *plus* which gave *plein* [full] and plenitude) designates only a large quantity of elements in a given totality, whereas one of the meanings of *multiple* explores the activity that consists of forming numerous folds and of forming them in a way that is different each time. Put another way, the plural belongs to a quantitative and arithmetic logic: the cumulative logic of signs adding themselves to other signs. Multiplicity, for its part, cannot be understood in this model of addition of numerous elements forming a totality. It does not proceed from the juxtaposition or coexistence of "constitutive" parts of a whole, but from an activity of modulation and sometimes of molding. Whereas the plural is an operation of composition or assemblage of diverse or identical elements by adjunction, possibly a point of saturation (which can in no way account for an activity involving muscular tension), the multiple thus understood in no way consists of adding, nor even of moving elements from one place to another, but rather, in a movement of gesturing, walking or dancing, of forming, deforming, transforming, in short of creating constantly new forms. Multiplicity is not accumulation (of signs or of goods), but tension. It is not so much totality (of assembled, combined or recombined elements) as intensity and rhythmicity. It calls for a mode of knowledge that is no longer structural but modal and, as concerns the body more particularly, a mode of knowledge that is no longer anatomical nor even physiological but—as we shall see—choreographic.

If the *multiple* is distinct from the *plural*, it is also radically opposed to the *single* [*simple*], in its dual meanings: that which is formed of a single element; that which is folded but once. A thing is *simple*[2] if it is alone and suffices unto itself in its homogeneity and compactness. That is the meaning of the verb to *simplify*, which literally signifies to make only a single fold or to fold in only a single manner, and which is opposed to *complicate* and to *complex*, which designate multiple folds or multiple manners of folding. Let us finally note that very close to the words derived from the Latin *plicare* is *plectare* (which we encounter precisely in the terms *complex* or *perplex*), which tucks away an eminently physical meaning: the act of braiding or intertwining, or the meeting of two bodies in the process of interlacing.

The multiple involves intensities and modalities, which pose the question of time. There exist involuntary folds. Some are of a geologic nature, formed through accidents, undulations and folds of the land. Others are physical and leave on the body what we call wrinkles. Both result from exertion that takes place over time. As for voluntary folds, they are produced through a movement, it too temporal, which consists of producing a bend, however light, upon paper (that we crumple), cloth (that we crease, pleat, wrinkle) or even upon the face (in the activity that consists of furrowing the eyebrows).

Anthropological thinking about the body must not be about being, but other than being. Nor must it be about the single, but rather about the multiple in the sense just given. It is a thinking that is elaborated in the movement (*métabolè* and not *kinésis*) of duration and becoming. It implies successiveness, and not simultaneity. It is not a thinking of concomitance (of elements united in a totality) but of intermittence. It is also incompatible with theoretical models that engage in a cutting up of units of meaning and that have for effect a stabilization of the sensible, which is thereby disqualified and reduced in an authoritarian manner to what it is not.

The body in itself is nothing—or rather, to continue to say "the body" as though it consisted of a set of functions or of surfaces identical to one another is to condemn oneself to say nothing. We begin to understand what it wants to say (or silence) by being attentive to the *manners* in which it is affected: what stirs it emotionally, touches it, shakes it, hurts it, the manners in which it reacts not expressively but performatively to that which affects it. It can cry out (in fear, joy, rage), weep, jump, be startled, pivot, squat, curl up, shrink, twist, extend, relax, unwind, luxuriate. Thus, the movement of Popeye in Faulkner's *Sanctuary* at times evokes something metallic and mechanical, at others a sort of elastic pliability.

Indeed, there do not exist bodily behaviors outside of experiences that are those of temporality. These may be extremely past-dependent (for example with tiredness) but also extended toward the future (in dread, fear, expectation, patience). There is no corporeality in itself but rather acts oscillating between slow and fast motion, acts prone to repeating themselves but also to being improvised in a singular manner at each occurrence. Such as the act of running. The subject may force herself, at extreme speed, to desperate efforts such as at the end of the film *Rosetta* by the Dardenne brothers, where the heroine is literally breathless. One may be dragged into a mad race like the young couple in Cassevetes's *Shadows*, who flee through Central Park to the vibrating rhythms of a piece of jazz by Charlie Mingus. He may also, like in Buster Keaton's *The General*, reach a second state when, colliding with reality, the outside literally takes hold of him. This last example undoubtedly constitutes the fullest critique of the body reduced to the conventions of its social functions.

What counts for speaking the body in all its states are not substantives but verbs and their moods, which can describe the precision of Lieutenant Fontaine's hand gestures as he digs out of the cell in which he is locked (in Bresson's *A Man Escaped*) or, in a completely different register, the agitation of the characters interpreted by Gena Rowlands in Cassevetes' films. Mostly in response to the assaults of Ben Gazzara, the actress resists, defends herself, gesticulates, loses her breath, falls, slumps, then sits up again. It is, in this cinema of feeling, through veritable physical struggle that embraces begin, kisses are wrested away, and the female characters begin to let themselves go before pulling back.

Subject through history to successive social injunctions, the body is prone to resistance. Granted, if it stomps, leaps, rushes forth, rises up, or if it tramples, parades, trots, ambles, it does so on the basis of accepted or proscribed modes of socialization (what American anthropologist Linton calls "models of misconduct", already evoked with respect to the *malandro*). But it would not be possible to draw up an inventory of differentiated forms of these behaviors that could then occupy a place in an all-encompassing totality. The parcelled-out body, the dissected body, ready to be analyzed and found to conform to a paradigm (that of functionality and social instrumentalization or, on the contrary, deviance) risks looking like what's left when the coroner has finished his work.

Body, Paradigm and Syntagma

It is necessary here to examine the relationship between the two meanings of the word paradigm: in the sense of Thomas Kuhn (1962)—which designates a dominant epistemological model—and in the sense in which Émile Benveniste defined it (1971), in order to distinguish it from syntagma. In the precise linguistic meaning, a paradigm allows for studying the *syntactic* organization of words in a *language* [*langue*]. It concerns the relations of the whole to its constitutive parts (phonemes, morphemes, lexemes) and forms a *system* giving rise to synchronic analysis. Now, this precise but narrow meaning of paradigm only concerns statements, and never modalities of enunciation. It in no way allows for providing an account of the thickness of our physical behaviors, such as the different ways in which the body can be, for example, subjugated, or on the contrary, may try to liberate itself. The social and political constraints exercised on the body are all the more imperceptible because individuals have collectively internalized them and they end up by seeming natural, even "innate". This process of repression/internalization is completely missed by an approach that grasps the social as but a system of relations between preexisting signs. Similarly, what can an exclusively semiotic approach say when we are concerned with, in the musical, theatrical and choreographic creation of Latin America, different manners of restoring the body-subject to its rightful place, in countries where, from the beginning of the Conquest, it has been humiliated and at times even killed—and in domains where it has been (almost) systematically ignored?

These examples in no way confront us with *paradigmatic* relations between elements of a *language* [*langue*], but rather with *syntagmatic* relations as studied for the first time by Ferdinand de Saussure (2001: 170–77). Syntagmatic relations do not occur in the discontinuity of *langue*, cut up abstractly into a *plurality* of prior units (words), but in the continuity of the flow of *langage*. The movement, and more precisely the *multiple* transformations of the body, can then be considered, in the manner of a *sentence*, no longer as propositions but as processes of enunciation. I must specify here that it is by no means for me a question of reducing physical processes to spoken language [*langage*] and even less so to written. But it is very much, on the other hand, the physical impossibility that we experience of finding ourself in two places at the same time or of pronouncing two words and even two sounds at the same time that leads us to show epistemological humility: the successive and progressive modulations of the life of the body, which never ceases transforming itself, are of a completely other nature than the formal relations between elements and a totality. The body-subject evolving from one state to another calls for an analytic model (a paradigm, but this time in the sense of Kuhn) which must not be of simultaneity as with structuralism, but of successiveness, of time, and of history.

What I propose, in order to orient us toward such a horizon of knowledge, is to challenge the logic of paradigm (in the sense of structural linguistics, which in its reduction of *langage* to *langue*, has the effect of spatializing thought) by experimenting with the fecundity of that which is syntagma (a chain or more exactly flow of associations) and paradigm (in the sense of Kuhn) at the same time: a model I will call choreographic.

Topos and *Choros*

The classic epistemology to which we still have recourse tends implicitly to think the social in terms of the Greek *topos* and not *choros*. It is much more of a topography than a choreography. *Topos* is the location, the site of one who remains in place, or who moves only in a space that is stable and finite. For speaking about *topos* we more readily have recourse to the Spanish or Portuguese verb *ser* (formed from the Latin *sedere*, that is, to be seated) than to the verb *estar*. Granted, *choros* also designates a space, but it is more precisely an interval supposing not only spatial mobility but transformation in time. "It is difficult to say whether we should go from the notion of 'group of dancers' to 'location prepared for dancing', or the reverse".[3]

The notion of choreography (and no longer of topography) has the advantage of leading us to understand (but first of leading us to feel, look, and listen to) the being-together of the choir, which refers at once to the place where one dances and the art of dancing. *Chora* is that place-in-movement in which a type of link that is physical is elaborated. But to apprehend the minute modulations of the body as it transforms itself, its aptitude to become other than what it was and, more precisely still, to feel the presence in it of all that comes from others, it is necessary to introduce a final notion: not just *chora*, but *kairos*, which is the instant in which I am no longer with others in a relationship of mere coexistence but where I begin to be disrupted and transformed by them.

Whereas in a topographical approach we take, we seize, we appropriate an object, in a choreographic approach, and more precisely in the time of *kairos*, there is no longer an object that can be regarded as a radical outside. The verbs' tenses and the verbs themselves are no longer the same: no longer take, seize, appropriate, but surprise and be surprised like in the *duende* of Flamenco. *Kairos* is the precise moment where we surrender fictions of the "other", of the "stranger" and where we achieve an experience which is that of strangeness.

An anthropology of the body must be built not in topographic terms, in terms for example of tables (the way we speak in medicine of "nosographic tables"), but in choreographic terms. It requires thinking about temporality in a manner that is attentive to the modulations of the sensible. A form of thinking about dance that cannot be resentment, vengeance, but is rather approval of life. That is the reason why, in opposition to Socrates' and Saint Paul's disdainful discourse of metaphysics and idealism that treat the body with abhorrence, Nietzsche favored another language. And this other language, which is no longer that of the humiliation of the body and the defamation of the real, Zarathustra announced while dancing.

It is therefore a matter of thinking about time in its becoming, but here is where the difficulty arises, since time is neither divisible nor repeats itself. It does not lend itself to cuts immobilizing the flow of movement. Bergson is no doubt one of those who most contributed to liberating thought from reduction to the spatial and the solid, and to challenging the stereotypes (*stereo*, in Greek, means to consolidate, to make strong) of spatial, static social identity "theory". But this does not mean that one must give up all analysis. By inventing chronophotography at the end of the 19th century, Marey broke down movement. He made *explicit* the *multiplicity* in action of steps, jumps, strides. Contrary to Claude Bernard's method, the effect of which is to stop time, it allows us to understand, by allowing us to perceive them visually, the infinitesimal transitions that make up the act of walking.

In order to study movement, theoretical and critical thinking about the body and the sensible must, itself, be in movement, which is not at all possible if we confine ourselves to an implicit or explicit conception of *langage* based on the primacy of signs, on the idea of an essence of the sign as the sign of a meaning, *a fortiori* of a single meaning. In the social sciences, however, we continue to be confronted with the persistence of a model that is resolutely dualistic and hierarchical and which opposes meaning and *langage*—envisaged as a simple utilitarian vehicle serving to transport information from one point to another—the body being but the instrument that allows for the "transmission" or "expression" of emotions.

In order to delimit and pin things down as clear-cut, clean, proper, explicit, and exact (but to the detriment of precision), this paradigm favors discontinuity and stability of sign, giving only secondary attention to rhythm. It deserves to be reexamined.

3

Pains and Pleasures of the Binary: The Dichotomy of Meaning and the Sensible

I am against Hegel. Thesis? Antithesis? Synthesis? It seems too convenient. My dialectic is no longer ternary, but binary. There are only irreconcilable oppositions.

PIER PAOLO PASOLINI

man is not truly one, but truly two. I say two, because the state of my own knowledge does not pass beyond that point. Others will follow, others will outstrip me on the same lines; and I hazard the guess that man will be ultimately known for a mere polity of multifarious, incongruous and independent denizens.

ROBERT LOUIS STEVENSON

Most forms of thought, action and writing are still today distributed on the basis of the terms of an alternative: playful and serious, subject and object, form and substance, imagination and reason. And each time we present ourselves, each time we are asked to expand on our "identity", everything takes place as if we absolutely had to identify the camp to which we belong: the subjective *or* the objective, individual flights of fancy that can be "interesting" but are only personal opinions *or* speech about the world that may be the object of consensus. We are far from through with this dilemma about which there remains impressive unanimity, as though we had no other choice but to analyze raw facts, real ones, by means of adequate "representations" of reality, or else let ourselves go with digressions.

The elaboration of the rules of method (Cartesian, Baconian, Durkheimian) is clearly founded on the elimination of subjectivity. And this produces consequences that for a long time managed to be held back, but which increasingly nourish contemporary thinking. The subject who writes an academic article or book should be absent from what he writes. It is as though there were no author or as though a part of the author, in writing, melted away. What he feels should be eliminated or discarded into separate texts, published for example under a pseudonym. They would contaminate objectivity.

This definitional position is the most consequential of any that can be held. It is the one that Wittgenstein upholds in the only work he published while living. But this proposition has been pushed so far that a significant part of what was written in the twentieth century can be regarded as revenge, retaliation, in any case, as reaction to it. Wittgenstein would spend his whole life reacting to the *Tractatus Logico-Philosophicus* (1921/1981), demonstrating its insufficiencies.

Dismissing a part of the self or separating it scrupulously, eliminating from a scholarly text all wandering, feeling one's way, hesitation, fear of the risk of the contamination that has just been mentioned, is where semi-modernity has led us. It constrains us to separate "creations", it pushes us to hate a part of ourselves, it forces us to lead a double life.

This logic of pure disjuncture, untroubled by temporality, indifferent to ethics and politics, also draws departmental boundaries: to the scholars, the facts; to philosophy, meaning; to poetry, sounds; to novels, stories; to the bourgeoisie, comedy; to French intellectuals, films by Garrel. Ah, the movers have arrived: put this in this room, this in the living room, these slippers in the storage closet, don't mix them up, good evening dear, don't get the boxes confused. Each discipline, according to Paul Veyne, is comparable to a fishbowl. "Once one is in one of these fishbowls, it takes genius to get out of it and innovate" (Veyne, 1988: 118).

Fundamental Oppositions: The Sensible and the Intelligible. Puritans and the Debauched

Since Plato we have been arguing within fundamental oppositions from which all the others flow: the intelligible and the sensible, the latter necessarily inferior to the former, and only ever capable of being muddled, deceptive and illusory, like all that transforms itself and does not remain in place. These separations are Greek, then Scholastic, then Cartesian, then Kantian. They condemn us to being tossed about between the poles of a tenacious dichotomy: the mind and the body, the one and the multiple, reason and passion, necessity and chance, order and event, rigorous but frigid logic and festive possession. The history of this thinking has spoken to us for nearly 2,500 years about the impossibility, or at least the danger, of putting one in the other, and the genuine difficulty of going from one to the other except (Saint Augustine) by conversion—and without the possibility of return. This incompatibility of knowledge and pleasure, of science and love, is such that we are astounded to find the following penned by a semiologist and a sociologist. Barthes: "We shall never be able to say how much love (for the other, the reader) there is in work on the sentence" (Barthes 1989/1984: 352). Bastide: "To do good sociology, it is first necessary to love Man".

If such pronouncements are capable of surprising us, it is because we have been (mis)shaped by this idea that the scholar's greatest trait is detachment. Were he to find himself tempted by pleasure, it could only be with flutters of infidelity. Of course, our intention here and elsewhere is to say that this ascetic ideal of pure scientificness, self-sufficient and self-legitimating, is worn and concerns only a scientism that has become increasingly defensive and limited, which we recognize is not science but its counterfeit, its caricature.

Nevertheless, a principle of watertightness continues to impose an absolute separation of genres. The writer is supposed to use images, whereas the scholar, for his part, is supposed to affirm the necessity of subordination (Plato) to ideas. It is supposed to be on the basis of images, or more exactly in the language of the imaginary, that the former aims to depict reality, whereas it is in the name of concept that the latter seeks to break with fiction.

Writers seek to free themselves from the real: they are the debauched. The scholars obey it: they are the puritans. This completes the earlier list of antinomies, which in the name of the great divide of knowledge and existence opposes precision and elegance, mourning and enchantment, sobriety and inebriety, asceticism and enjoyment, spontaneity and self-control, all ways of naming reason and unreason.

Grasped in these terms (of which one is always the measure of the other), there is no (scholarly) reason why the two universes shouldn't, not so much join—which would be, as we shall return to, to misapprehend both in the confusion of a catch-all conjunction—as encounter one another. If this does not happen it is because we consider that the one group must remain impassible precisely in order to guard against the other, who are a tad delirious and very ill-mannered: they refuse to comply with the rules of method. The case seems to be settled: one group are renouncers, borderline martyrs, while the others are living it up. The former demand proof while the others so badly need tenderness. The former probe texts or works of art—works of art which, incidentally, tend to shy away, to withhold themselves like a woman pursued by a man whose advances are too eager: they wish to protect their ineffability.

This conception of the relations between "science" and "arts" (which concludes that there is no possible relationship or, more indifferent still, concludes nothing at all) finds itself accentuated by the existence of an attitude that became the delight of an entire tradition in the eighteenth century: libertinism. This is the character of the uninhibited aesthete, capricious, shifting, flighty, who cherishes walks in the woods or thickets, *flânerie*, and love affairs. The libertine writer is a man of distraction, wandering, confusion of feelings. He is a talented artificer, but irresponsible. His writing is strong, but his thinking is wrong.

It is because of this dispute that there are serious doubts about literature, which is always more or less suspected of pillage. The relations between it and science are often ones of incomprehension. They never go out together, are not on familiar terms, never call one another nicknames the way two farmers dripping with sweat in a beet field might, for example. They do not want to hear anything about one another which is normal, since literature aims to pulverize the rules of method. Their relations are also ones of preeminence and of power. The classic and contemporary distinction between scientific discourse and literary discourse is governed by the (entirely Platonic) separation of *knowledge* and *art*. Science discovers (the truth) whereas art creates (illusions). Only the former is imbued with a veritably cognitive function, giving it its unwavering critical reputation. The latter, on the other hand, ought to remain confined to the realm of public entertainers. It is made to please, amuse, entertain (exhausting efforts required by the first). Purely ornamental, it is located or rather is placed (by the scientist, of course) on the side of rhetoric.

For these two poles around which social as well as individual existence never cease oscillating do not enjoy the same legitimacy. It is "science" that is appointed by "society" to determine the place and the status of nonscience, of art in particular. It is the former that traces the boundaries of knowledge (the general and the intelligible) and nonknowledge (the particular and the sensible), obliging the latter to demand its rights: the autonomy, rather than the former heteronomy, of forms of discourse. Art may be a recognized and admired activity, but it nevertheless very often continues to be considered subaltern, marginal, ornamental, relative to that which has "importance": the content of knowledge. We see this very clearly when a painter, a filmmaker, a writer is mentioned in a work of social science: it is nearly always as an illustration, in the form of incidental material used to confirm (almost never to refute) the theory of the researcher who most often retains the last word.

Literature is a synonym of unreality and approximation and he who associates with it or devotes himself to it is, as Paul Valéry wrote, defining the intellectual, an "attendant of vague things". What is it that we say? "Separate fact from fiction". "It's theatrics". Or also: "He's being dramatic" or "putting on a show". These expressions say a great deal about the status given in our society by common (and even more so by uncommon) sense to artistic exploration of the world, while we never say (or never with disgust on our lips) "It's gymnastics", "It's business", "It's camembert". Indeed we judge people much more based on what they "consume" and in particular what they eat than based on what they read. "It's fiction" can be translated to the writer as "you make us dream, that's very nice, keep on doing it", and to the reader as "but you, don't pay attention to it!"

Through the grand dualisms of this way of thinking—it is sufficient to state a single one, it conjures all the others—that march in tight rows forming two long horizontal lines (in front, the kings, behind, the jesters), it is also, or rather it is especially the question of language that is posed. Reality and appearance, depth and surface, mind and body (which are for that matter three manners of causing the question of occultism to arise), the inside and the outside, the rigor of reason and joyous or tearful sensuality, cannot advance without form and substance, which will be joined—later in this story, which is the official, non *métis* part of the History of Europe—by language, the *patois* dialects, denotation, and connotation. The first terms—which affirm in the major scale what the second sketch in the minor—must do so much. They must ensure that the principle of seriation is not threatened by the effects of its own logic, which is that of reversal and inversion (as would indeed happen with Nietzsche). They must battle on all fronts in order to always further reduce the other to the same (which amounts to expelling it from the self) and to do so, make the confused clear, the opaque transparent. We are the inheritors of the logic of cascading separations just invoked, to which can also be added the oppositions between written and oral, the heart (impulsive, "irrational" and therefore more feminine) and reason (calculating and resolutely masculine).

This conception of the world evolved, took shape, and led to a hardening of each of the protagonists's positions and the likely reassuring reconfirmation that spaces (social, cultural, but also mental) should remain compartmentalized. Despite the disproofs inflicted, positivism is far from dead. The premise of objectivation as the paradigm of science is still there, humming along routinely in what Kuhn calls "normal science" (Kuhn 1962). It cannot but constantly comfort and nourish the movement of *romantic revolt* so characteristic of the second half of the nineteenth century and which finds several of its expressions in the once again *separate* fields of art as well as in differentialist movements.

Of course, in even the most unforgiving periods of the religion of reason, all this ferment of subjectivity hardly remained inactive. It was for the secret passions of the campaigners of Progress and the heroes of Science to silence affectivity and imagination. Kierkegaard, Dostoyevsky, then André Breton, to cite only them, set reason in opposition to passionate intensity [*amour fou*]. Between the two World Wars, surrealism thus constituted the rallying point for Europe's nonscientific culture, and offered a true epistemological alternative.

But what we are witnessing today is very different. It is at once a return of subjectivism *and* of reactions in terms of identity. This reflux of the past that is mounting in our throats, this surge of roots and of origins, a "flood so powerful that we can no longer observe its source" says Michel Serres, is our own *mal du siècle*. We are in the process of paying the price for five centuries of rationalocentrism. Recycled into positivism, this had consisted of eliminating a certain number of "objects" from the field of knowledge (the body, sensuality, love, passion, death, magic) which, in the name of the division of knowledges, took refuge in a state of partial secrecy or were rejected into culturally separate—and socially devalued—domains.

But these "objects" that have been so scorned and disparaged succeeded in transforming themselves into subjects, and here they now are rising up and showing themselves everywhere. They demand power be given to them alone. One of the crises that we are living through at the moment is the difficulty of calmly recognizing ourselves as *the children of Descartes and*

Cervantes. It is at once a crisis of separation that has led us to where we are (*schizophrenogenic dualism*), and a crisis of nostalgia: that of sorrow over lost unity, of the hopeless quest for synthesis, of reconstituting the whole from one of the two poles whose separation has only been accentuated since the Renaissance (the temptation of *totalizing monism*).

The latter tendency—of recombining in one what had previously been cut in two—is worth lingering on. Differential oppositions (of life and death, of the divisible and the indivisible, of the psychic and the physical, of subject and object, of form and substance, of meaning and style), which can lead as far as lines of fracture, are not without problems for the very attitude that calls for them. Thus, part of the effort—a considerable part—in this form of thinking consists of mediating them and first asking: how to attempt to link? For example the sensible and the intelligible by means of what Kant called schemata. How to reconcile the contradictory? How to escape a static face-off?

One of the most systematic attempts at reunification is certainly religious in the word's etymological sense. It is deployed in the different modalities of the Christian response: the reconciliation of the human and the divine in the Incarnation. One of its fullest theoretical realizations is in the Hegelian dialectic, where negation is prone to overcoming (*Aufhebung*), as well as in totalizing thought-systems: the system, synthesis, closed explanatory models, complementarity . . . in which this time the logic of conjunction prevails over that of disjunction.

These endeavors, which do not always cause the wound (at the heart of the European question) to scar over, are sometimes extremely violent toward the turbulence of the sensible. But they may also be seen in a less dramatic light as reality effects, fairly outdated "language games" (Wittgenstein). Since all these ideas of reduction to Unity (on the basis of Reason, History, Progress, Desire, Sex, the Brain, Celestial Bodies, Nature, the Nation . . . regardless, God always sneaks in through the cracks of these catch-alls) have, despite constant watering, gone totally yellow. We must nevertheless guard against them regaining their colors in another mode of totalization that consists today of saying *everything*, showing *everything*, claiming to know *everything*, spreading *everything* out in a close-up camera shot.

Benjy's Story: Saying the Sensible?

Against the fiction of the unity and totality of seeing and knowing, of feeling and saying, there exists a text of rare complexity, that demands careful attention, undoes habits (in particular habits of reading) and has, in my opinion, no equal in all of literature. It is *The Sound and the Fury* by Faulkner (1995/1929) and in particular, at the beginning of the novel, the long monologue of an idiot, Benjamin Compson. What this character, whom everyone calls Benjy, experiences conveys an exceptional degree of sensory acuity. He intensely senses cold, the absence of love, the approach of death (like the two dogs Dan and Blue), the often minute sounds made by rain when it falls on the roof, the smell of chamomile and honeysuckle, and, through all these tiny, precise sensations, the inescapable flow of a family's decline and a society's disintegration—that of the state of Mississippi.

But here's the thing. He cannot manage to say what it is he senses. He is torn between the fullness of sensation (oscillating between pleasure and pain) and the difficulty, impossibility, even, of speaking it. He cannot but, in a synesthetic frenzy, "try to say". Benjy, deprived of speech, is not able to understand what he experiences. Hence the confused and difficult to understand text imagined by Faulkner, who has no "key" to understanding to offer, no "message" to deliver, no "cause" to defend.[1] The author gives up holding the reader by the hand, of chewing in a certain sense the work for him, of telling him authoritatively what he ought to understand from a character who does not understand himself.

Benjy's narrative echoes scene v of Act V of *Macbeth* in which Shakespeare gives us this definition of life: It is a tale told by an idiot full of sound and fury, signifying nothing. It is a shattered, unchronological discourse, the discourse of an idiot but more still an idiotic[2] discourse in the strict sense of the term, which is to say a singular discourse. What are we told by this discourse, which is idiotical and therefore irreducible to the generalization and clarification of a well-organized discursive order? It speaks to us of desire, distress, defeat, and degradation. The desire to appropriate a young girl, Caddy, the sister of the "innocent" character, who also has two other brothers, Quentin and Jason. The distress of the character, but also of the narrator and of the reader who clearly perceives the immediacy of the sensations experienced but finds himself deprived of mediations that would allow for attributing them a meaning. And finally of defeat and degradation: the degradation of the Compson family and through them all the inhabitants of this South of misery, hatred, and abjection, defeated by the North and forgotten by history. The defeat of this South left to waste, but also, through it, the defeat, brought up hundreds of times in the work, of meaning, which is inexorably undone.

Nevertheless, the malaise produced by the impossibility of correspondence between sensations (sounds and perceptions) and words will give rise to other attempts to say that which obsesses Benjy's idiotical brain. It will spur other discursive regimes, each recounting how he felt about what happened during a wretched day that "began with the picture of the little girl's muddy drawers, climbing that tree to look in the parlor window with her brothers that didn't have the courage to climb the tree waiting to see what she saw". "I tried", the novelist adds, "first to tell it with one brother, but it wasn't enough".[3] That is the reason why this same story—that of Caddy Compson— will have to be told again. A second time by Quentin, who will commit suicide out of love for his sister. A third time by Jason, who pours out a long monologue of racist imprecations. A fourth time, finally, by a narrator who is not part of the family, but whose point of view has nothing omniscient about it either. These different discourses are successive attempts brought on by the failure of the preceding narratives, but which do not seem to succeed any more than the last in relating a meaning to a sensation.

It is nevertheless in the last part of the book that a semblance of order seems to appear out of this general chaos, with the appearance of Pastor Shegog, a man of words if ever there was one, and even a man of the Verb in the Christian sense of the term. His climb into the pulpit triggers a reflection not previously present in the novel, on the relations between knowing and seeing, meaning and sensing. Contrary to what the text "tried to say" through the three successive monologues of Benjy, Quentin and Jason, which are flows of sensation related in an ambiance of strangeness and even unreality, Reverand Shegog's speech is direct, dogmatic, unequivocal. It is a form of speech constituted of *signifiers* in the pure state, the opposite of Benjy's monologue, entangled in a flow of *signifieds*. This speech reestablishes order in chaos. It is explicitly aimed at making sense, although the narrator has just described the pastor as an "insignificant looking man" (Faulkner p. 249).

The scene in question is characterized by the pastor's aptitude for changing voices and more still the effect his "two voices" produce on the faithful who have come to hear him. When, after having introduced himself to the parishioners, he pronounces a few words of thanks, his voice seems insipid. Comparing it to a "cold inflexionless wire" (p. 249), the narrator writes that the voice "sounded like a white man" (p. 249). But his voice transforms itself radically when he stands in the pulpit. He speaks then in a voice that "rang ... with the horns", while his "intonation ... became negroid" (pp. 250–251). Of this second, piercing voice, that touches the deepest recesses of the heart and provokes psalmodic reactions on the part of the members of the congregation, the narrator tells us that "[i]t was as different as day and dark from his former tone, with a sad, timbrous quality like an alto horn, sinking into their hearts and speaking there again when it had ceased in fading and cumulate echoes" (p. 250).

The distortion that unhinges meaning and sensation in the three preceding narratives is not however abolished. The preacher, whose speech is cluttered with expressions ("Jesus", "Mary", "de blood of de lamb", "de Lawd", "po sinners") gives us very little to understand, but so much to see and to hear. He sees "the thief, en de murderer", the third thief of the Calvary, "the shadows", "de resurrection", Judgment Day, "de light" ... He hears "de boastin en de braggin", "de golden horns shoutin down de glory, en de arisen dead". ... And what he sees and hears—physically, since it is "with his body [that] he seemed to feed his voice" (p. 250)—far from imposing a logic on the sensible, an order on disorder, provokes highly emotional gestural and auditory reactions in those who listen. They begin, shudderingly, to intone with a single voice a plaintive and monotone chant that for the Whites of Mississippi probably has no immediate significance but undoubtedly retains a primitive and somewhat mysterious character. The sounds they emit in unison, felt more than thought, are sounds "beyond the need for words" (p. 250). They in no way lead to reflection or reasoning, and even less to a transformation of sensations into the abstract. They are also visual perceptions, like in Flaubert, which suggest (more than they explain) to the reader what the characters are experiencing: "[a]s the scudding day passed overhead the dingy windows glowed and faded in ghostly retrograde" (p. 250).

This Faulknerian tragedy can be read, or rather listened to, as a tragedy of language posing the question of the relationship between sound and sentiment, the sensible and the meaningful, the non-sensical and that which is difficult to signify but by no means insignificant. Although it is indeed noise ("the sound") that gives the *the* and provokes feelings ("the fury"), it is not for that reason that a coherent unity is established between that which relates to the sensible (auditory but also perceptive) and that which would be on the order of a meaning preexisting it. The sounds and the feelings are very real, but they do not make sense or at least do not immediately and directly make sense. It is thus, preceded by Benjy's long roar, that this strange story of life and desire will end. Of life snatched by death and of desire thwarted by destiny. Benjy, deprived of speech but not of voice, begins to bellow. His voice "mount[ed] toward its unbelievable crescendo". It "roared". What could be heard through those "cries" was "horror". Not meaning, "just sound" (p. 271).

The Sound and the Fury ends with a return to an order without speech and even without voice. The author will not have the last word, since discourses gives way to images: images of the village landscape of the South, which is the novel's true protagonist. But none of the tragedy's characters, any more than the narrator, and with them the reader, succeeds in connecting sensations and meanings. Nothing comes to fill the gap that separates the sensible and the sayable, since it is this gap that is constitutive of the tragic character of social life and in particular the life of language. The various questions posed—How can we speak about the South's contradictions? How to speak the hereditary evil that gnaws at it and begins with nonrecognition of the other and in particular with slavery?—cannot be responded to directly, only through the mediation of the art of the novel, that is to say the creation of a language of fiction, of which one of the characteristics is to be not resolutive but interrogative. That is the reason why, even in the final return to an initial order, meaning is far from having divulged itself. It continues to be evasive. It is up to the reader, like Benjy, to "try" to understand this non-sensical story.

Disjunction, Conjunction, Translation and Modulation

The much-decried end of the twentieth century and beginning of the New Millenium do still have, despite what is said, good sides. They allow us, when we succeed in extracting the lessons from texts that were ahead of their time like the one just discussed, to be wary of these stultifying games of for or against simplifications, or these tricks consisting of casually dangling yarns to make us hate Southerners (not Northerners), "Westerners" (not those who aren't), or vice versa, it does not matter. They also allow us to realize that it is not dualism that is evil but its opposite, monism, which leads to totalitarianism.

What I favor, following many others, is to open passages, to attempt to bring face-to-face languages that are unaware of one another, fields of knowledge that do not mingle, trying at the same time to account for the interstitial spaces and the differences between the attendant protagonists, which can be regarded as parts of ourselves that had never really met.

This is not without difficulties; if the task has often been described but never, strictly speaking, accomplished, it is because our dominant epistemological traditions resolutely obstruct it. The first may be called *rationalist*. It goes back, as we have seen, to Plato, who opposed the world of essences to that of appearances, truth to simulation, mind to body, intelligence to madness. The second is Kantian and establishes a separation between what can be known by pure reason and what can be believed by practical reason. The third, finally, which has already been evoked, is Hegelian and is aimed at the reconciliation of that which had been separated. We can find traces of it even in Breton's search for the famous "point" of convergence.

The mode of knowledge of what I propose to call a *modal anthropology* has been operative in film since Murnau and Stroheim, for whom the work of constructing a shot is done in an alternating play between shadow and light. Watching these directors's films, we understand that the contradictions in the sensible and the social can be perceived other than in a binary manner: not as relations between two preestablished universes with nothing common, not as an outright and contrastive heterogeneity of two heterogeneous natures, but as variations of degree and intensity.

This perspective frees us to no longer envisage the local as against the global, the periphery relative to the centre, women relative to men, the madman relative to one who is normal, the future relative to the past (or the opposite). The question, which cannot be resolved through the logic of thesis and antithesis, nor even of synthesis, is sparked by the neither totally White nor totally Black (which is the subject of the film *Shadows* by John Cassavetes), neither exclusively man nor only woman, not completely sick yet not in good health, neither past nor future in itself; the presence of the Third World in the West (the south of the Bronx in New York, so as not to give a French example) and the West in the very heart of the Third World (São Paulo); the hybridization that gives nature-culture, science-politics, artificial intelligence; "mediumship" but also the cat-fish, the feathered serpent (Quetzalcóatl), the spider-woman and especially the werewolf, who is not a full-time wolf. Let us refuse, in what follows, to allow ourselves to be locked into the terms of this alternative struggle that becomes a tired refrain (either/or), yet not yield to illusions, logic of conjuncture, and politics of consensus.

Thus, the idea that criticism takes place to the detriment of emotion and emotion to the detriment of criticism supposes a fairly curious idea: that there is a work of art only where there is no thinking, or thinking that does not think about itself. Art as a sort of initial thinking that calls for subsequent thinking capable of teaching it what it thought without knowing it, so to speak. Diderot reacts to this oddity in his fable *Les deux amis de Bourbonne* in which he shows that critical comprehension does not destroy pleasure. Something Umberto Eco expresses today, in his own way, when he says that even gynaecologists can fall in love.

Interpreting a text, giving it a critical reading, in no way abolishes the pleasure of reading. One can easily be both a critic and a creator (Blanchot, Kundera, Octavio Paz, and before them Diderot, Baudelaire, Huysmans, Proust), a scholar and an artist (Leonardo da Vinci, Mandelbrot), poet and theoretician of language (Mallarmé, Meschonnic), filmmaker and critic (Eisenstein, Antonioni, Godard, Glauber Rocha), search for a writing of the world and a writing of the self (Montaigne). The idea that we can be competent in but one narrowly defined area is not so much a "scientific" requirement as the expression of a technocratic ideology founded on the division of labor, which lends increasing importance to specialization and the assessment of "experts". "Today", as Brazilian philosopher Marilena Chaui writes,

> one of the principal aspects of the fight against exclusion is to succeed in breaking the discourse of competency. I realized this in working with people who were already excluded from work and economic life: the discourse of experts also excluded them from political, cultural and intellectual life.[4]

All of the authors just cited have shown, each in their own way, what was artificial about the separation of the soul from the body, of form from substance, of reason from experience, which in fact never cease to "mix" (Montaigne). All these authors, proving movement by walking, so to speak, inspire us to become aware of the instability of genres and to relinquish the very idea of well-drawn contours, neatly defined and, even more so, definitive boundaries between an "inside" and an "outside", between what is original, adopted, adapted. They invite us to think through temporality, logic, the self and others jointly—which does not mean simultaneously.

The games of binarism, which are no longer any fun, exacerbate two postures that, granted, do correspond to one another, but in a mechanical fashion, leaving us with no other alternative than the solemnity of the sanctuary and the frivolities of the cabaret. This couple of pure reason and art for art's sake—let us make clear that the latter, even more than its adversary, genuflects to itself and is repelled by the idea of entering the *mêlée*—constantly bicker. Their fights are reminiscent of the show of rivalry between two well-known bands about whom opinions are divided. What should they be called? Cortázar called them the Cronopios and the Famas,

Macedo Fernandez the Hilarantes and the Enternecientes. In Faulkner's universe, they are the Snopes and the Sartoris, and on French television in the 1970s, the Shadoks and the Gibis.

Are we condemned, for lack of a third term, to a flood of images or a drought of concepts: how would you like to die? Between the reaction of the impressionists, who short-circuit all mediations and suck you into those muse stories, of inspiration, of ineffable genius, of soul, of identity, and who knows what else still? and the foolishness of positivism, its insensibility, its indifference to language, why should we be constrained to choose? Why must we always conclude, in the manner of Aristotle, with logic against existence, or romantically, with passion against reason? Why, finally, must an argument for objectivity against subjectivity or on the contrary subjectivity against objectivity always be made? The latter is constructed *with* and *by* the subject, *within* language. All scientificity is human, and therefore anthropological not theological.

It seems possible to me to live in a manner that is nonreligious, I mean without deifying one of the "poles" of the "real", without postulating a justificatory noumenal world, like in Diderot's fables but paradoxically also in Brazilian Candomblé ceremonies. Everything that was neglected by rationalocentrism—in particular its project of detemporalizing existence—is not *relative* compared to reason, but progresses in *relation* to reason, which is in no way an idealized and incorporeal authority situated outside history. Reflecting on this turbulent relationship, which is impossible in the absence of a reflection on language, and is a process constituting itself in language, is the task modernity must keep returning to.

It so happens that subject is still often confused with subjectivism and even with individualism, indeed narcissism, which are but possible strayings of which one of the major expressions is found in romanticism. But the subject is no more on the side of affect than of concept. It engages the totality of sensibility and intelligence in acts of language (verbal but also non-verbal language, conscious but also unconscious language). It does not have much to do with incantatory discourses, with the hopeless self-admiring sentimentalism that vaunts its beauty, inundates you, spreads pathetically, often with the best intentions in the world. Indeed the idea that the subject is limitless emotion, affection, affectation, life and desire, whereas thought is pure idea without desire, is not only a fiction but a fraud that turns the clock back to a pre-Freudian psychologism. The subject cannot be reduced to the arrogance but also obscenity of an egological striptease, to this "expanding self" in which Canetti (2005: 185) sees "wretched self-deception about death". It is infinitely richer in possibilities because it is unswervingly action and knowledge, affection and reflection.

It can be envisaged other than in a mode of grievance or nostalgia for a humanistic civilization as irremediably lost like the time when the milkman still plied the streets with a horse-drawn carriage, leaving bottles on doorsteps. The subject is caused not so much to *return* (to this period, to the narcissistic initial phases of personality development) as to *become* a "heteronomic" actor and author, in the sense of Fernando Pessoa, which is to say virtually multiple. He is made of others but is not completely social or rather is not, as we will return to in the following chapter, totally socializable. In addition, while his psychic evolution is clearly apprehendable, he is not exclusively psychological. Thus, there is no psychology in Kafka's writing, and yet the subject (constantly threatened, it is true) is no less present. Lastly and above all, while *langue* (learned and therefore wholly social) in large part constitutes the subject, what he himself constitutes is *langage* as a singular activity of speech or writing taking shape within a history.

To understand the singularity of "language as activity of subjects within a history" (Meschonnic 1985: 40), it is necessary, along with numerous precursors—not just Baudelaire, but Humboldt, and beneath Humboldt, a part of what was already germinating in Aristotle's *Poetics*—to radically question the simultaneously desubjectivating and dehistoricizing dichotomy between *content* (conceived of as reliable information, stable, identical to itself) and *form*, treated as an instrument used to transport (today we increasingly say "communicate") messages. This conception, which we can refer to as "expressionist" or "expressive", postulates that an already constituted, preexisting meaning has ontological priority over what is referred to as form: speech, voice, writing, musical or theatrical interpretation, cinematic images that do nothing but "express", "reflect", or "represent" that which we aim to "transmit".

This language of telecommunications applied to History, to histories, to narratives and in particular those of novels or films, is a hoax. It leads for example to considering Dostoyevsky's *Crime and Punishment* as a mere "document" giving us information about student life in St. Petersburg at the end of the nineteenth century. What is rejected on the side of "style" in this instrumental logic sees itself relegated to a relation of grotesque domination. It is as though there could exist a mind independently of the body (spiritism) or in music a meaning that would not also be sound. When meaning emerges, it can form itself in music only through creation, interpretation, and audition. It is not only auditory material (that could exist somewhere), but a way of playing or singing, act in the process of signifying.

The Sensible, Sounds and Images:
The Contribution of Cinema

The idealized character of meanings that could have an autonomous existence independently of sensory experience appears clearly in the historical depreciation of the relationship to images. Condemned by Plato (for epistemological reasons) and forbidden by the Mosaic and Islamic laws (for ethical reasons), images were long considered to be of a lesser reality and to be sources of hallucination, at best of distraction. In this perspective, thinking is in a sense thinking against images, or at least without images, to abstract oneself from them in order to reach the purity of the idea (or of divinity), in short to deny that there could exist a thought-process in images. We are reminded, in this regard, that Alain's *Propos* recommended a classroom with white walls, a room in which the authority of the texts studied and of the master's speech were to suffice.

The reflexive energy of thinking in images seems to continue to go unrecognized today; it still finds itself emptied out and reduced to what it is not. No doubt out of fear of its potential for bringing doubt and disorder, it is most often apprehended solely from the viewpoint of the order of discourse. This is clear whenever cinema comes up. Everything takes place as though the idea (the already written text), the intent, the message, even the thesis, preexisted the image. The latter is then solely envisaged as a means, instrument or format that allows for telling a story, and through it, illustrating a certain content. Everything takes place, in sum, as though there were an inert meaning (to decipher or decode) that preexisted its production, a script ready to be interpreted.

But such a preexistence and preeminence of discourse is totally inapplicable in cinema. They really do not have, even in films by Hitchcock (who, like Antonioni, is first and foremost a visual artist), any relevance to cinema. The cinematographic image does not say. It shows (and hides), but it does not say. It is irreducible to the *logos*.

Cinematographic thinking, a form of sensory thinking if ever there was one, since it is constructed with only fragments of images and (from 1927 onward) moments of sound, is a resolutely aconceptual and adiscursive thinking. It is interested, like ethnography, only in concrete singularity. What is resolutely prohibited in cinema—as in ethnography—is generality of concept. It does not speak of "Man" or "Woman" in general, but shows what is unique about this woman, that man, this actor, that actress. Making a film consists of opting between a multitude of possible perspectives. The cinematographic unit has nothing to do with *langage*, less still with *langue*, which only recognizes stabilized statements. It is elaborated through the construction of a shot that is filmed and recorded at a certain distance, for a certain amount of time, and from points (which are also always singular) of view—or, more exactly, "of looking"—and of listening. Then comes the moment of editing which consists of a process of organizing (it too singular) relations between the two sensory modes of image and sound.

What is interesting about cinematographic art—an art of resistance to the simplification and commercialization of television and advertising images, as well as high-budget Hollywood, French or Japanese films—is that it draws our attention to the critical potentialities contained within the task of re-articulating sensory linkages, at a time when concentration and reflection are diminishing. Re-scripted through a frame, or more precisely a process of "framing",[5] the micro-events of daily life are better seen and heard. Cinema, by assembling and modulating images and sounds, arouses, or awakens, our sentience [*sensibilité*]. It allows us, against the hijacking of the real in the context of visual and auditory totalitarianism's triumph and the eradication of small sensations, to relearn how to see and listen. It shows us the underside of the visual, the other, the outside: *Muriel* (1963) by Alain Resnais, or the unseen-unspoken of the war in Algeria; *Wanda* (1970) by Barbara Loden, or the other side of the United States; *Games of Love and Chance* (2004) by Abdellatif Kechiche, or the flipside of stereotypes concerning the housing projects in the French suburbs. But cinema is much more precise still. With Murnau, Stroheim, Antonioni, Satyaijit Ray, Oliveira, we are more able to perceive tiny nuances, minute details of facial expressions, skin complexion, or the different textures of wood, glass, metal or stone, or better still, of this wood, that glass, this metal, that stone.

We perceive these nuances and details in a refined manner only when, paradoxically, we no longer feel the work of the director, crew and actors. The work of organizing sounds and images that begins on the set and continues with editing is obviously there but it has become invisible and subterranean. Without this element of the inexplicit, the elliptical—even of ambiguity and misunderstanding—without all that evades univocal interpretation, there would be, strictly speaking, no art, only technical skills. Technical skills that, nowadays, are increasingly in the service of filling seats and obscenity.

Nothing is more concrete, but also complex, artisanal, and theoretical at once (I'm thinking in particular of the critical contribution of Canudo, Krakauer, Bazin, Bresson) than the art of organizing sequences of sounds and images. The vast majority of cinematic productions do not involve the always singular process of thinking about the form of this organization. But there is nothing less abstract, conceptual and logocentric. Everything that is of the order of discourse, of enunciation (the orality at play in recountings, interviews, dialogues, replies, narrations) and *a fortiori* of statement may well be elements of cinema, but they are not properly cinematographic. To reduce cinema to speech, making it a "narrative art", or to deport it to the realm of "image arts" (the work with light, color, lines, and masses that it shares with painting and photography) is to speak of what is not characteristic of the sensations and emotions that we can experience in cinema.

Temporalities and Cross-Cutting Paths

The social sciences, which are still far from having realized the potentialities opened up by cinematographic knowledge, for the most part still adhere to a "Balzacian" conception of society. In *The Human Comedy*—and even more in Zola's work—the reality of raw facts uncomplicated by ambiguities is initially given, or rather postulated. Presupposing relations of causality and deductibility, the writer endows the characters with clearly defined personalities: each reflects the milieu to which he belongs.

This conception of the subject, compact, homogenous, in total harmony (with the optimism of the liberal society of the July Monarchy), began to fissure with Flaubert during the 1848 revolution. It then cracked with

Proust, who was an analyst of early Third Republic society, which no longer had the same stability as before.

What one realizes, very progressively, and in an extremely slow manner, through the reading of *In Search of Lost Time*, a book of associations and digressions, is that the social is not what explains, but what needs to be explained. Explained in a history that is also that of the subject in search of himself in writing. What is questioned is the permanence of social types, of differences established once and for all and given as irreducible, and by correlation the constructedness of the unitary, uniform, self-sufficing subject, who in fact discovers himself, plural and collective, to be, in the successiveness of his states, different each time from what he was: "I was not a single man, but the parade of a composite army where there were men who were lazy, indifferent, jealous—several jealous men of which not one was jealous of the same woman" (1954, t. III: 489).

What appears at the beginning of this quest, of which one of the prominent aspects is surprise—in other words, what will happen to the narrator and the characters is of an undeductable nature—is that clearly opposed semantic units are a myth. Indeed, everything seems to separate the bourgeois universe of the Verdurin from that of one of the most illustrious families of the French aristocracy, the Guermantes. They are two worlds that do not rub shoulders and which are extremely topologically and even directionally distant one from the other. Two doors can be taken out of the Combray house. One taken to go "the way towards Méséglise-la-Vineuse, which we called also 'Swann's way' because to get there one had to pass along the boundary of M. Swann's estate" and the the the other to go "Guermantes way". "If the Méséglise way was fairly easy", the narrator continues, "it was a very different matter when we took the Guermantes way, for that meant a long walk" (Proust 1992: 188).

It is in the *Search*'s temporality that this opposition is progressively overcome. The narrator learns much later, and very incidentally, during a walk with Gilberte, that the two sides were not as contradictory as they initially appeared. They can be joined together by a "cross-cutting path", a shortcut, in sum, that allows for reconciling the two itineraries, one leading toward the bourgeois and the other toward the aristocrat. This passage, a spatial one if ever there was, is also a passage caused by the workings of involuntary memory that produces not nostalgia (missing a time passed), but melancholy (the feeling of time passing).

In the first volume of *In Search of Lost Time*, the individual tends to be equated with the social class from which he originates, the distance separating the Verdurin and the Guermantes seems unmeasurable, as vast, the narrator insists, as "that separation between the mineral world and that of humanity". In a nutshell, the limitations that the bourgeoisie imposes upon itself as much as they are imposed upon it, are the forever inaccessible heights of the name Guermantes. But over the course of the story, we realize that these two blocks are not so heterogeneous as we thought since there exist links between them. The characters' lives acquires their meaning progressively in the exceedingly evolving relationships they entertain with all the others, and in particular with the social environments from which they do not come. It is in *Sodom and Gomorrah* that the social edifice of the Faubourg Saint Germain (these *hôtels particuliers* that constitute the recent urban emulation of the aristocracy's landed residences) begins to fissure. A few bourgeois are admitted into the salons of the aristocracy, and the narrator, through the intermediary of the Baron Charlus (who himself frequents the "small group" of the Verdurin, though not without a certain amount of shame), is invited to the Guermantes'. There he meets Orianne, his second love. The reader, at the end of the book, is confronted with the narrative of an even more unexpected evolution. This *petite-bourgeoise* of a Madame Verdurin becomes princess of the Guermantes, something which appeared completely inconceivable in the beginning. But she does not cease, in so doing, to be dual and contradictory. What found itself separated in a logic of firm disjunction (the bourgeoisie and the aristocracy, being and appearance, the sensible and what Proust calls "intelligence") is prone to meeting, but without then coming to coincide in a merely conjunctive present that would stabilize each of the protagonists.

4

The Semantic Obsession

Making meaning is very easy, mass culture does so all day long;
suspending meaning is already an infinitely more complicated
enterprise, it is, if you will, an "art"; but "making nothing" of
meaning is a hopeless project, proportionate to its impossibility.

ROLAND BARTHES

Distinguishing, classifying, and organizing every existing thing is by no means exclusive to the rationalocentric mode of knowledge. Every society effects systems of opposition. The societies once called "traditional"—and which are less so every day—are no doubt moved by an even stronger passion for the logic of classification of the living. Mixing is for them a calamity, and they ceaselessly prevent masculine and feminine, heaven and earth, dry and moist from mixing, or rather from mixing in an uncontrolled manner, ensuring rather that they remain rigorously separated even as they can ally themselves, connect, and fertilize one another at certain moments, according to precise ritualities. It is therefore contemporary societies that, under economistic domination and the audiovisual culture of everything as "communication", tend rather to lose their bearings (often, even, in their general indifference), while we witness the increasing disintegration of what had constituted them: the political sphere of which the Nation State was the symbol.

The Optical and Spatial Determination
of the Real

What is characteristic of the form of knowledge elaborated on the basis of classic European rationality is therefore not—or not only—the full exercise of categorizing and classificatory thinking. It is the deculturalization of meaning, first named then distributed, and by a process of packaging, numbered, polled, controlled, regulated, normalized. The dogmatism of dating, of remorseless clean breaks, of neat and incorruptible borders, does not merely divide. By assigning and apprehending, it captures, reifies, subjects, appropriates, manipulates. It subjects the continuity of the sensible to contortions. A logical operation such as this one, which is eminently conservative, resembles what Spinoza called a "sad passion". It passes off as natural that which is historic and cultural, such that the oppositions constructed within a system end up appearing as though given. Finally, it supposes an optical, even optic, conception of the real. It is an operation by which what is separated must first be not only identified, but clearly authenticated (*what is it?*) under the light of day so that no mystery remains. As Hercule Poirot might say, "with me, mysteries never last. It never takes long before I've solved them".

What in other cultures or for other individuals from the same civilizational area may be apprehended as a continuum marked by degrees, sees itself transformed here into a perfectly stable *object*, placed clearly before us (that is, in passing, its etymology: ob[in front of]-ject[thrown]), and endowed with specific and consistent properties that allow for, in each instance, locating regularities. The indeterminable, the imponderable and the unobjectifiable are, under these conditions, considered to be veritable catastrophes, attributable to an error of judgment. What count are only clear and distinct differences, which suppose contours, contrasts, even walls, as well as an ensemble of distinctive traits capable of reproducing themselves and which are so many guarantors of truth. Let us not presume, however, that this perspective is uninterested in the life of the senses. However, sensations must first be sorted, filtered, purified so that only the clean, the proper and the explicit is left. Only perfectly identified notes (not "noises"), photogenic faces, clear colors like flamboyant red or navy-blue—at the expense of the continuity of more "indecisive" colors that oscillate between red and blue, such as purple and garnet—are worthy of interest.

As for the other pole allowing for the identification of the object, that is to say the subject of discourse (discourse in the literal sense of that which interrupts the course), anthropology itself, for a long time, resisted speaking about it or, since Malinowski's *Diary*, did so in separate works presenting themselves as "outside the text". Everything takes place as though this subject, compact and constant, could, in turn, be but objectified and neutralized, and in so doing dehistoricized, or inversely, in a reactive manner, cherished and cultivated.

The Social Catch-All

What counts for the moment is to question the treatment received by other subjects when they are transformed into objects. Very often in the social sciences individuals are considered merely as vehicles—and practically interchangeable vehicles—for an order: one of type, culture, or structure. They tend to be thought of like chameleons and become practically caricatures of the realist novel of the late nineteenth century. Indeed we rarely speak of subjects but rather of (social) *actors*, (social) *agents* who occupy "roles", "statuses", or "functions". These agents are vectors (but not truly authors) of "social practices", of healing, educational, dietary, religious, sexual, "practices" (everything, nowadays, has become a question of "practices").

In this positional reading, taking place in what we call "a field", what matters is the position of the "agent" within the spatial configuration of a system. Thus, in a large number of ethnological works, the subject who has become a member of a whole shows no personal desire. He tends to evolve in a confined manner, separated from the rest of humanity (but rarely divided against or in conflict with himself) and in mimetic uniformity. He follows one of the inclinations of sociological naturalism, which consists of becoming a monk among the monks, bearded among Cuba's bearded men, Black among the Blacks of Harlem, gay among the gay men of San Francisco, a marquis among the marquis at court, a professor at the university, a parent in the family, a citizen in the nation, a horse in the merry-go-round and a camel in the desert. We only want to see one face.

This individual is not totally a subject since he was conceived beforehand as socialized or at least socializable through and through. He must, in order to be studied, become a homogeneous element belonging entirely to the milieu in which he develops and the group into which he inscribes himself.

In this idea of reproduction, where the ideal consists of finding exact copies each time, the only things to exist are conformity to the social order or major social deviance such as criminality, incest and, above all today, pedophilia, not to forget the major disorganization constituted by madness. The individual, whose autonomy and self-sufficiency are negligible under these circumstances, as though he were not potentially multiple, tends to become a mere vehicle for a process of total socialization or desocialization. Everything takes place as though within a given group one cannot but be identical. This process is so impeccably logical, and we know just how far it can lead us. If all Jews are the same, they are all replaceable, displaceable . . .

The idea—capable of becoming an ideal—of flawless correspondence of the real and the social with the rational, or to put things differently, of a totally socialized society enveloping each and every person in a seamless garment of normalized behaviors, is nothing other than fascism, that is to say, totalitarianism. The latter proceeds on the basis of an excess of culture and forced hypersocialization. Its efforts are directed at constantly fashioning and refashioning the homogeneous and the compact, by any means, in order to obtain, through obedience, unanimous agreement. It does not tolerate the slightest deviation, which must be corrected, punished, condemned, even eradicated.

That which resists this process, which leads to what Robert Musil calls the "copy-man" or the "character man", to whom he opposes "potential man" or the "man without qualities" (Musil 1967), are the minute differences that can be perceived in the slight bends of the sensible. Not the absolute other (the Black, the madman, the animal), or what doctors sometimes call a "real sickness", one which can be perfectly identified. In romantic jealousy like in religious syncretism—Umbanda in Brazil, New Age in the United

States—what is sought is possession, fusion, the enjoyment of the other as a homogeneous and undifferentiated totality. And correlatively, what is denied are differential deviations, those intermediary spaces that are infinitely blurry and floating but which lead us to be attentive to what is going on at the margins and the edges. To incite us for example to try to think about the distinct that is not very distant (the encounter with Romania for an inhabitant of Western Europe), the distant which is not very distinct (the French for the the Québécois, the Québécois for the French, Argentines and people from southern Brazil for Europeans).

Sense Saturation. The Tricks of the Ideology of the Present, of Presence, and of Representation

The great ideal, or rather the great obstinacy, of our society is not only oversocialization, the nightmare of a life that becomes entirely social, but the ideology of being as presence: fullness, plenitude without any leftover, the saturation of all situations by words, sounds and images. Today any need must be absolutely met, any gap filled. As soon as something is seen or heard, it must absolutely have a meaning and be named. What this society and this moment find horrific is emptiness, absence, the vacant, vacuity, wandering, blundering, floating attention in which one looks at nothing in particular, like Monica Vitti in Antonioni's *Eclipse*. What is repugnant is the subject divided from himself, or at least who is no longer driven by the unbridled need to stick entirely to current events. It is thus the failure, the defection, the deficiency of presence, put differently the absence (of meaning) that, on the basis of events, or be it only incidents, is indeed apt to undo these fictions.

The semantic obstinacy at work in contemporary societies is of great brutality: it seeks obstinate mastery of everything (and everyone) and, in a strategy of domination, knowledge in an annexational mode, meaning at all cost in language's instrumentalization, that is to say of the subject in its historicity, which, as Henri Meschonnic (2002: 12) reminds us, "is not only situation but the undefined capacity to get out of it and to continue to act".

This pseudo-universality which passes itself off as reason but is in fact what Horkheimer and Adorno called "instrumental reason", is a dehistoricized universality, constructed for the satisfaction of seeing the machine idle away. It is a curious universality, or rather a curious manner of conceiving of the universal: neutral and dispassionate, capable of engendering a certain contemplative pleasure but remaining fairly indifferent to both the ethical and the political.

The language that is mobilized in the simulacrum of meaning, rigged, produced and reproduced in excess and aimed at functionality and the integration of the subject, attributes itself various roles. Clear denotation (*this is a cat*) to enunciate what is seen. Connotation (*this is a gray cat, always the same gray*) to carry out an over-enunciation, like added value, and to contribute to a sort of semantic stuffing of statements. This process is one of extreme linguistic violence: it feeds the illusion of solidarity between the seen and the heard, the perceived and the said. We expect the second term to reproduce reality not just fully but fanatically, in high fidelity, live. In this authoritarian imposition of what ought to be called a bluff but which takes the appearance of something natural, as though there were no other choice, everything fits together easily like in mechanics, everything flows perfectly in the liaisons of a settled writing, without a bump or gap.

This de-realizing fiction is one of a preestablished harmony between stimulus and sensation, emitter and receptor, a previously encoded message capable of being decoded, and totally decoded, a cause and an effect ... The purified and made-up ideality of "meaning" is credited with every quality and in particular transparence and reiteration. It retains but one dimension of sensible experience: the present of a clear percept, untroubled by affect and less still by decept,[1] hard and fast difference, never what elaborates itself in a deferred temporality.

This ideology is the ideology of representation, an empty notion but one which always affirms fullness. Representation repeats, reproduces, copies. In the word itself of representation is the term *presence*, which goes so much in the direction of the dominant current in our society, which mainly sees positives that it would suffice to spell out, presence in the raw state, but only with greater difficulty the movement that nevertheless makes for the richness, the charm, and also the strangeness of life in society, and not identity in the present and given once and for all sense, and which it would suffice to "represent". There isn't "meaning" to one side and prefabricated words responsible for "expressing" it to the other. There are but snippets of meaning that are like you and I: they appear, they disappear, they move constantly and are far from being "present" at all times. The ideology of representation[2] does nothing but enunciate, monotonously, presence and the present. It resolutely adopts a frontal, not lateral or oblique, view and never envisages, so to speak, that in our sensible experience of the real there might be things outside of meaning [*hors-sens*] the way they can be off-screen [*hors-champ*] in cinema, as we will see shortly. In this optic, in the literal sense of the term, there can be no place for critical thinking, of which one of the characteristics is to be unfashionable, or as Nietzsche says, "un-timely". Critical thinking, indeed, cannot be elaborated without negativity, that is to say, particularly, without resistance. This "philosophy of no" (Bachelard 1968/1940) cannot go in the direction of fashion. What it challenges, against the period and the society in which we live, is an unquestioned or insufficiently questioned anchoring in the present, which gives rise to an attitude of hypnotic adherence and even adhesion.

The Off-Screen[3]

Cinema—or rather cinematography, in the sense of Robert Bresson—which is a practice with great critical potential, is capable of awakening us from this torpor. To begin with, it teaches us that there is never a single preestablished frame, but a large number of possible frames, never a definitively closed (or open) system, but only the progressively closed and the progressively opened. Any framing arises from a choice, and what is shown on the rectangle of the screen can vary from the greatest saturation (of characters and sounds) to extreme rarefaction, like in the films of Ozu and Bresson himself. The frame may empty itself in order to focus attention on a single character, or face, even, like with Dreyer, part of a face. It can introduce heterogeneity and contradiction into the same shot through depth of field techniques, as is often the case with Orson Welles or Jean Renoir, or in Mizoguchi's *Ugetsu*: a primary scene takes place in the foreground while a secondary scene takes place in the background. Finally and above all, just as there is no frame without an effort to frame, deframe, reframe—which can be done, since the invention of portable motion-picture cameras, on ground level, from below, from above, from high to low, from low to high, laterally—there can be no camera shot without an off-screen.

And a large part of contemporary anthropology seems to me comparable to the very earliest days of cinema: it still favors a single, frontal point of view. Granted individuals move, but it is most often in the vacuum [*huis clos*][4] of a fixed and confined space. If everything is said and shown in the present of the shot, it is as though there were no off-screen, the absence of which has the effect, we shall see shortly, of eliminating time. What we call the cinematographic screen is but the visible part of a vaster space: filmic space, which is not limited only to the screen's frame. The off-screen is an invisible space that is in permanent relation with the visible surface of the screen. In cinema, indeed, characters (but also voices, sounds) are constantly entering and leaving the screen's field. Those that have not yet entered, like those that have already exited, exist nonetheless. And yet the spectator could not say with certainty where they are, whereas in theater, with some exceptions (Beckett), we know that they are waiting in the wings. That's what distinguishes the theatrical stage from the cinematographic screen; it is this relationship between the screen and the off-screen that in cinema creates dramatic intensity: what is acted out is not only acted out inside the frame, but in relation to the outside, the outside of the screen or the off-screen as outside.

It is the reason for which the spectator has but a partial view. He cannot know on the basis of what is shown to him (if the film is any good) what will happen. An important part of cinema's charm comes from this expectation, less of what will enter the screen than of what is engendered by the unexpected or at least strange encounter between a story that has begun to be told and an off-screen of which we know almost nothing. It is the unpredictable character of this encounter that provokes the spectator's perplexity and uncertainty, causes him to waver between several possible hypotheses. It is from off-screen that surprise appears suddenly, from the off-screen or perhaps the edge of the screen that, for example, a doorknob will start to turn. Fear, threat, horror, and all that constitutes the pleasure of suspense—especially developed in fantasy film, crime film, the cinema of the unexpected (Hitchcock, but also Bunuel), which play off this oscillation between what has begun to be shown and which still remains hidden (either to the spectators, or more rarely to the characters themselves who, in Hitchcock's cinema, know less than the spectators)—all mount off-screen.

The joy—but also the dread—that cinema provokes can be related to the game Freud called *Fort-Da*, which consists of a small child throwing a spool of thread, then making it return to him by pulling on the thread. In *Beyond the Pleasure Principle* (1953), Freud writes that the child "compensated himself for it [his mother's absence], so to speak, by *himself* re-enacting this same disappearance-reappearance scenario with whatever objects fell to hand" (Freud 1953: 14). Hitchcock, in an interview for the *Cahiers du cinéma*, offers this reflection: "take babies, for example. Mothers, to entertain them, hide themselves. The children cry, thinking themselves suddenly abandoned. Then the mothers reappear. The babies cry with joy! Spectators behave the same way" (Bazin 1954).

If the spectators, like babies, have their eyes fixed on the doorknob, it is also because the actors are also constantly looking outside the screen's frame. A film's characters, unlike television presenters, seem to be attracted by the strangeness of this outside: everything in these sideways glances and these voices that speak to interlocutors that find themselves on the side, but that we do not see, suggests that what is most important in cinema does not happen on the screen. Cinema does not stop at the screen's edges, unlike theater (even it was filmed theater). It operates at the edges, the fringes, the outer limits, the intermediary or transitional spaces, where sounds and images can enter and leave, gain or lessen, alternatively, in luminous and acoustic intensity—and not at boundaries which would act as a confinement. The frame of the cinematographic screen, contrary to that of a painting, paradoxically does not separate. It permits, on the contrary, permanent movement and exchange between the screen and the off-screen. The strangeness of cinematography comes from this encounter: not only sounds and images, in which we believe and which become for us, at least for the duration of the film, reality, but as the cinematographer Pascal Bonitzer writes (1999) "ghosts and voices that haunt and hallucinate the edges of the image".

It is in the off-screen (which is not reducible to either the wings of the theatrical stage, or to what is not said by characters in novelistic narratives) that processes take shape, but that we do not see, yet which will cause the event, however small it may be. It does not consist only of the entry into the scene (and not on stage) of new characters, but of characters already encountered who are no longer quite the same as at the moment when they left the screen's frame, and also the strange eruption of the past in the present, like in *Eternity and a Day* by Theo Angelopoulous.

The notion of off-screen appears very much operative in the domain of the social sciences. It contains potentialities for renewal that are extremely fertile for understanding the movements, of greater or lesser intensity, of which the life of the senses is constituted, and through it—a point to which we will return—social life. Contrary to syncretism, which seeks to fill up, to occupy all of space, to fill it so that no one is missing, the encounter between the on-screen and the off-screen creates a tension of mixing [*de métissage*], a movement of alternation between presence and absence, appearance and disappearance (of characters, voices, and images on the screen). It allows us to sense/think that which is not shown, is not illuminated but kept in reserve, does not allow itself to be perceived directly but only foreseen. Indeed, many of contemporary social science's theoretical difficulties come from the fact that they have mainly envisaged, until now, the almost always exclusively visible and present (and consequently capable of being appropriated) character of reality. Yet that which does not enter the visual field in the present moment, everything which is outside the frame, does not cease to exist: the present of the screen refers to an absence, but also creates forgetfulness, in the fissures of which a memory takes form.

A large part of what comes into play in our perceptions and sensations, like in cinema, is on hold and comes from elsewhere. The off-screen is what does not allow itself to be seen, what momentarily hides itself, but it is also the virtual. It is not exactly that which keeps itself off-screen, but the outside that does not stay in place, that does not stop moving between the light (of the screen) and the darkness of what is not strictly speaking a place. This outside of the screen, this other of the screen, this other of space is in fact time in motion. And this time in motion is still largely the social sciences's *terra icognita*.

Apprehending the Sensible: To Take, to Detach Oneself, to be Surprised

The social sciences have achieved considerable progress in making the shift from thinking about substance (*what is it?*) to thinking about relation (*what unites us and separates us?*). The latter is nevertheless often conceived in a differentialist manner as a relation of identification or opposition, of convergence or divergence, of affinity or repulsion, of alliance or hostility between two preexisting poles, that is to say already constituted units of meaning. We do not really escape the dominant paradigm—the discontinuity of signs or the recollection of symbols—through alterations of what has been previously hardened, rigidified, and definitionally fixed in semantic categories that we hold to be clearly determined: the same and the other, the indigenous and the foreigner, the "inside" and the "outside" as though the "inside" were primary data that could not be worked on and more exactly dug into (in the German sense of *graben*) from "outside".

Let us begin by noting that in the process of dividing the real into categories, designations or assignments are necessarily made from a center. And that, even in establishing relations between terms distinguished beforehand, at the end we find only what had been possible in the beginning. "Traditional philosophy", writes Adorno (2001: 149), "imagined it could recognize the unlike by making it like itself, but in so doing it only recognizes itself". But relational thinking—evoked here insofar as it has not yet sufficiently freed itself of substantive thinking—invites a still more radical critique, which we have but outlined. There is often something mineral, something rigid, stiff, motionless in the manner of conceiving the terms between which exchanges are supposed to take place. These terms are signs, only signs, endowed with the features of purity, unequivocalness and stability. To speak of type, system, structure, and even culture when the latter is the result of an immobile cross-section constituting a discontinuous unit, exaggerations are required. Exaggerations that analyze the social and the political solely in the major mode of solidity, generality, and regularity. It is through this attitude that the social sciences in their beginnings maintained a predilection for the heavy and the compact: Comte's three stages, Marx's social classes, Tönnies's community and society, "the crowd" of Tarde and Le Bon . . . This approach to the social, characterized above as Balzacian, never proposes to understand the singularity of each social relation.

Now, it is possible to envisage that which is opposed or connected—and which is thus also susceptible to disconnecting itself—other than in terms of relations between preexisting groups and a fortiori between preexisting "traits", "elements", or "components" forming a totality. Other, also, than in terms of "place" and "position". The questions often posed today— "where do you locate yourself?", "what is your relationship to . . .?", "what is your position on this subject?"—are akin to injunctions to situate oneself spatially. Not that it is unnecessary to "take a position" within social relations that are indeed made of oppositions, struggles, and in particular class struggles. But it is also necessary to be attentive to that which derives not only from spatial configurations, arrangements (of the places of various individuals in a whole), structuration within a "field", as well as intersections, but from growth, maturation, and decline.

And to give an account of this dimension of life in society, it is not sufficient to tone down, attenuate, dilute (like in what we normally and lazily call "métissage", which is often but syncretism or eclecticism), to ease or else to soften, dampen, relax and fluidify that which had previously been solidified or rigidified. There exist other choices than the one consisting of accentuating or on the contrary toning down, which are in fact two manners of exaggerating, polishing, policing, making roughness and irregularity disappear. We cannot come to a compromise with the hardened thinking of the exclusivity of signs, especially today when everything or almost everything can increasingly, and unreasonably, be bought and above all measured (in square kilometers, demographic density, gross domestic product, interest rates or audience ratings). In this process, our epoch alternatively favors addition, multiplication, subtraction, that is to say the logic of numbers in which the complexities of conduct reduced to behaviors can be deciphered. This logic, which is accompanied by the elimination but also, more perniciously, the control of useless fractions (dreaming, imagining, creating), is that of exchanged signs, with winners and losers. It makes good bedfellows with the logic of capitalism. Indeed nothing in the unequivocal character of semantic categories carved into the real opposes the law of the market. Objects and subjects alike, or rather subjects that have become objects, treated like merchandise and now producing nothing but goods, even where they are immaterial and "cultural", can be subjected to the utilitarian demands of liberal commerce. They can become a conscriptable labor force and prey for prostitution rings.

This process of reification—of which one of the salient features is what Simmel referred to in his time as a "tragedy of culture"—invites an analysis that is not only economic, but epistemological, political and aesthetic (in the Greek sense of *aisthésis* which designates the study of the sensible). Such analysis must question the idea that there exist, ontologically and chronologically, poles (be it only, as is increasingly the case today, ends or fragments), and that movement allowing for shifting between them should arise accessorily, afterwards. That is however how relations between the individual and the social (the collective), or what we continue to call "objectivity" and "subjectivity", often continue to be conceived of, as though the subject were not made of others. Each time we postulate a preexistence of semantic units we cannot envisage thinking of duration other than as a path from one space to another, that is to say as a predetermined journey.

It is entirely possible not only to envisage but to analyze social life in a very different manner. There exists in particular, as we began to see in the preceding chapter, a theory of the social ahead of its time, elaborated, or better still composed, when sociology had not yet affirmed itself as an autonomous university discipline. It is a theory in which the relations between groups, far from being weighed down by social origins, on the contrary ceaselessly move. At the same time Durkheim was elaborating the notion of social *anomie*, Proust, by multiplying the perspectives, introduced relativity and dynamism into the understanding of social relations between the dominant classes. *In Search of Lost Time* is not only one of the greatest works of literature, it is a social history, of France from the 1880s to the 1920s.

The work of Proust the social analyst is the very opposite of a narrative of social origins. What he shows through the study of the respective positions of individuals, which evolve so considerably over forty years as to give rise to veritable processes of permutation, is the instability—sometimes even blurring—of social bearings, what he shows is the destruction of coherent wholes. What he shows us, more precisely, is the ephemeral character of power, the decline of the Parisian aristocracy that in his youth the narrator thought as durable as stone, whereas now "a thousand foreign bodies penetrated it, depriving it of all homogeneity", and above all, through the collusion between two worlds, it is the ascension of the bourgeoisie, which is no longer strictly identical to what it had been. Everything that has just been said however remains very insufficient, since it does not account for the artists—Vinteuil, Bergotte, Elstir—who inspire the narrator's quest. It does not account above all for Albertine's impromptu arrival in the novel, which adds further uncertainty and turbulence to the text and opens an unprecedented social space which, unlike the others, is weighed down by no past. The elusive and unpredictable *petite-bourgeoise* moves between the different *milieux*. She puts on a third culture, less confined, that comes neither from the muffled, even airtight universe of the *salons*, nor the provincial one (Combray): a resolutely new culture for that time, with yet unfixed contours, the seaside culture symbolized by Balbec. It is in the sociality of the beaches that the young libertarian, or at least libertine heroine emerges, then evolves. She contributes, through her strange mobility, to further developing the Proustian social vision, which is not one of class struggle, but struggle over classification.

In order for what has been stabilized and subjected to a regime of virtual glaciation to come back to life, it is necessary to show availability and even hospitality (cf. Derrida 2000) and above all attentiveness: what Alfred Schutz (1999: 10 and 115) calls "attentiveness to life" and more specifically to the "world of daily life". Granted, a part of the social sciences is well aware of this, but often it does not look and does not listen enough. And, not listening enough, it does not hear the rhythmic character of living things. This is not intellectual ineptitude but, on the contrary, lack of sensory appetite.

It seems indispensable to begin with ethnographic description, which is the method of the infinitely small, of attention to small details and details of details, the minute variations for example in the manner in which people prepare meals, meet, touch, avoid one another—which requires not only acuity of sight, but an awakening of all the senses. In order to do so, what is needed is not so much to illuminate as to lighten by disengaging our perceptions from a rhetorical sheath of comments, glosses, and paraphrases. In this type of observation, it is not so much the result that must preoccupy us, but the process, the outline, the act, the energy of outlining that consists of scratching out, making mistakes, hesitating, and not fixing, stabilizing, marking (today we speak of "identity markers"), decoding, indexing. This is the reason for attempting, whenever it is possible, to use gerundive verbal constructions and to abandon the genitive constructions (the students *of* the professor) characteristic of the logic of capitalism.

What I favor is not grasping, seizing, accepting, but rather detaching, defamiliarizing, surprising, not resisting, being astonished. What Husserl calls *épochè*, that suspension (and not negation) of judgment. It is an attitude that does not consist of affirming or denying, but of doubting, questioning, distrusting, in particular the routine of syntactic linkages in irreproachable grammaticality. To suspend and surprise is to apprehend things differently, it is to move, to destabilize, to decenter, to make problematic, especially the relations between subject and object.

This attitude in which there is *suspense* and surprise, and which introduces doubt and uncertainty into the semantic machine, does not seek a frontal and performative delegitimization (or, in other words, a trial) of knowledge that classifies in a notarial fashion, that orders, organizes by scrupulously separating reason and emotion, and believes it arrives at certain and irreversible conclusions. It shows, more modestly, that there is legitimacy in waiting, that there subsists a gap between what is seen and what is said or written, between seeing, believing, knowing, believing one knows, making seen, making believe. Like in Eric Rohmer films, something escapes us. We are rarely confronted with raw facts but rather with events, however small they may be, which call for narratives, that is to say interpretations. Like in Orson Welles's *Citizen Kane*, the ethnographer does not know part of the facts. And he therefore must search for what he still does not know: not only what is said, affirmed, shown, but also what is silenced, denied, hidden—or is simply *elsewhere*.

Such an approach must be carried out without precipitation, which supposes that we accept having to often stop, or at least slow down, before explanatory or interpretive excess (of links regarded as settled) is reestablished. It is thus possible to advance in the activity of knowledge without finding oneself subject to the canonical oppositions of the inside and the outside, of subjectivity and objectivity ... It is not a matter, strictly speaking, of abolishing these oppositions, but rather of cracking them, splitting them— and certainly not of melting them in an illusory synthetic or dialectic manner. To split these categories is to suspend them (provisionally), and to catch them out, not in lack but rather in excess, in explanatory and resolutive overabundance. What is not exactly a weakening but rather a vacillation begins to take place when we relinquish the emphasis on "meaning" (given, lost, found again) in favor of the fact that there exist today but fragments of meaning that begin to appear, withdraw, sketch themselves out, then slip away in scratches and stutters more than outright silence.

What is needed is not to performatively overturn, but to blur, giving experimentation back its full place. What is often called deconstructing consists of taking apart by questioning the stability of relations between object and subject, the distance between observer and observed, while the boundaries (in particular of exclusion) are far from being cracked. What Roland Barthes calls "designifying" and François Jullien, about Chinese painting, calls "depicting" [*dépeindre*], "unrepresenting" [*dér'eprésenter*] and "de-ontologizing" consist of disrupting the fiction of a state where no event can burst in (Jullien 2009).

The "exit" from categorizing and classificatory thinking cannot be an exit from language towards a complacent "unspeakable". Although we owe it to ourselves to refuse certain language that is compliant, finite, controlled, that imposes, but in which complexity is eliminated, it is only through language that we can succeed, not in attacking this language, exactly, but in showing its simultaneously imprecise and insignificant character. Our effort must be focused on words, of which no two are equivalent—and we should be sad about a certain forgetting, in the present, of the playful and humorous alliterations, anagrams, spoonerisms, portmanteau words and other games invented particularly by the surrealists, which contribute to subverting the order of serious discourse. But above all on the sentence, its construction, its momentum. The sentence can behave differently than an arrow aimed at a target and hitting it. The flow of the sentence, its intensity (of writing, of reading), allows, by stretching and specifying, for nuancing the rigidity of reasoning that is in appearances perfect. It may also, by interrupting itself at a moment when we do not expect it, produce jolts, or at least tremors. The search for a logic other than of conventions takes place first in a syntax (of oxymoron, contradiction, included middle, ellipsis, parataxis) that is suspicious of all that tends to fix in place (*paradigm*), and gives back its full place to the life of associations that are in the process of taking place (*syntagma*) or being undone in stories and narratives.

The logic of subdivision tends above all to lead us to think only of relations between a limited number of finite products. It retains but a part (and not the most interesting one) of the social: *ergon* (work) rather than *energeia* (process), play in the sense of the English word *game* (configuration and reconfiguration of signs) rather than in the sense of *play* explored by Roger Caillois, which designates an interpretation that is a transformation in time.

What characterizes time is its irregularity: the past and the future (which exist only in the present) are not symmetrical and, what's more, cannot be outrightly separated, though they are not capable of being connected in a synthesis either. Difficult though it is to comprehend, this logic, which is neither of radical disjuncture nor voracious conjuncture, exists none the less. We encounter it in what Primo Levi (2000) refers to as the "gray zone", an improbable place, but one that is scandalously real, where in the time of the camps, the clear distinction between victims and torturers disappears. It is at work in Marrano thought (Cervantes, Montaigne, Spinoza), in what Gilles Deleuze (Deleuze and Parnett 1977) refers to as a "disjunctive conjunction", Homi Bhabha (1994) as a "third space", Florence Dupont (2002: 41–54) the "included alterity" and what we proposed with Alain Nouss to theorize under the term *métissage* (Laplantine and Nouss 2001).

To analyze these notions—which are echoed in what Henri Meschonnic calls rhythm, in what François Jullien, following Chinese thinking, calls breathing—we cannot remain within the Greek, then Scholastic, then Cartesian logic of separation, yet we cannot yield to the idea of fusion through indistinctness and indifference. What is stimulating to thought today is studying intermediary and cascading states: not dark and clearly contrasting colors, but rather the pale, the pastel, the faded, the blurry, the drab, the gloomy. No longer the generality and regularity of settled, arrived, foreclosed "meaning", ready to be "grasped" and explained, but singularity, irregularity, disparity as well as the lone character of a significance (and not a signification) in movement. This singularity cannot be that of objects, but must rather be that of subjects, such as the names of families (Swann, Guermantes, Verdurin . . .), the names of people (Odette, Gilberte, Marcel, Albertine . . .) and the names of places (Balbec, Combray . . .) that resonate throughout the *Search*.

Yet the singularity of the sensible continues to be no less conceived of by scientific rationality in the manner of Aristotle, as that which slows, delays, handicaps access to the intelligible. It is either rejected, pushed back, forgotten or, inversely, absorbed. In this perspective, there can only exist cleavages (between, for example, absence and presence), never continuous modifications, even though these attest to the fact that the people we study and we ourselves are still alive. We confine ourselves primarily to distinctive traits and not processes of erosion, maturation, withdrawal. Everything takes place as though there were only alternatives: empty *or* full, written *or* oral, language [*langue*] *or* speech [*parole*], the *logos* of Plato's world of ideas or the *pseudos* of the unknowing inhabitants of the cave, being *or* non-being, though this last question, it is true, is outmoded in the present day when what counts much more is to have *or* not to have. Yet what forms in the movement of the *between* and the *in-between* exists no less. Between the true and the false, reality and fiction or lies, are appearances, false appearances, semblances of truth.

The significations of what we are searching for rarely appear (or show through, and sometimes even disappear) in discontinuous, definite and determined content (the generalizing character of the concept), but rather in the always changing manners of signifying (the rhythm of the sentence—less in fact the rhythm of the phrase as the retelling, with a different tonality, of what appears to have already been outlined: thus, the preceding paragraph, which a purist would describe as "repetitive", is deliberate). They can appear only in a differentiated temporality that moves like a melody, rising and falling. They form in the continuous movement of crescendo and decrescendo, in fast-forward and slow-motion more than on-off. These movements are also movements of contraction and expansion of that which grows, thickens, shrinks, spreads, lengthens, gains (blushes) and loses (blanches) in alternation (and not the alternative) between colors.

Passages, Smugglers, Precursors

At this point in our itinerary, two questions present themselves. Does it fall to anthropological rationality to think through these imperceptible gradations, and not rather to art? Are there not cultures or time periods that are more subtle and more sensible? The China about which François Jullien speaks? The Japan that Barthes, in *Empire of Signs*, is conscious of having partly reinvented?

I will direct my attention to the second question first. It seems to push us toward a search for "de-Westernization", which indeed was the attitude favored by Roland Barthes, who invited readers to "leave the Western enclosure". This is also the temptation of culturalism, which considers the difference between "East" and "West", Europe and Africa, Amerindians and other Americans to be irreducible. It often affirms not only that there exists an absolute alterity, but that the Orient (for example) allows for detaching oneself from the West or at least correcting its didactic tendency toward the explicit. The Orient is then a sort of inverted West. Asia (or Africa) becomes a place overflowing with meanings and beauty that calls for being considered in itself, either *against* Europe, or *without* Europe. Under these conditions, the elsewhere (or the other time) is hypostatized into an absolute and self-sufficient source of "meaning".

We must beware such easy anti-ethnocentrism, which assigns a role of absolute alterity to societies different from those in which we are born, and of which one effect is the mystification of signs (alternatively positive or negative when we speak of the Orient, Indianness, Latinity). This alterity is not absolute. It cannot be envisaged as the unthought-of that would allow, for example, in the manner of Warburg (2003), to speak an emptiness, an absence, a nuance unknown in the observer's society.

The first question, which would call for a longer development, far from taking us away from our initial inquiry, brings us back to it. The extremely tenacious system of authority in which what we call knowledge [*savoir*] is the measure of all forms of understanding [*connaissance*], language is the vehicle of thought, art is one of its ornaments, science is the norm, literature the margin (and within literature, poetry the margin of the margin), could lead us to renounce the whole culture in which it is inscribed and claims its place. But it is within this same culture that we can also perceive what Deleuze calls a "tiny little heterogeneous line", urging us to first be modest. It is a Russian novelist, Turgenev, who whispers in our ear: "My business is to paint horse thieves, not to recall that it is bad to steal horses. That is the business of magistrates". It is a North American author, Melville, who writes in *Moby Dick* about Captain Ahab that he should be thought of not as a gospel but a panorama. It is one of the most European writers, Kafka, who notes in his *Journal*: "I do not want men judging one another . . . even with you, Eminent Gentlemen of the Academy, I have contented myself to relate" (Kafka 1972).

It should first be recalled that the civilizational area that takes form in Europe—the name of a young Phoenician girl found and kidnapped by Zeus on a beach of Asia Minor, and a word that for the Ancient Greeks evoked a space outside of Greece—has nothing monolithic about it. It is made of tendencies, of currents and counter-currents that cannot be reduced to the alternative of rationalism and irrationalism any more than to that of dualism and monism.

Although a whole part of Greek culture, transmitted through Cartesianism beginning in the seventeenth century, constitutes an epistemological obstacle to comprehending sensible thinking, which is a thinking of the language-body in movement, many authors may on the contrary help in constructing mediations.

It is in the horizon traced by Ferdinand de Saussure (1857–1913) then by Émile Benveniste (1907–1976) that a demanding thought process no longer of category, but of energy, life, and in particular life of language may be constructed. Many misinterpretations (for which Bailly and Sechehaye, who transcribed the *Cours de linguistique générale*, are principally responsible) have been imposed on Saussure's work. It has been treated simplistically. It has been read through Lévi-Strauss and Chomsky. It has been made the uncontested precursor of formal linguistics and structuralism in anthropology. What has above all been retained from his research is the invention of oppositions now famous in the social sciences (*langue* and *parole*, synchrony and diachrony), when in fact it consists of something entirely different: the exploration of two levels of understanding of language that are by no means mutually exclusive. Beyond the poles that were hardened by phonology, which undertook the task of breaking down vocal continuity into distinctive units (phonemes), it is necessary to reexamine the radical novelty of Saussure's approach, in which *langage* cannot be considered an object since it is "form, not substance", *langue* (which can give rise to an analysis in terms of a system), but also speech [*parole*], that is to say movement and history.

It is in this perspective that Benveniste's research may be regarded as a considerable contribution to reflection on language [*langage*]. The author of *Problems in General Linguistics* radically shifted the discipline, from the study of the word to that of the sentence. He shows that "a sentence constitutes a whole which is not reducible to the sum of its parts" (1971: 105). With the sentence, he believes, "we enter into another universe" (1971: 110). "The sentence is the unit of discourse" (110). "The sentence, an undefined creation of limitless variety, is the very life of human speech in action" (110). It is the act of the subject engaged in a temporal and historic process of enunciations [*énonciations*], which the author distinguishes from mere statements [*énoncés*].

The not only linguistic [*linguistique*] but phraseological [*langagière*] approach of Saussure and Benveniste is rich not only in epistemological consequences but also ethical and political ones, which is also the case when we adopt a Spinozian (and no longer Cartesian) conception-perception of the human being in his or her intelligence and affects, and society in its dynamism. The links that begin progressively to weave themselves between the sensible and the social require the reintroduction of temporality and historicity into thought. I will turn now to the notions of rhythm, intensity, modulation (and no longer of separation), of resonance (and not only of reasoning), of tonality (and not of totality). This approach can be refined through a rereading of a certain number of authors whom I believe were significantly ahead of their time: first Spinoza and Rousseau, then Georges Bataille and Roger Bastide. But it is first necessary to examine the notion itself of sensibility, along with the neighboring notions of life and energy.

5

The Sensible, the Social, Category and Energy

The term *sensible* is a polysemic term lending itself to confusion; it has at least five meanings.[1]

1   A media-centered meaning almost always used to designate "sensitive neighborhoods" and the "the youth of the *banlieues*".[2] We obviously will not make use of this stigmatizing connotation.

2   To mean attentiveness, listening, an attitude of hospitality as in the expression "to be sensitive to".

3   The crossing of a threshold, like when we speak of a perceptible change (for example in temperature).

4   Fragility or vulnerability: a "sensitive person".

5   Finally, the term is used to designate the life of the senses: the relations that we entertain with the three families of sounds (voice, noise, and music, which is organized sound), with odors, tastes, and visual and tactile sensations. It is this latter meaning that we shall retain.

Reflection on the different meanings of the sensible oscillates between rationalism's violence and empiricism's platitudes. A rationalist (or intellectualist) attitude, without denying that there exist data from sensory experience, is preoccupied essentially with what organizes them: what Kant calls the "a priori forms of sensibility" and the "categories of understanding". What is given priority is the rational order that discerns an intelligibility hidden behind the apparent disorder of sensations and emotions. Everything takes place as though rationalism were called upon to judge and subordinate amidst the polysemy of the word *sense* [*sens*], which designates at once the sensible and the sensical, sensation and signification. What Montaigne called the "undulating and diverse" universe of sensibility is not only organized, but risks being neutralized, even discredited. In short, there is clearly, in one of the traditions of European thought (and only in this tradition, which is found in no other society), a conflict—supposed to be resolved through a hierarchization—between the multiplicity of the sensible and the universality of the intelligible, between the body and thought, and in particular between social and political thought.

Empiricism (or sensualism), for its part, aims to limit itself to the immediate certainties of what we perceive: images, sounds, odors, tastes, colors. There exists in this perspective an obviousness to the sensible, or more exactly an impression of obviousness, which is that of a presence in the world, to oneself and to others. This impression of obviousness merges with the feeling of being *alive*. It is an ordinary experience of everyday life. But of this experience there is little to say, so irrefutable does it seem, or rather little to say scientifically.

The revelation of the real by way of an improbable morning freshness is always in fact a psychologically, socially and culturally constructed experience. It can therefore be "deconstructed", which is to say not destroyed, but displaced by the work of the language, or re-scripted by that of cinema.

This chapter proposes to sketch a confrontation between thinking about sensible life and thinking about social life. This confrontation is often truncated for two opposing reasons: either we consider that there are only two possible models, two models that are completely foreign to one another. Let us call them psychophysiology and sociology. Or, on the contrary, we arrive, but in an untheoretical or insufficiently theoretical manner, at an illusory reconciliation between the two horizons of knowledge.

To engage in this confrontation, it is first necessary to agree on words and in particular on the word *life*, an "all purpose word", as Barthes noted in 1978 (2008: 47). For the sake of clarity, a certain number of distinctions shall be made: life [*la vie*] and the living [*le vivant*], the living [*le vivant*] and the lived [*le vécu*], experimentation and experience, category and energy.

The Ancient Greeks had not one but two terms for designating life: *zoè* and *bios*. *Zoè* signifies the fact of living that is common to all living beings: plants, animals, humans, but also gods. *Bios*, for its part, aims to define manners of living, modes of life, forms and in particular forms of social life. *Zoè* is a notion that is much more unitary and also much more universal than *bios*, which designates the living [*le vivant*], but through the living, living beings [*les vivants*]. *Bios*, it seems to me, more than *zoè*, introduces the multiple and the diverse into the idea of life.

A second distinction apt to help us is provided this time by the German language, which differentiates *das Leben* and *das Erleben*. *Das Leben* means life, but life without consciousness: animals live, but do not think about what they live through, at least so we suppose. *Das Erleben* is used, for its part, to designate the *lived* [*le vécu*], that is to say, in Dilthey's (1991) expression, "life that grasps life", which is capable not only of thinking about it, but of experiencing as opposed to *comprehending* it. Comprehension, according to the author of the *Introduction to the Human Sciences*, does not listen to life, but turns away from energy in favour of category.

It is this last distinction that will now, and at much greater length, retain our attention. The categorizing thought process—in which terms anthropology took shape—differentiates plant life, animal life, and human life. It proceeds to divide up the "kingdoms", and, in the animal kingdom, distinguishes mammals, birds, fish and reptiles, which does not, let us recall, fail to raise the question of the ostriches that, from the beginning of European classificatory systems, have always resisted entry into a single one of the categories.

Life and Category

The merits of category thinking need not be demonstrated. It has allowed us to situate and orient ourselves in the study of the living. However, it does not allow us to account for organic life in the sense of the definition given by Bichat in his *General Anatomy Applied to Physiology and Medicine* (1800). The more we move toward that which is not (or not exclusively) organic, toward psychological life and social life, the more the boundaries are mobile, or in other words, living.

In order to understand the meaning and limits of category thinking when it is confronted with the energy of life, it is helpful to return to Aristotle's first treatise on logic, the *Organon*, in which the category is defined. We are in the presence of a device for the determination, distinction, and distribution of all existing things into separate classes, endowed with what the philosopher calls "pure attributes". The category—in fact, the process of categorization—is a simultaneously logical, ontological, and linguistic process that consists of saying something about someone or something in a manner that attributes properties. It is a process that is eminently tributary of language (in this case, of the Greek language). It tells us as much about the language of the person who engages in these operations as it does about the objects he seeks to designate. And, through language, it is tributary of the Greek metaphysics of being in its permanence, that is, the logic of identity and the excluded middle.

Thus the first of the ten categories defined by Aristotle is essence (*ousia*), excluding a priori any change, event, accident, or even just an incident, capable of disturbing it. This first category, foundational so to speak of the nine others, is subject to an in-depth treatment, later deepened even further in the *Metaphysics* (which in the strict sense means *after physics*). The ninth and the tenth categories on the other hand—respectively called *acting* and *suffering*, which necessarily pose the question of the living, that is, of what grows, ripens, perishes—do not have, in the eyes of the author of the *Organon*, the same legitimacy.

Aristotle postulates that, contrary to an intuitive approach, a discursive approach (*dianoia*), characteristic of science, knows and thinks by reaching "a state of rest and com[ing] to a standstill" (*Physics*, VII, 3). This Aristotelian notion of "stabilization" of movement and, as a consequence, of the living, is at the heart of the *Physics*, and of the treatise *De Anima*. The author (and, basing itself on him, much of medieval thought, both Arab and Latin) establishes a necessary connection between the precise knowledge of science (*épistémè*) and the act of stopping or stopping oneself (*sténai*). Through categories that are what the scholastic philosophers call "universal", life is grasped, as Aristotle writes, "at rest". The question that under these conditions does not fail to arise is that of the legitimacy of the relationship between the process and the particularity of its object. Can precise and rigorous knowledge fix its object in categories when this object (the living) itself has no fixity, but is evolution, transformation, variation?

The language-universe of the category, insofar as it carries out a stabilization of the living [*le vivant*], and *a fortiori* the lived [*le vécu*], appears refractory towards this question. Finite, definite, definitive, it distributes all that exists into unbreakable physical, biological, psychological, but also chromatic and musical categories. To put things differently, the time, the tempo, the tension of the rhythm that begins with breathing, that drive of human and animal life, are not conceivable in the categorizing and classificatory thinking of signs, signs alone. For this thinking, there can only ever be a drawing of an ensemble of traits characteristic of a class, a family, a genre, a species, never processes of withdrawing. We cannot conceive and first of all perceive that which is formed, deformed, and transformed in between appearance and disappearance, presence and absence, opacity and transparence, darkness and light, solid and liquid, the contracted and the dilated, the calm and the cruel, acting and suffering, genius and idiocy, dementia and coma.

Category thinking eschews that which is formed in crossings, transitions, unstable and ephemeral movements of oscillation. It opts, in a drastic manner, for the fixity of time, movement and the multiple, and it opposes, in so doing, the tension of the between and the in-between. Yet, these exist. Between presence and absence, there is melancholy and its Lusitanian inflection that bears the name *saudade*. Between darkness and light, there is the *chiaroscuro*. Between the retracted and the rolled out, there is the movement of loosening. Between wakefulness and dreaming, there is dreaminess. Between the expected and the unforeseen, the suspected. Between trust and mistrust, slight doubt. Between the certainty of that which is named and designated (the definition) and refusal to speak is that which can be suggested (Mallarmé) or shown (Wittgenstein). Between life and death, there is the spectral: ghosts, or as they say in Haiti, Zombies, revenants as well as survivors.

Although a whole part of Greek culture, transmitted beginning in the seventeenth century by Cartesianism (in particular with the invention by Descartes of the "body-machine" which becomes La Mettrie's "human-machine" in 1748), constitutes in my view an epistemological obstacle to the comprehension of the living in its temporality, many authors nevertheless belonging to the same civilizational area may come to our aid. Two among them shall particularly retain our attention: Spinoza and Rousseau, who are veritable precursors of an anthropology of *life* and the living, two terms which imply a third: the *vital*—on the basis of which will be posed the question of what is alive and what is essential, that is, the question of *values*—and even a fourth: the *social*.

But before examining the contribution—significant for our purposes—of Spinoza and Rousseau's reflection to the elaboration of this anthropology, it is necessary to recall that the "moderns" are not the only ones to have opened a dynamic perspective in philosophic and scientific thought: the pre-Socratics, initially, had contemplated it.

The Rhythmic Character of the Living

Several pre-Socratic philosophers who, long before Aristotle, paid extremely close attention to the life of natural phenomena, have the merit of having introduced the notion of rhythmicity into knowledge of the universe. Rhythm (*rhutmos*), as it was understood in particular by Heraclitus, then combatted by Plato, is form (*morphè*) as it is transformed by time, that is to say the work of uninterrupted movement. For the Ionian philosopher, nothing is stable, "everything passes" (*panta rhei*, from the verb *rhéo*, meaning to flow, from which was formed the term *rhythm*). To live is to become or rather to return, since the primary element, fire, transforms itself into air, which itself becomes a humid element before returning to fire. Rhythm, in its phosphorescence but also its fluidity and plasticity, involves the question of the relationship to the sensible (*aisthésis*), that is to say that which in part escapes the intelligibility (*noésis*) of reason.

Those are the terms of one of the major debates that runs through Ancient Greek thought, in which the Ionian and Heraclitean conception, which is that of change (*métabolè*), opposes the Attic and Platonian conception, which aims, in order to understand it, to stabilize change in a suprasensible form that belongs to the *order* of reason (*logos*). In this debate, several pre-Socratic philosophers, far from espousing the Parmenidean conception of being that has always existed and will always exist in the same way,[3] introduced a two-part distinction: that of rhythm (*rhuthmos*) and of pattern (*skhêma*), that of movement as *kinésis* and movement as *métabolè*.

Democritus opposes rhythm and pattern. Whereas pattern is the result of a mental operation aimed at fixing the trajectory of atoms, at subtracting them from their movement in a fixed configuration, rhythm is a process. The former gives rise to shapes, but the second is prone to transforming them.

The pre-Socratics therefore had two terms for designating movement: *kinèsis* and *métabolè*. They used *kinèsis* to define the journey or the trajectory between two extremities in space, and were conscious of giving an account, in this way, of but one part of the experience of time and life. *Kinèsis* is a mere motor movement that does not profoundly modify the person who follows a route. Thus, we can arrive (almost) identical to what we were, from one point to another. Transformation (*métabolè*) is something else. It is not attributable to a location. It is a process through which all that lives becomes other than what it was.

The difficulty created by Plato, a philosopher of the subject envisaged in particular in its movement of rising up toward the world of suprasensible "ideas", that is to say the conversion toward the "above",[4] and no longer a pre-Socratic thinker of the "below" (for example of geologic vibrations and maritime fluctuations), comes from the presupposition that leads to devaluing what lives, and consequently what transforms itself (*métabolè*). The author of the *Phaedo* only envisages movement (*kinèsis*). And he envisages it only based on order (*taxis*), just as he conceives of form (*morphè*) only as it is formatted by essence (*ousia*). Form, in its aptitude to transform itself, thus finds itself essentialized. He does accept the existence of rhythm, but only to the extent that it submits itself precisely to measurement (*métron*). To Heraclitean mobility, the Athenian philosopher opposes the stability of determination and delimitation, and, in so doing, he paves the way for the search for recurrences, regularities, periodicities, and laws. Proceeding to stabilize rhythmicity in the Ionian sense, he substitutes for it the measurement of movement (*métron kinèseos*), its reabsorption into a metric order, and the determination of proper proportions (*rhusmos*), which must organize the equilibrium of both the psychic order and the order of the city. Thus does the rhythm of the living become passive. It is objectified and analyzed in the framework of fixed forms (*skhêma*), and ultimately denied since, Plato believes, far from everything is in movement. Above movement and the living there is reason (*logos*), which is another name to designate being. This *logos*, and it alone, has the aptitude so say all this, to account for, to be right.

This debate reveals that one trend in Ancient Greek philosophy furnishes a certain number of tools for thinking about the living in its rhythmic process, whereas another trend resolutely opposes it, as Platonically inspired philosophy does up to the present day, maintaining an arrhythmic understanding of the world. Although a large number of pre-Socratic philosophers principally thought about eurythmy, in other words the right rhythm (a conception that would be taken up in the twentieth century in Rudolf Steiner's theosophy), and in no way envisaged that there could be conflict, discordance, and dissonance, their contribution to the construction of a theory of the living is nevertheless decisive. It is a thinking about that which forms, deforms, and transforms itself, and it calls, consequently, for a mode of knowledge that is one of becoming. In this mode of knowledge, movements of flexion, of curving, of turning (*tròpe*) are more relevant than either a firm affirmative or negative position (*thésis*), or the reference to a foundation with which Ancient Greece is very often credited.

From Category to Mode: Spinoza, or Life as Intensity

With Spinoza we enter a whole other horizon of knowledge—that of classic rationalism—and we shall see how the question of life and the living are radically reactivated. Spinoza (1632–1677), let us first recall, is no less of a rationalist than Descartes. He is even, as the latter's (unfaithful) disciple, an uncompromising rationalist who constructs his thought on the basis of logical sequences (*concatenatio*). But he elaborates a thinking about life that is inseparable from language. Whereas Cartesian thinking, which is still dominant today and was, from the beginning, a conquering form of thinking, separates body and soul, concept and affect, and cuts out categories that will have the effect of constituting disciplinary and subdisciplinary fields, Spinoza, in the height of the classical century, elaborated a thinking of continuity where affection, reflection, language, theory of knowledge, ethics and politics can no longer be envisaged as distinct fields. To understand what this thinking can bring to the questions we debate today in the difficult task of constituting an anthropology of the body and the emotions, it needs to be examined as a critique of Cartesianism, or at least orthodox Cartesianism.

Cartesianism's force and richness is to have liberated knowledge from occultism. But its other side is to have created two universes closed to one another: the body, incapable of thinking, the mind (which Descartes calls the "soul"), incapable of feeling. What characterizes the former is exclusively "extension", spatiality, mass (answerable to a measurement process), whereas the mind is purely intellectual but also spiritual since, let us not forget, in Cartesianism it is God who holds the whole edifice up.

It is this epistemology of purity and disjunction (of a passive body without any relationship to thought, and of an active but immaterial thought, one that does not mix with affectivity), that creates the impossibility or at least the difficulty that is still often ours today, of perceiving a continuity between the different dimensions of the living: organic life (reduced in Descartes to the mechanical), psychological life, life in society.

Spinoza is the first to combat—but using rationalism's method—this dualist, intellectualist, and idealist (in the precise philosophic meaning of the term) conception of the human being. The human being is for him what he calls *conatus*, in other words desire, movement, energy, involving the whole of intelligence and sensibility. The *conatus* moves "all the efforts, impulses, appetites, and volitions" (2001: 147). It is the "effort by which each thing endeavours to persevere in its own being" (2001: 105). The author of the *Ethics* criticizes, in so doing, not only the separation of the mind and the body (and consequently the idea of an interaction between two initially separated instances), but also the division of the human being into distinct faculties: understanding (*intellectus*), sensibility, imagination, memory. He believes that life cannot be apprehended in terms of category, but rather intensity and modality. To the "faculties" in Descartes' philosophy, he opposes what he calls in the *Ethics* "modes" (2001: 105), and in the *Political Treatise* "manners of being" (1966: 12). The entire third part of the *Ethics* (entitled *On the Origin and the Nature of the Affects*) is devoted to the study of what we call since Darwin (2009/1890)[5] the life of the emotions. What characterizes the emotions is that they are apt to change. Joy is the free and voluntary transformation of suffering into acting, of passion into reason. It "grows" desire whereas sadness diminishes it.

Everything in Spinoza's reflection on the living is a matter not so much of models as modalities, modulations and "fluctuations" between terms—which are never postulated as original data—as well as between tenses,[6] that is to say verbs. What we understand in reading him is the importance of the notion of passage and transition for apprehending the living, which is characterized by germination, maturation, aging, decline, and death. As he writes in the *Political Treatise* (1966: 124) "human understanding, naturally inclined to abstraction, takes as unchanging properties what are but a passing manners of being".

Spinoza, against theology, establishes the foundations of an anthropology, one that for the first time is re-situated in life in the biological sense of the word, as well as in the life of language, and which has ethical and political implications. It is an anthropology that deploys itself in a plane of immanence for which there is no longer any back-world, any principle that is prior, exterior, or superior[7] to what the *Ethics*'s author calls *nature*. In this nature, contrary to Cartesianism ("animal-machines") then Kantianism ("animal-potatoes"), humans are endowed with no preeminence. They occupy no anthropocentric position. They are "a part of nature" (1966: 16) along with the "living creatures that we say are deprived of reason" (1966: 193).

If this anthropology gives a preeminence of some kind, it is to activity, and not to thingness. With Spinoza we abandon mechanistic thinking about the thing, about substance, and enter a staunchly modern thinking in which the subject is individual and collective indissociably, affection and reflection, act of sensing and of thinking. This solidarity of what we cannot call categories or instances is nevertheless not without conflicts, of which Spinoza knew something himself, given the marginal Marrano position he occupied in the seventeenth-century Netherlands.

In the construction of an anthropology of the sensible, Spinoza, we see, can provide extremely valuable food for thought. Yet still today, in many respects, we have remained Cartesian, we have not become Spinozists, which for a long time was a term of insult for designating atheists.

A Botanical Rethinking of the Social: Jean-Jacques Rousseau

With Jean-Jacques Rousseau (1712–1778), we cross a further threshold in the elaboration of this anthropology, and as we shall see, this threshold is decisive. Rousseau, more still than Spinoza, seeks to reintegrate life and the living into the social. And, thinking about the *social* through the *living*, he is also the first author not only to announce ethnology (as distinct from philosophical anthropology), but to begin to constitute it.[8]

The Rousseauian revolution, which was already germinating in Spinoza, consists of no longer studying the social independently of the living and *a fortiori* against the living. To analyze society, but also to reform it, to revolutionize it, even, it is necessary, Rousseau believes, to cease separating culture and nature, and in particular humanity and animality. In a pre-Rousseauian epistemology, apart from Spinoza, as soon as the notion of nature is posed, it is opposed to culture. For Rousseau, on the contrary—who proclaimed himself at once a "man of nature" and a "citizen of Geneva"—we are not beings who dominate nature and can by virtue of that discourse *on* nature. We are *in* nature. Nature is in us.

For the author of the *Discourse On the Origins and the Foundations of Inequality Among Men*, the eighteenth century's policed civilizing process, in particular its exaltation of art,[9] which is made but of artifice, consists of a *negation* of nature. He opposes the *fact* of this negation to the *law* of the social as anti-nature.

For Rousseau, the "state of nature"—which is for him a *lived* experience—cannot be rediscovered either speculatively, prehistorically, or spiritually (since he refutes all revelation and confines himself to what he calls a "natural religion"). This "state of nature" can nevertheless be recognized then gathered in emotions, sensations, feelings, and more precisely in the experience of solitude in the *forest*, by letting what connects us to the living, and in particular to plant life, express itself.

It is especially in *Reveries of a Solitary Walker* that the author carries out this experiment. Rousseau was then aged 64. He gives up on his initial project of complete self-knowledge and shows himself to be more reserved than in the *Confessions*. He also abandons his tendency toward extreme dilation of his personality in nature. It is also a more discreet, more concise, more precise text than the *Confessions*, one in which the ideas, leaving aside "sad papers" and "piles of old books" (2011: 51) have become sensations. What primarily occupies Rousseau in this work is the infinitely small kingdom of plants, what he calls the "*petitesse*" (1983: 117) ["*littleness*"] of the constituent parts of plants. Following a German botanist who "once wrote a book about a lemon rind" (2011: 51), he undertakes to write on "every grass in the meadows, on every moss in the woods, and on every lichen covering the rocks". He enters the forest "a magnifying glass in hand" wanting "every single blade of grass and atom of a plant to be fully described" (2011: 52).

This work of collecting specimens, which allows him to make, unmake, and remake his herbarium day after day, beginning always "with pimpernel, chervil, borage, and groundsel" (2011: 70), requires extreme care: on the one hand to the particularity of each species, but above all to the continuity of the living as well as of the lived. These are made up of imperceptible "degrees" between which "I could not distinguish" (2011: 57). He goes on,

> Everything on earth is in a state of constant flux. Nothing keeps the same, fixed shape, and our affections, which are attached to external things, necessarily pass away and change like the things. Always beyond or behind us, they remind us of the past which is no longer, or foreshadow a future that often is not to be: there is nothing solid there to which the heart might attach itself (2011: 68).

The originality of the Rousseauian enterprise is that it consists of reexamining the social through the *mediation of the botanical*. In other words, Rousseau's project of reintegrating the "energy"[10] of the living into the social by proposing a new contract (*The Social Contract*) is constructed by going not toward the *Church*, but toward the *forest*. To put it differently, it is by turning away from society that he seeks to change society.

Vitality and Sociality: Lumière, Freud, Bergson

Every period can be characterized by a dominant tendency, a current of thought which although greater legitimacy is given to it, does not preclude the existence of counter-currents. Classical Greece poses the question of being (or of substance), the Middle Ages the question of God, the Renaissance that of nature, and the nineteenth century is traversed by two major preoccupations: the social (Balzac, Saint-Simon, Auguste Comte), but also life (with Romanticism).

Twentieth-century thought is marked in France by two major directionalities: one runs from Durkheim to Bourdieu, the other from Bergson to Deleuze via Foucault. Obviously, in the social sciences, it is the Durkheimian tendency that appears to have triumphed. But at the same time, since the 1970s, Durkheimianism (with its principle of objectivity through objectivation) as well as structuralism (with its formalist theory of systems of opposition and relation between invariants) has been questioned. Durkheim, like Lévi-Strauss—but also like Sartre in *Critique of Dialectical Reason*—are logicians. The questions they pose and the methodological instruments they devise are not at all aimed at thinking about modulations of life and the living, that is to say their processes of genesis and maturation, of the transformations by which they progressively (and not structurally or categorically) decline, wither, and disappear. To put things differently, an anthropology of the life of the senses cannot easily operate in the framework of an approach that, beginning in the early 1950s, has tended to reduce gradual and often almost imperceptible change to the order of structure or culture, paying almost no attention to the collective rhythms of the body and the emotions.

In the years that followed the Second World War, the firmly rhythmic orientation of the research of Mauss, Halbwachs, Leroi-Gourhan, Granet, but also Evans-Pritchard, saw itself rapidly covered over and abandoned. It is thus both by directly re-reading these authors, but also by going outside the dominant trend in social and cultural anthropology, that we must search for the waymarkers that will make possible the construction of an anthropology of the sensible; on the one hand in dialog with the biological sciences (guarding against sociobiology's strayings), and on the other in a thinking often described as vitalism, which, from Schopenhauer to Foucault and Deleuze, is often marked by Nietzsche's thought, as well as by part of the surrealist movement's experiment. At the turn of the nineteenth and twentieth centuries, three discoveries—which are rigorously contemporary—contribute to (re)introducing life into thought: the invention of cinema, psychoanalysis, and the philosophy of Bergson.

Cinema comes from a technical transformation: the invention in 1885 of a machine similar to a sewing machine, capable of pulling film, something Edison's device, the Kinetoscope, which only permitted viewing images, could not do. What is characteristic of this invention is its processual, in other words temporal, character. Contrary to painting, in which everything is shown in simultaneity, in cinema not everything is shown, not everything is said, not everything is heard from the outset, but rather *little by little* (the title of a film by Jean Rouch). Cinema's successiveness is opposed to painting's simultaneity, just as the latter's wholeness is opposed to the fragmented and discontinuous character of the former.

It is the assemblage, through the process of editing, of these fragments of space-time that creates movement, or more exactly sequences. These sequences, as we began to see previously, are by no means constituted by ideas, but rather by images, then (after 1927) of images and sounds, in other words pieces of the sensible. To film is to film the sensible, that is, the emotions of the body. To film is to film the body in a group, that is, in minuscule social interactions like in *Coffee and Cigarettes* by Jim Jarmusch (2003). To film is to film the body in movement, that is, to create duration.

There is a radical antinomy between cinematographic duration (the narrative, as tenuous as it may be) and abstraction, whereas there exists a close relationship between the sensible, duration, and cinema. Filming (that is to say transforming) social reality allows us to grasp that lived social reality (distinct from the life of the film) is never a state, but rather a potential for transformation.

The discovery of psychoanalysis,[11] for its part, takes place based on the notion of drive (*Trieb*), which Freud calls "life drive", to which the "death drive" will come to be opposed in the theoretical elaboration of this new method for investigating the unconscious. Demolishing the fiction of a subject that is homogeneous, transparent, and identical to itself through time, Freud distinguishes three instances (id, ego and super-ego) as well as three levels of interpretation (dynamic, topographical and economic). And he shows that psychic life is not reducible to a system of relations between preexisting poles. For him, affective life has flexibility. It is malleable, moldable, ductile, and capable of multiple metamorphoses.

Bergson (1859–1941), already in his doctoral thesis (*Time and Free Will: An Essay on the Immediate Data of Consciousness*, 1889/2001), proposed to study the relations between what he calls "theory of knowledge and theory of life" (2005: xxiii), which he considers to be "inseparable". To know the living consists for him of seizing "absolutely invisible" (2001: 111–112) intensities and movements. It is necessary, in "attentiveness to life" (1991: 173), to no longer apprehend time or more precisely becoming—which Bergson calls duration—in the same manner as we perceive space, as a juxtaposition of elements but not a gradation. To do so, Bergson writes, it is necessary to discard the "confusion of duration with extensity, of succession with simultaneity" (1889/2001: xx). Believing, in *Creative Evolution* (1907/1944), that "our logic is, pre-eminently, the logic of solids" (1907/1944: xix), he comes to distinguish what he calls solid concepts (which he compares to off-the-rack clothing) and fluid concepts (that he compares to tailored clothing). And he suggests, in a manner that could retroactively be characterized as Bastidean, that solid concepts are not fit for studying all situations and all societies.

The ideas developed by Bergson (and also by Proust who began writing the first volume of *In Search of Lost Time* in 1908) are very far from the research being conducted at the same time in the social sciences. There was one sociologist who was the first to introduce the notion of "social life", but he explicitly considered himself a Bergsonian: Georg Simmel (1858–1918). Within the perspective of the Bergsonian "vital force", Simmel distinguishes the *categories of the living* [*du vivant*] and the *dynamism of the lived* [*du vécu*]. What the author of *Inquiries into the Construction of Social Forms* calls the "fluidity of life" or again "the concrete experience of the lived" (Simmel 2009) challenge the Kantian (Kantian, Durkheimian then Gurvitchian) separation of material contents from the formal frames of knowledge, which are held to be atemporal, unchanging and staunchly universal. With life, Simmel believes, these forms are inclined to become fluid, to deform and transform themselves.

Let us guard, however, against making social life an application of biological life. There exist highly differentiated social rhythms: for example, in Brazil, a slowed temporality in the *sertão* and an accelerated temporality in the city of *São Paulo*. Today, social, economic and political rhythms tend to perturb "natural" rhythms (like the alternation of wakefulness and sleep), to contradict them, indeed to transform them. The totalitarian State may even go so far as to destroy democratic rhythms, made up of periods of confrontation and refutation, which may at times get worn out by power. We see here, as in the opposite example to Benjamin's figure of the *flâneur*, who tries to escape the rhythm of the market economy, that there is no biological continuity in the social.

Life in the Field, From Social Facts to Social Acts

Having been re-elaborated in terms of category thinking, anthropology is extremely reticent to adopt energy and rhythm thinking, which it sees as containing the risk of a possible irrationalist drift. It is nevertheless through the mediation of the *lived*, and more precisely of *lived experience* in the field, that any anthropologist is confronted with the dynamism of social life. He is not engaged in *experimentation* (as it emerges from the biological procedure of Claude Bernard) but in *experience* (properly ethnographic).

To put things differently, ethnographic experience, if it is a form of experimentation, is *in vivo* and not *in vitro* experimentation.

It is this concrete and at each instance singular experience (from the Latin *experiri*, that has the same root as *periculum*, a term signifying an attempt, then peril, danger) that leads the ethnographer, on the basis of the *life* of the field and the *events* capable of occurring there, to consider the life of the senses. In this experience, which is an interaction that, through the play of transfer and counter-transfer, as Georges Devereux was the first to show in 1951, transforms the observer as much as it does the observed, social facts can no longer be considered in a Durkheimian manner as "things", but rather as processes. I have personally never encountered in the field what we continue to call "social facts", only social acts [*le faire social*], or more precisely, fragments of the social in the process of making and unmaking themselves. There is action and therefore energy in social acts as well as in the person who studies them.

At this point, three series of difficulties nevertheless present themselves, which it is now appropriate to make explicit.

The first concerns the notions themselves of energy or vital force, notions that, as they are among the words and phrases that need "to be watched" (Barthes), must be constantly questioned. What needs to be questioned here is Bergsonian intutionism, which postulates "immediate data of consciousness" and is capable of leading to the abandonment of a method that has recourse to mediations. If an anthropology of the sensible as an anthropology of the living, attentive to the experience of the lived, is not reducible to the logic of concept and category, it cannot construct itself in an unproblematic rehabilitation of affect or energy. Yet it is this problematization that is singularly absent from all the atheoretical postures that believe they can do without the mediations of language or, a point we will return to, a process such as that of the cinema, which introduces doubt and uncertainty into the supposed "givens" of sensation and in particular of images.

The second difficulty with which the anthropological study of sensations and emotions finds itself confronted comes from a tension, at the very heart of our discipline, between two paradigms. Is anthropology, along with biology and zoology, a science of nature, as Radcliffe-Brown and Lévi-Strauss conceived of it,[12] or is it, with history and sociology, a science of culture, or as is more often said, a social science (an expression that appeared for the first time in the seventeenth century, in the writing of Malebranche)?

There is no doubt that the process in which researchers in social and cultural anthropology are engaged takes shape in the epistemological matrix of naturalist forms of knowledge, descended from Jussieu, de Tournefort, and Cuvier. When, in 1787, Chavannes proposed to add a new discipline that he called *ethnology* to zoological, botanic, and mineralogical knowledge, it was indeed conceived of as the natural science of human customs. It was much later—through reflection on the dual question of meaning and values as it began to be posed by Dilthey and Rickerts at the end of the nineteenth century, but above all by Max Weber, in 1919, in *Politics as a Vocation*—that a veritable fracture between the objectivity of knowledge and the subjectivity of values opened up. That's when it was realized that a physicist conception of the living emerging from the model of the natural sciences risked leading to a naturalization of the social and of the individual.

We cannot but, in the context of this book, lay the terms of a debate otherwise more complex than its binary simplification: on the one hand nature, on the other culture; to one side organic life, to the other that of the mind, intelligence, consciousness. Today the confrontation between the life sciences and the human and social sciences is reinvigorated by questions of eugenics, cloning, and genetic modification. These call for bioethical reflection, which is reflection not just on facts but law. And this reflection causes antagonisms to appear between science, conceived instrumentally, and law. In an anthropological optic that is attentive to heritage [*patrimoine*] (of a cultural, animal, botanical kind), it is obviously not the living that needs to be altered, but rather the process that aims to know it and, knowing it, to respect and defend it.

Finally, some of the theoretical difficulties with which we are confronted seem to me not just epistemological, but syntactic. They often come especially from the language's non-gerundive[13] constructions, which tend toward a stabilization of language—a process of substantialization and of reification that also occurs when substantives or attributes are no longer sufficiently enlivened by verbs. Indeed, in animating the narrative, verbs are capable of setting in motion concepts that are not also affects.

Norbert Elias provides an example concerning wind and a river. It is preferable, he says, to use the verb *to blow* rather than the word *wind*, which fixes and thingifies; the verb *to flow* rather than the substantive *river*. There is no direct access, as we can see, to the life of the senses "in general", only through singular modalities for observing sensations, diverse methods for analyzing them, and manners of speaking, and speaking about them.

6

Two Precursors to an Anthropology of the Sensible: Roger Bastide and Georges Bataille

The life of the senses, we have just seen, inscribes itself into the continuity of the living. It poses the question of human beings' animality, a question which is not just delicate but incongruous for an anthropology that took shape in an idealist (Durkheim) or rationalist (Lévi-Strauss) frame.[1] Such an anthropology, insofar as it is an inheritor of the humanist tradition in philosophy (that of a sovereign and autonomous, constituting subject) is anthropocentric and logocentric. It introduces not only a distinction between life and death conceived of in terms of animated being and nothingness, but between nature and culture.

This question of discontinuity, of the border between humanity and the rest of the living, and within the latter category animals in particular, is not in my view just any question, since it involves not only an epistemology but an ethics. And what offends the anthropological idealism grounded in Descartes's philosophical mechanism (Man as "master and possessor of nature", incommensurable with the object he possesses) and Kant's thinking (in which, as already noted, "animals are like potatoes"), is the idea that there could be some sort of resemblance, an affinity no matter how small, between the human and animality. It is a given that to become human is to cease to be animal. This is the reason why, in this perspective, still today, to call a human being an animal (an "ass" or "jackass", a "bitch", a "pig", "vermin") is an insult.

This fascination-repulsion with the branch of the living constituted by animality tends to take shape following one of two modalities, both of which operate according to the same (psychological and social) logic. First, totally domesticated, subjugated, and denaturalized animals, which it is claimed are pampered but which are nevertheless reduced to things. Second, in the singular-general (as though there were only one and above all as though we were not it) the "animal" is also referred to as beast, a term coming from the Latin *bestia* (from which also come bestial, beastly, bestiality), which is opposed to *homo*, and which emphasizes either animals' stupidity[2] or ferocity. In the latter of the two cases, an assumption, which can be regarded as a taboo, is constantly evoked by the (strategic) disdain for animals, the manner they are treated in industrial farming, slaughter, and therapeutic testing: humanity and animality, in the constitution of objective knowledge of the living, must be radically separated.

The rhythmic rather than semiological character of the life of the body and the affects was anthropology's blindspot during the period of its early development. This was what Georges Bataille called, as we will return to, "the accursed share".[3]

This system based on a strategy of dissimulating the living's permanent transformation nevertheless began to be reshaped by one researcher, Marcel Mauss, on at least three occasions: in the pioneering text cited above (Mauss 1973) on the "Techniques of the body", presented in 1934 to the *Société de Psychologie*; in his *Manual of Ethnography*, where he affirms that "Man is a rhythmic animal" (2009: 84); and especially in his encounter with the notion of *mana*. The latter contributes to blurring and destabilizing classic theories of knowledge constituted on the basis of binary systems: the pure and the impure, the sacred and the profane, the earth and the heavens ... *Mana*, which can be understood neither archaeologically nor teleologically, is an elusive object we can just manage to name (calling it energy, force, life), without being able to say what it is. The surplus of signification it produces is as difficult to reduce to function as to structure or culture. It introduces uncertainty and worry into what we believe we know, and leads to a problematization of categorization, which is unsettled by thinking in terms of energy. Only here's the problem: the turn taken by the Maussian agenda relative to the strictly Durkheimian framework would, for a long time, have no effect. Marcel Mauss's work constitutes a considerable step forward in the exploration of life and the living, but many who claim to follow it continue to work in a perspective of near fixity.

Confronting sensible thinking with social thinking, as elaborated in sociology's threefold Weberian, Durkheimian, and Marxist matrix, is obviously delicate and problematic because the paradigms may well be incompatible. That is the reason why a certain number of points of departure for the constitution of an anthropology of the body and sensation must be elaborated outside the framework of official anthropology, in its margins, at its boundaries, or through the complexification of existing models.

Two exactly contemporary (born one year apart) but exceedingly different authors, Roger Bastide and Georges Bataille, are in my opinion capable of aiding in the construction of a social theory of the sensible. The teeming anthropology of Bastide and the heterodox anthropology of Bataille indeed open pioneering avenues of research for elaborating the anthropology of the moving and the living.

Roger Bastide: Category Thinking Questioned by Energy Thinking

It is no doubt less the notion of living, strictly speaking, than that of vitality, and more still fertility, that could characterize, as a whole, the work of Roger Bastide,[4] a resolutely innovative researcher who for fifty years studied the processes of transformation emerging from the encounter between three continents: Africa, Europe, and the Americas.

To understand the pioneering character of this *œuvre*, it is necessary to situate it in its period and to recall the epistemological framework in which the generation of researchers who were in their thirties at the beginning of the 1930s learned to work. Classic ethnology at that time favored the monograph (and not at all the polygraph) and continued, following Malinowski, to systematically recommend the study of groups in an isolated milieu:[5] "traditional societies", in which order and purity were taken as coming first ontologically and chronologically, and the blurring caused by *métissage* was envisaged as a sort of disorder. This ethnology favored stability in space (which is divided in advance into homogeneous units) over the dimension of time. It said nothing about the dynamics of interaction between groups, and even less of social and affective processes that form (for example in dreams), deform (in madness), and reform (through trance in religions of possession). In the early decades of the twentieth century, time was resolutely bracketed by French and English anthropologists, and history was excluded from the disciplinary horizon. We are of course in the presence of a "methodological" neutralization and exclusion. History was abrogated because it was the bearer of disorder, and it is this disorder that stood in the way of a discipline conceived, in Radcliffe-Brown's expression, as the "natural science of society". This relationship to time founded on the negation of time and distrust toward history (which was not yet totally emancipated from the historicist mold of the nineteenth century) expressed itself among the period's European anthropologists in a simple proposition: to achieve objectivity, it is necessary to neutralize historicity. This first proposition is articulated with a second, on which Durkheim insisted a great deal: to arrive at objectivity, it is necessary to neutralize affectivity.

Relative to this stabilized understanding of isolated cultures, protected from the turmoil of life and history, and for whom intrusion of the other is understood as a threat of alteration, two researchers (once again, very different from one another) contributed, in France, to transforming ethnology. Both introduced a break in the until-then static conception of what was beginning to be called the "Third World". They laid the foundations of what I have called a dynamic anthropology. These were Georges Balandier, beginning with his doctoral thesis *Sociologie des Brazzavilles noires* [*Sociology of the Black Brazzavilles*] (1955) and, slightly before him, Roger Bastide. It was with them that the study of processes of encounter between societies and their transformation relative to one another began, in France, to be considered an integral part of anthropological research.

A second characteristic of the perspective introduced by Bastide is that, for him, the movements of interaction between cultures play themselves out in affective life and call for being studied in terms of the subjectivities of the actors involved: "It is not", he wrote, "civilizations that are present to and act upon one another, but individuals belonging to those civilizations" (2003a: 203).

This position was about as marginal as it was possible to be relative to French social science research in the 1950s and 1960s, a time when sociologists and ethnologists almost always lacked knowledge of what psychiatrists, psychologists and psychoanalysts were doing. It naturally met the multidisciplinary needs of an even more isolated researcher: Georges Devereux (1908–1987), author of the *Essais d'ethnopsychiatrie générale* [*Basic Problems of Ethnopsychiatry*] (1970) for which Bastide wrote the preface.[6]

The difficulty some have (much more in France than Brazil) in understanding Bastide's thinking is that he moves very freely (but also very methodically) beyond the established pathways of both anthropology and classic sociology, and in particular Durkheimian sociology. To grasp all that separates the Durkheimian approach from the Bastidian approach, it is necessary to bear in mind the fact that Durkheimian rationalism is firmly Kantian: Kant affirms not only the primacy but the immutability of the "categories of understanding" and the "a priori forms of sensibility" (space and time), which organize experience. For Durkheim, as for Kant, the forms of rational knowledge are atemporal and universal. They may certainly be the object of a study in variation, but always within the confines of a frame that remains invariable. The Durkheimian subject remains the impassible, distant, conscious, vigilant, coherent European male subject of classic philosophy. He is a subject of total stability, allowing for pure objectivity: the objectivity, in particular, of social phenomena that occur only as determined by the order of understanding and a priori forms of sensibility, both of which are universal and immutable.

Durkheim aimed to constitute a new discipline—sociology—that would not be merged with either with psychology (hence the "exteriority" of social phenomena, untroubled by affectivity) or history, and which would finally emancipate itself from philosophy. Yet it is precisely the preservation of what Bastide calls "the metaphysical foundation of Durkheimianism" that constitutes the point of divergence between Durkheim's thought and Bastide's approach. Durkheim the sociologist remained marked by the teachings of Renouvier, a neo-Kantian philosopher. What he proposed to found was a sociology of knowledge conceived of as the "skeletal structure of intelligence".

Bastide was never totally Durkheimian, even when he referred to Durkheim's method, but did find himself compelled by Maurice Leenhardt's earliest field research as well as the work of Lucien Lévy-Bruhl. Based on his observations conducted in New Caledonia beginning in 1934, Leenhardt published *Do Kamo: Person and Myth in the Melanesian World* (1979). He shows in this work that members of Kanak society consider themselves to be fully part of the living environment. They are so integrated into their environment (plant environment, in particular) that the kidneys bear the name of a fruit, the intestines are similar to forest lianas, and a single term designates both skin and tree bark. There is no doubt that Bastide would recall Leenhardt's lesson when he too found himself physically confronted, in Brazilian Cadomblé, with an analogous conception of the continuity of the living (mineral, plant, animal, human).

The encounter with Lévy-Bruhl's work would also play a very important role in constituting Bastide's approach. In a letter addressed in 1957 to Henri Gouhier, he wrote about the study of religious thought that it was necessary to "pick up the debate at the point where Lévy-Bruhl left it". Lévy-Bruhl, although historically connected to what is called the "French School of Sociology", was in fact very distant from Durkheim. He discerned that much of the social, and in particular the dimension of the social constituted by the religious and in which the sensible and the affective are mobilized, is not reducible to the categories of understanding. But, very unlike Durkheimian sociology's intellectualist inflection, he proceeded to radically separate two "mentalities". He did not aim, in the manner of Durkheim (then Lévi-Strauss), to reduce the multiple to the singular (the order of reason), but separated it in two: the logical, and the affective, which he calls "pre-logical".

What Roger Bastide did, assisted by Leenhardt's early ethnographic work, was reconsider from the ground up that which had been recognized (but resolved dogmatically) by Lévy-Bruhl. It is this reconsideration that led him to reject every one of classic anthropology's paradigms. He then reexamined the logics—for him, diverse in the extreme—of what Descartes had called "obscure and confused" thought, which expresses itself in particular in dream and mystical experience, and which "clear and distinct ideas" had excluded from the field of rational knowledge. And, to study this thinking, which he sought to analyze in its multiple metamorphoses, he was required to construct tools, pursue avenues that did not exist before him. It is this exploration that he undertakes in the second half of *Le rêve, la transe et la folie* [*Dream, Trance, and Madness*] (2003b). He read all that existed at his time on the subject. He carried out ethnographic observations in Brazil, then from Brazil went to Africa. He progressively realized that apparently wild, frightening, spectacular manifestations of affect are in fact "an admirably ordered bodily liturgy".

The fact that Bastide began, practically alone, to undertake a portion of Marcel Mauss's agenda for the anthropology of the body discussed previously has not yet been sufficiently underscored. He studied reactions to skin color, culinary tastes, and the physical forms of trance. He distinguished two mystical forms: one, ascendant, like Teresa of Ávila's path toward the sacred through levels or "dwellings", but also like the voyage of a shaman; the other, descending, like in the case of the Ghanaian Hausa Jean Rouch filmed in *Les Maîtres fous*, whom the spirits penetrate from below, via the feet.

What is complex and disconcerting (especially for a number of French intellectuals, who are fond of classifications) in Roger Bastide's approach is the impossibility of connecting him to any school whatsoever, be it even to name his nonetheless extremely robust thinking. He resists all academicism. Neither a structuralist searching for "laws" and "constants", nor a functionalist preoccupied by the "social order", nor a Marxist (a conception of the world that very early on struck him as a secularization of Messianism), and even less a structural-functionalist or a structural Marxist, he advanced against the flow (in particular of the infatuation with the paradigm of structure). Hence the lack of familiarity with him on this side of the Atlantic, which contrasts with the place he is given in Brazilian universities. Roger Bastide is probably the French researcher with the greatest influence in the social sciences in Brazil. But he is perhaps even better known—along with with Pierre Verger—in Candomblé religious centers. In all those I frequented, and in particular the one where I underwent the first level of initiation, Roger Bastide was spoken of with esteem and affection, and I was shown his books. It seems to me that it is the nonsystemic character of Bastide's perpetually alert thinking that has led all those in France who so love -isms to distance themselves from him. It is the atypical and firmly iconoclastic character of this scholar, who was alternatively (and not, in my opinion, simultaneously) Professor of Sociology at the Sorbonne, a Cévennes Protestant, and a believer in Candomblé. It is too much for the various orthodoxies.

Bastide was neither a rationalist (like Lévi-Strauss) nor an empiricist (like most of the Anglo-Saxon anthropologists). He is not a rationalist because he considers that the study of concrete human beings cannot be resolved into either structure or function (there exists for him the nonstructural and the dysfunctional). He is not empiricist since he transforms lived phenomena into constructed phenomena, taking into consideration, in particular, the unconscious, which most often operates without social actors realizing it. What constitutes the originality of his thinking is that his not entirely Durkheimian understanding of the social does not lead him to pursue what could be described as the vitalist option, as for example in Simmel. His approach, made up of "rigor and fervor" (Henri Desroche), is never impressionistic. He is admittedly a thinker of life, but certainly not of immediate life that can be grasped by intuition (Nietzsche, Bergson). A theoretician of mobility but more still someone who experimented with it, nothing is more foreign to him than a formless conception of flow (Bataille, Deleuze). He patiently constructed (never ceasing to refine) meditations in the rigorously analytic Gurvitchian[7] framework of social morphology.

By distinguishing formal frames and material contents, Bastide appears to situate himself in a Kantian and Durkheimian perspective. But his great innovation consists of, in a manner that breaks with Durkheim, showing (which had never been done before him) that forms (in the Kantian sense) are liable to deform and transform themselves. Thus the indistinctly social and sensual transformation of African religions into Brazilian Candomblé, then of Candomblé into Macumba in Rio de Janeiro, and finally into Umbanda. Bastide specifies how this "change in form" occurs: "A complete re-elaboration of the *Gestalten* takes place, which modifies perception, memory, the process of thinking, and metamorphosizes sensibility". "In the beginning", he further writes, "the new material is thought of in the old forms, then it breaks them, because of the incompatibility of the *Gestalten* that order it" (2003a: 148). Here we realize the full novelty and flexibility of the Bastidian method. Without renouncing the analytic approach of the reflexive philosophy, then sociology, in which he was trained, his Brazilian experience led him to have recourse to the gestaltist notion of configuration, which he rethinks in terms of configuration in motion.

Along the way, Bastide situates himself—or rather, moves—within a perspective that is totally opposed to that of the formalist purity of a Lévi-Strauss. He prefers, over the "mineralogical" knowledge of structural anthropology, that of the "organization of plant life, like living lianas". What interests him in the movement of exchange and permanent to-and-fro between the same and the other, the near and the far, are not the systems of relation (which lead Lévi-Strauss to think that empirical objects are, all in all, interchangeable), but the meaning and living values of that which circulates and transforms itself in circulating. This does not prevent Bastide's approach, in several of his works, from framing itself in a mode of thought that, while no longer being classificatory, remains categorical: to be able to understand Candomblé religions, "it was necessary for me", he writes, "to change logical categories". These new categories become logical and affective categories, or more exactly schema in the Kantian sense,[8] but schema of social life caught in processes of encounter and transformation, capable of accounting for a thought process of "participations, analogies, and correspondences" (Bastide 1995: 223).

In the Bastidian universe, constantly open to the complexity of the real and never forming a system, the question of contradiction never ceases to be posed—and in particular the contradiction of a researcher who moves "between science and poetry", between the Cévennes Protestant faith and belonging to a Candomblé *terreiro* in Salvador de Bahia. But he seems to me to respond to contradiction through cohesion and coherence. The cohesion and the coherence for example of African and Afro-Brazilian thought. The Bastidian universe is an optimistic one: it is one of "balance", "rebalancing", of "compensation", "integration", "incorporation", "interpenetration", that is to say of affirmation and proliferation (born of the creative intermingling of cultures), of the abundance of affects, which can be seen even in pathological conduct. It is not at all one of negativity, absence, lack, loss, forgetfulness, decline, disappearance, withdrawal. We are in the presence of what Desroche called a "sumptuous anthropology", very far from the skeptical and disenchanted vision of Lévi-Strauss (that of *Tristes Tropiques*) or the pessimistic vision of Devereux, which was that of Freud.

I believe that it is on the basis of the anthropophagic metaphor of Oswald de Andrade and the Brazilian modernists that we can truly understand the transformation of Bastide's thinking: the Brazilian anthropophagic movement would renew the Tupinamba Indians' act of devouring Europeans in order to appropriate their vital force. In the beginning, Brazilian society appeared to be an ideal field site to the French professors (Braudel, Lévi-Strauss, Monteig, Bastide . . .) who participated at the end of the 1930s in the foundation of the University of São Paulo. But this society turns out to have a capacity to metamorphosize, to progressively "Brazilianize" those it receives. And Bastide more than the others. An important part of the French scholar's sensibility and intelligence, by means of the processes of anthropophagic transmutation that he had himself studied, became Brazilian.

But it is not just any Brazil that is concerned here. Discovering the vitality of Africa in Brazil, Bastide did not so much become Brazilian as African (or Afro-Brazilian, as he himself wrote in Latin at the beginning of *The African Religions of Brazil*: "*Africanus sum*"). What was in fact decisive for him—and which constitutes something like the backdrop [*hors-texte*] of his scholarly work—is the first trip he made to the Nordeste in January and February 1944, which foreshadowed his initiation (in July 1951) into a *Nagô* Candomblé *terreiro* in Salvador where, as a follower of Xangô, he acted as an *Ogan*.[9] This was a very sincere spiritual conversion, but also a methodological conversion that does not fail to evoke Griaule, with whom he is at once very close (seeking understanding from "inside") and very far (Griaule did not study contact between societies).

His "veritable passion" for Salvador and its Candomblés opened up for him, as he said to a Brazilian newspaper in 1944, "new paths that he had not imagined". It is as a scholar but also a believer in Candomblé that Bastide encountered the domain of the living and what he would himself later call ecology.

It was sensually, not intellectually, that he discovered this religion, organized around the notion of *axé*, the life force, the energy active in the bodies of the *Loas* in trance. This energy travels through or more precisely animates the continuous flow of the living, be it animal (in sacrifices), plant (in the herbs that must impregnate the body of the initiate in the *bori* ritual), or mineral (in necklaces soaked in blood but also the divinatory game involving cowry shells brought from Africa).

In Candomblé, which is a nutritional religion, the notion of ingredient prevails over that of element, and the *atabaque* itself, that percussion instrument full of power with which the *Orixas* (divinities of nature) are called, can no longer be considered an element in a symbolic system but rather material energy capable of making the *terreiro* vibrate. It is therefore a thinking of rhythm, not easily analyzed and broken up in the scholarly terms of a system of signs or symbols, that Roger Bastide found himself not only confronted with but drawn into. In *Images du Nordeste mystique en noir et blanc* [Images of the Mystic Nordeste in Black and White] it is clear that he is working with energy and no longer with categories, and that he was brought to reconsider much more than before the anthropocentric presuppositions not only of Durkheim's intellectualist sociology, but of Mauss's anthropology.

Bastide at that point became aware that in anthropology it is necessary to take into consideration tonality and not just totality. In the context of the Candomblé *terreiro* to which he belonged, he knew and above all physically felt the extent to which energy thinking is capable of submerging and subverting category thinking. Nevertheless, as a sociologist who knows to always remain reasonable, he believed that through the surging and apparently unruliness of life, particularly in the tumultuous experience of trance, there existed rules and processes of social regulation.

From Bastide's immense work, I suggest that we retain a certain conception of the social scientist, which is not that of an external observer, but rather of a committed actor. Being neither Weberian, nor Durkheimian, nor Bachelardian, he does not separate life from the intellect, affectivity from rationality, fervour from rigor. He believes on the contrary, as already mentioned, that "to do good sociology, it is first necessary to love Man". It is this conviction that led him to an ethnographic approach fairly close to that of Leiris toward the Ethiopians, or more still that of Griaule toward the Dogon, and above all that of Leenhardt among the Kanak of New Caledonia. Bastide was driven by the requirement not only for scientific knowledge but action, as can be seen in his *Applied Anthropology*.

What is surprising when reading his works (certain passages of which by now obviously show some wrinkles), is that we are in the presence of a thought process in perpetual experimentation, which constantly reintroduces the question of the life of the senses and of values into the heart of research work and permits us, in turn, to free ourselves of a stabilized and solidified conception of the social. This thinking is, today, an invitation to follow many myriad paths that, practically alone in the French university system during his time, he so firmly but in so undogmatic a way was able to clear.

Georges Bataille: Category Thinking Submerged by Energy Thinking

From the economic to the religious via the political, no field of inquiry or research was unknown to Georges Bataille,[10] whose preoccupations were infinitely diverse. Yet his work is traversed by a constant that amounts to a veritable obstinacy: the question of the life of the senses, which can be broken down as follows: the living, the lived, the vital.

Bataille's thinking, like his existence, is marked by the unreserved acceptance of life in all its forms, including, and perhaps especially, at its most horrible, abject, and scandalous: everything that comes from below, which he opposes to the mystification of surrealist evasion toward the high and the beautiful. In December 1924 in a Parisian brothel on rue Saint-Denis, Bataille and Leiris, in reaction to the nihilism of the Dada movement, established the foundations of a what they called a "yes" movement, defined as a "perpetual acquiescence to all things" (1976: t. VIII, 170). The approach of the author of *Story of the Eye* (Bataille 1928) is a resolutely anti-idealist and anti-intellectualist one that, distrusting the "peeping of ideas", concentrates its attention on the "tumult of the living" and the "intensity of sensations" and never ceases to remind us that humanity is also animality.

It is with a chapter entitled "Animality" that *Theory of Religion* (1992/1973) opens, after this quotation from Alexandre Kojève: "human reality can be formed and maintained only within a biological reality, an animal life". Bataille's work, of which one book (1955) is devoted to the animal frescoes of Lascaux, was tormented by the "unbridled immensity of animal life" and is shot through with a veritable bestiary—tigers, pigs, rats, horses. It also bears mention that the author always kept a horse's skull near him while writing (that those close to him nicknamed the "*cheval de Bataille*"[11]), which evoked for him both his childhood in Auvergne and, more still, the horses that fell by the millions on Europe's battlefields during the Great War.

"The history of life on earth is principally the effect of frenzied exuberance" (1977: 85) Bataille writes, also speaking of the "general effervescence of life" (1977: 86), "outbursts", and "excesses", excesses to which bourgeois society is opposed, in his view. What in his eyes characterizes the living is that it is in no way verb, speech, thought, but organism, and for certain species (animals and humans), body animated by an "overflowing" of energy.

We begin here to encounter the dual originality of *The Accursed Share*, a work that required of the author eighteen years to prepare: the most relevant but also the most unsettling and "paradoxical" manifestations of life must be sought in loss and waste, not in profit and accumulation; they call for being studied through a shift from a "restricted economy" to a "general economy", capable of producing a "Copernican shift, the turning upside down of thought—and morality" (1977: 76). What Bataille calls the "accursed share" is the part of the "general economy" that he describes as expenditure, that is, the excess energy put to work in those activities that have particularly interested ethnologists: ritual, festival, sacrifice, but also luxury, the construction of prestige monuments, gaming, spectacle, nonprocreative sexual activity, war.

A "movement of excess energy, translated into the effervescence of life" (1977: 58) drives these activities, which pose the question of how a society deals with an unproductive surplus. These are useless activities that consist of spending without counting, and which are at the heart of both the economy and religious behaviors such as trance (dear to Bastide), ecstasy, and orgy. But for Bataille the question of "excess energy" (1977: 75), which he also calls "waste of energy" (1977: 85) is at work in the entire field of the living. This energy is primarily cosmic—animal, plant, mineral, solar—energy. The example of the sun, which at once gives and loses energy without anything in return, is the very first example in *The Accursed Share*: in its "incessant prodigality . . . the sun gives without ever receiving" (1977: 79). The author then takes the example of the living organism, showing that what characterizes it is a potential for excess energy: "for living matter, in general, energy is always in excess" (1977: 72) Bataille writes, adding that "neither growth nor reproduction would be possible for the plant or animal not habitually having at its disposal an excess" (1977: 77).

The questions posed by the living therefore must, in this perspective, be investigated from the angle of proliferation, and cannot be resolved, or even stabilized, in balance (what in physiology is called the principle of homeostasis). It is excess, growth, that makes live. But we can also die, let us note, not from lack or rarefaction but by proliferation (of cells), as with cancer. For Bataille, life is surplus. It exceeds all measure, all limit, all form. It is what he calls the "formless". Neither substance nor relation, but energy, it cannot be understood in terms of social morphology in the manner of Bastide, a student of Gurvitch. It cannot be confined to frames, codes, rules that when they exist, he believes, call for being transgressed or profaned.

Through five types of tightly connected experiences—the mystical experience referred to as "atheological", eroticism, writing, political struggle, and effervescent community—Bastille experiences the intensity of the living. For him, knowledge of the living calls for a lived experience of the sacred, "that prodigious effervescence of life" (1992/1973: 36): what he paradoxically calls a "sacred sociology". The social, according to the author of the *Somme athéoligique*,[12] is of the order of the sacred (Bataille, in this respect, remains much truer to Durkheim than Bastide) and his research leads to the constitution of a tie that is not one of contract (Rousseau, Renan . . .) but "communialty". It was to the elaboration of this tie that he would devote a large part of his life through the founding several associations: Counter Attack (1935–1936); Acephal (from 1936 to the beginning of the Second World War), mirrored by a secret society of the same name in which a human sacrifice to bind together the members was verily envisaged; the College of Sociology—college in the sense of brotherhood—lead with Michel Leiris and Roger Caillois, devoted to making the teachings of Mauss and Durkheim effective and even activistic.

Bataille also created and served as editor of several journals, including *Documents* (1929–1930) and *Critique* (from 1946 until his death). The experiment of the journal *Documents*, created with Georges-Henri Rivière, and which had as a subtitle *Doctrines, Archaeology, Fine Arts, Ethnography*, is extremely stimulating for the study of the history of ethnology in France. Of resolutely anti-ethnocentric and anti-colonialist inspiration, the journal at once gathered writers and artists who were disappointed with or excluded from the surrealist movement, such as Robert Desnos and Michel Leiris, and ethnologists such as Alfred Métraux, Marcel Griaule and Marcel Mauss himself (whom Péguy nicknamed "card catalogue").

Bataille called these associations and journals "communities". They were elective communities, "convulsive", paroxysmal ones, in transition, continually changing, in constant contestation and revolt, in which the members cannot be called either "followers" or "disciples", form neither a "mass" (Canetti), a "crowd" (Le Bon, Freud), nor constitute a class (Marx), but were moved by a certain sense of collaboration, though not of common ownership. What was sought was another form of social bond than the civic bond of the nation or the confessional bond of religion: an ecstatic bond capable of extending beyond death and which Bataille experienced in the bond of love (with Collette Peignot) and friendship (with Métraux, Masson, Caillois, and Klossowski, but especially with Michel Leiris).

Community is a requirement for the writer: "carried to its highest point of effervescence", life's intensity vitally requires simultaneous sharing and resistance. He resisted on three fronts, against three clearly identified enemies: bourgeois society, which instead of really living just gets by; the various forms of fascism, which capture a part of life's forces but transform them into death; Stalinism, finally, which hijacks the energy of revolution.

The objective of Bataille (about whom it has not escaped remark that the name he bore and the life he led were all of a piece[13]) does not consist only, as we can see, of studying the sacred but of living it through radical action. "Bataille", Leiris wrote, "wanted to become a shaman", a phrase which echoes Leiris's own comment that "I'd rather become possessed than study possession".

What we observe in France between the two World Wars is that a sensible thinking was being elaborated within a textual network constituted by constant cross-references among a certain number of ethnologists, artists and writers who, at one time or another, believed that surrealism could be a rival epistemology to official science. We might conclude that in the constitution of this sensible thinking ethnology was the path of wisdom and the College of Sociology and Acephal the path of madness. However, that is not the case. Between the writer and ethnologist—Bataille the madman and Métraux the sage—Métraux was the one who committed suicide.

Finally, it is necessary to insist on the fact that "experience" (a critical notion in Bataille's work), which is always experience of the extreme, that is to say the greatest tension of both body and thought, is also an experience of writing. It concerns the life of language, which is not at all conceived in the manner of Geertz, as capable of being organized in a "social text". For Bataille, it is the exact opposite: there is certainly a sociality, but there is above all an asociality to literature, which does not make society but undoes the social in order to transform it.

This insubordination of Bataille's approach draws the author toward what we referred to above as vitalism: "My method, or rather my non-method, is my life. Less and less do I question in order to know. I don't care, I live, I question to live" (1945: 157).

Yet it is not at all a matter, particularly in the writing of *The Accursed Share*, of withdrawing existentially or aesthetically from anthropology—did Bataille ever even enter it?—but rather of attempting to think about the "share" that is obscured by anthropology. The horizon of knowledge—the *episteme* in the sense of Michel Foucault—in which Bataille is situated is a resolutely nonindividualist and nonpsychological one in which what is given from the start is not at all the subject's interiority, the "separate being" or what he sometimes calls "the Sartrian cogito", but social acts [*le faire social*], which "begin with conversations, shared laughs, friendship, eroticism". In this perspective, which is no longer that of humanism, there is always something that precedes and exceeds individual conscience: an outside, an exteriority, a "*he/it*" that escapes us (the flow of the life of the senses) but also an *us* that could be constructed (through social and political bonds).

The author of *The Accursed Share* therefore no more renounces Mauss's "total social fact", quite the contrary, than he does the Hegelian notion of totality taught to him by Alexandre Kojève. He radicalizes the "total social phenomenon", explores all of its dimensions in all of their intensity. But, in so doing, he puts into question the coherence and the cohesion of the Maussian concept of totality, which is destabilized. The "accursed share" is a critical part that introduces negativity into social thinking, which after Auschwitz no longer had, for Bataille, the solidity and stability with which it was credited. In sum, totality remained for him an anthropological requirement, but it is a divided totality, torn and irreconcilable with itself.

An abyss thus seems to separate Bataille and Bastide, despite the latter having devoted a large part of his research to extreme experiences: mystical ecstasy, madness, trance, possession. Although they cross much common ground and are united by the same passion for the sacred, they do not share the same perspective or personal history: Bastide, without ever reneging the Protestant convictions of his Cévennes youth, "converted" (his expression) to the polytheism of Candomblé. Bataille, after a period of seven years (from 1914 to 1920) of Catholic faith, became violently hostile to all forms of Christianity, while at the same time affirming that he was "furiously religious". The former is a man of measure, of moderation, of conciliation (as one learns to be in Brazil); the latter was a man of excess and rupture. Bataille's works are as injured, tormented and revolted as Bastide's are calm and balanced. They express a veritable fascination with the present and still more with the deflagration of the now, foreign to Bastide's path of understanding slow and continuous processes of societies' sensitive transformations relative to one another. They are insolent, animated by the breath of Nietzsche and the worrying input of Sade. Bastide does not experience this anxiety and tragic intensity. The contrast is at work in all the domains with which they were confronted and in particular that of politics. Resolutely on the left, Bastide is nevertheless a moderate in politics. He became a member of the SFIO (which would become the Socialist Party) in 1923 and was, from the 1960s onward, an honorary member of the MRAP.[14] Bataille, for his part, was an extremist. Between 1931 and 1934 he was part of Boris Souvarine's Democratic Communist Circle.

Both nevertheless opened the way toward questions that were little explored in their era, on life and the living, which are not easily reduced to the scholarly, as on the sensible relative to the intelligible and affect relative to concept. And we realize with the benefit of hindsight that both can be considered heterodox thinkers relative to the "French school of sociology", to which each claimed membership in his own way and, paradoxically, perhaps more Bataille than Bastide. If we wanted to push the comparison a little further, we might say that between what unites them and the official anthropology of their period, there is something of the difference that separates Pascal and Descartes. What both favor is not so much a participant observation in the usual sense of the term, as participant collaboration. If the theme of the life of the senses—which is change for Bastide and outburst for Bataille—runs through their respective *œuvres*, it is for both of them on the basis of lived experience. But once this experience (of the "wild sacred" and the "domestic sacred" for the former, of "mystic atheism" and eroticism for the latter) is encountered, it is elaborated by the authors in ways that could hardly be more different. Bastide studied with passion but also serenity the transformations of others, whereas Bataille, through a bond that he called "communial" or "sacrificial", dramatically experienced within himself something which in his eyes was not merely a transformation, but called for an insurrection.

I do not therefore think that it is possible to reconcile them. This does not change the fact that, without having ever met or even crossed paths, they passed very near one another. Giving up the simulacra of identity and welcoming the multiple, they are more divergent than opposed in their experimentation with what we might consider twentieth century anthropology's shifting orientation. Between them, Bataille and Bastide cover an important part of that shift, which is difficult to think about in this beginning of the twenty-first century without the two of them together. In particular they undertook, each as much as the other, a demanding and resolutely pioneering confrontation between energy thinking and category thinking. Each realized, to a certain extent in isolation, that the experience of life's continuity (which is flow and not just a plane or straight line, rhythm and no longer sign, tonality and not only totality, resonance and not only reasoning) could contradict modes of knowledge founded on discontinuity, such as culturalism or structuralism.

They certainly gave different responses to this contradiction. Whereas for Bastide, energy is given to inflecting and complexifying category without abandoning it, Bataille gambles reason in an energy thinking (that he calls "heterology") that is apt to submerge category. They were thus both, during the same period, obstinate precursors of an anthropology of the body and the sensible. They have become our contemporaries.

7

Living Together, Feeling Together: Toward a Politics of the Sensible

The Bearable Lightness of Being

The title of this chapter may sound like a gag or at least a contradiction. The political domain purports to be that of the rational organization of collective life by governing laws, whereas the sensible has a physical and affective character that is resolutely subjective. What relationship can exist under conditions such as these, between a domain—public if ever there was one—that aims, through action, to resolve conflicts and accomplish a project, and the singularity of a sensible (in the Greek sense of *aisthésis*), in other words affective but also aesthetic, experience?

If the political in its simultaneously rational, intelligible and general dimensions concerns everyone, then it is addressed to no one in particular. The law, perfect as it may be, and especially if it is perfect, is of an abstract and impersonal character. The political, through delegations of power, is made of distances and it tries to last. In comparison the sensible, which is intimate, diverse, ephemeral, and never completely constituted, seems to lack constancy and consistency. The political tends to orient the sensible, to control it, submit it to the point of eradicating sensibility, though it may also ignore it. As for the tendency of the sensible, which shifts between smells, colors, and sounds, and is made of desires and repulsions, it tends rather to avoid politics, to escape that which is of the order of programs, projects, and the organization of civic life. Aesthetic experience also appears to be backgrounded relative to politics, on its margins, even opposed to it.

Posed in an oppositional manner, the debate risks quickly coming to a premature end. If there is every reason to suspect that the two terms are reluctant to encounter one another, it is nevertheless necessary to reexamine the initial opposition, which goes back to Plato, and of which there are echoes to this day, for instance in the work of Habermas, who makes a strict distinction between idea and image, or if you prefer between the rationality and ideality of meaning and the senselessness, so to speak, of the sensible. It is this binarism that needs to be reexamined since, as we shall see, what is at stake in the critique of this principle of separation is what I propose to call, oxymoronically, a politics of the sensible.

The binarism in question not only concerns the opposition between sensations and reason (the former, in this perspective, perturbs the latter), but the distinction, about which European philosophy is unanimous, that consists of separating sensations and emotions, and more still sensations and sentiments. This distinction is absolutely not universal. For instance it has no relevance in the Candomblé apprenticeship I personally underwent in a *terreiro* in São Paulo. It is a tactile, olfactive, musical, chromatic, but above all food-based apprenticeship—an awakening of all the senses. It is a process of socialization (into the community that receives you) in which the *emotions* that you feel and the *sentiments* that you experience in no way consist of a secondary elaboration of an experience of extreme sensuality. It is only in the Eurocentric Cartesian construction of distinct "faculties" that the sensible is enclosed in a separate domain by relegating it to the side of instinct, drive, and impulse, that is, of animal life. In this perspective, and this perspective only, sensations are deemed to be devoid of psychological and *a fortiori* social signification. This status of exclusion in fact only concerns a very limited number of experiences, such as the reaction to heat, cold, day, night (which are not socialized and cultivated in the same manner in all groups and time periods). It becomes much more problematic with desire, aversion, disgust (an affect constructed on the basis of smell and leading to distancing), fear (which leads to flight), anger (which pushes us to destroy), and unease, which is no longer physical but psychological.

There is, of course, a resolutely physical component to sensations (furrowing the brow, shrugging the shoulders, shuddering, crying out, fainting . . .) but it is part of the oneness of life and affective thinking. This can be understood through the experience of Afro-Brazilian cultures, but also in that of European languages. Thus, while the English language may distinguish sensation and sentiment, it is also capable of uniting them in the notion of feeling. We might also recall what Robert Musil wrote in *Man Without Qualities*, which is a veritable treatise on affects: "in the sentimental, there is sentiment, and there is mental" (Musil 1967).

One of the merits of anthropological (and not just psychological) reflection on the sensible is that it may shift disciplinary categories, revivify and reorient our thinking and in particular weave new connections between the sensible, the social, and the political.

If the question posed by politics is the question of *how to live together?* then a politics of the sensible, for its part, is concerned with *experiencing together*, that is, of shared sensibility. Put differently, political togetherness is also sensible togetherness. A major part of social life consists of loving, suffering, tasting together. This togetherness [*vivre ensemble*] is elaborated, as Jacques Rancière puts it, through the sharing of the sensible, that is of the auditory, the tactile, the olfactive, the gustatory, the visible but also what cannot be seen. Sharing the sensible (sharing the dual sense of dividing and putting in common) is speaking together, drinking and eating together, listening together, dancing, playing music, going to the theater or cinema together. The political and the sensible can no longer then be considered in a binary and obsidional manner. They are not two separate spheres: one, public, indifferent or hostile to sensibility; the other, private, purporting to escape any relationship of power and maintaining a position of refusal, even hostility, toward the political.

If the connections that are beginning tentatively to sketch themselves continue to seem problematic, it nevertheless already appears that a conception of the political that has nothing to do with the sensible, regarding it as a kind of useless luxury, is restrictive, and that a conception of the aesthetic in terms of a desire to escape the political is illusory. Indeed, what would a "senseless", that is, unconcerned with what the subject experiences, politics mean? Inversely, what would be the meaning of a sensibility totally separated from the social and the political, for example an aesthetics in the pure state (Adorno) or art above everything (Tarkovski)?

Politics of the sensible does not mean that everything, all the way down to each individual's sensory experience, is entirely political, but that there exists a political and also historical dimension to sensory experience, which exceeds what individuals can consciously experience. Put differently, the political without the sensible risks being an abstraction. But the sensible without the political has all the features of escapism.

If reflection on the sensible often gets cut short, it is that we are not able to go beyond this contradiction between tastes and discourses, sentiments and arguments or, to put it differently, between an empiricism that only observes and a logicism that so orders things as to end up dissolving its subject. The difficulty in the search for the rational status of the sensible comes from the fact that knowledge (and *a fortiori* scientific knowledge) presupposes the existence of a *permanent object* and a *constant subject*. Yet sensibility cannot concern an *object* (be it sonorous, tasteful, colored), but the necessarily unstable *relationship* a subject entertains with objects (as well as other subjects), in an experience that is itself singular and rarely reproducible. Sensations never stop transforming themselves. They appear, disappear, show through, reappear. Contrary to the political, they do not, strictly speaking, have any consistency. They are not substantial and therefore not substantializable. They resist generalization to the level of concept, even less do they form essences. Thus there exists no color in itself but a whole range of colors capable of oscillating between different tones. The same is true of heat, warmth, blandness or softness, which we would have the greatest difficulty in stabilizing into categories. Put differently, the sensible—which is not muddled intelligibility but complex intelligibility in a state of becoming—is *inessential*. But *it is precisely this inessentiality that is reality*.

We get upset, as heirs of Plato and St. Paul, with reality, we are angry at life every time we feign to complain about how the polymorphous universe of sensations cannot be reduced to unity (the unity of reason, of conversion, of the city, of the family), nor brought back to the straightforward positivity of a (clear) intention or a (precise) direction. After grand explanatory narratives of history collapse, there nevertheless remains a residue, which reasoning about identity in terms of oneness and sameness has great trouble ridding itself. *The body is this "leftover"*. It is at once that which is most obvious and that which constantly escapes analysis. It is that which resists being said.

This is what is stimulating about the sensible, which is another word for designating the body in all its states and multiple metamorphoses. It resists being apprehended, fixed, enclosed, stabilized, generalized. It shatters the fraud, or at least fiction according to which the real is in consonance with the rational. It is by no means the added value, the suit, the clothing, the bark, less still the vehicle or the instrument serving to "express" or transport ideas. It is the living sap of thought and language. It is by no means the variable *form* of a *meaning* endowed with an immutable content. This operation of dehistoricization—but also depoliticization in which the subject finds itself dismissed or at least subdued—invites a radical critique: meaning is relative to the sensible and not the other way around, the political only really acquires meaning through the sensible in action.

The Continuity of the Sensible and the Political

The refusal to consider a portion of the population as political individuals is ordered by the hierarchizing distinction of the sensible and the intelligible, of emotion and reason, and more radically still of sound and speech, and *a fortiori* writing. If the category of "*metics*" did not have access to political life in Greece, women in France until 1945, as well as young people under the age of eighteen until 1960, and if still today Indians in Brazil have difficulty being recognized as citizens, it is because their mouths are considered to emit sounds not speech, at least not sensible speech. These different categories—metics, women, adolescents, Indians—are perceived and heard as having to be cast onto the shores of instinct and of childhood in the strict sense of the term: those who do not speak.

What must be proposed in order to move forward in this anthropologically democratic endeavor is an epistemology of continuity that allows for thinking together about domains most often considered as separate: aesthetics, the political, ethics, history. A mode of knowledge such as this, which engages the totality of affectivity and intelligence, opposes the sequential breaking up of reason and emotion, of meaning and sound, of content and form, of the West and the East, one of the finalities of which is to legitimate policies for maintaining law and order. It opposes the semantic equation of disorder, sound, the sensible, and the senseless, capable of threatening the order of speech, reason, and civilization.

Among those who blazed the path for this type of thinking, which cannot be considered as exclusively intellectual or purely sensorial, there is, as we have seen, Spinoza, who ceased to oppose the mind and the body, the sensible and the intelligible, affect and concept. There is also Baudelaire who, refusing the theory of art for art's sake showed that the aesthetic is revelatory of that which is at stake in politics. Spinoza, Baudelaire, in very different registers, allow us to do away with the threadbare acts of duettists like the logicism and irrationalism duo that oppose the structured and the invertebrate, the hard and the soft, the serious and the playful.

What I propose to call the politics of the sensible is the recognition of the inscription of politics, ethics and history into sensibility, that is to say in particular in the temporality of the life of the subject. This politics is not without a *poetics* (in the Greek sense of creation), which is not unrelated to what François Truffaut and the young filmmaker-critics of the mid-1950s called the *politique des auteurs*: the filmmaker as author, not simply subordinate to the scriptwriter and producer, who takes back the creative and reflexive initiative. He chooses, takes sides.

While a thinking of continuity allows us to free ourselves from the division (of feeling and acting in separated spaces and temporalities), it nevertheless does not imply a reconciliation and less still a fusion, but rather a movement of tension, as this new example indeed attests. A difference in sensibility cannot be taken as equivalent to an opposition in principle. What is *played* at the theater (for example the aesthetic of the Greek tragedy) echoes what is *said* in the Assembly (the constitutive discourses of political life of the Athenian city), but cannot be reduced to it. If the aesthetic and the political are not found without one another, they rarely make good bedfellows, and are in fact often prone to conflict. Thus, Griffith's *Birth of a Nation* is a resolutely revolutionary film in its aesthetics, but utterly reactionary in its politics. The life of Leni Riefenstahl is even more revealing in this respect. She displayed genuine artistic talent (notably in directing *The Blue Light* (1932) with Bela Balazs), but she employed that talent in the service of the Nazis, of whom, in passing, many were extremely receptive to art, and in particular music. A final example is given to us by Eisenstein. The filmmaker's ideal was to go beyond the dualism of reason and emotion, and to try through editing to reconcile intelligence and sensations. But he realized, progressively, the contradictions that exist between language and images.

These contradictions must not, however, lead us to relegate reflection on the organization of the city and the life of the senses to categories that are impermeable to one another. If politics is a matter of administering, that which is of the order of law, norm, rule and regulation nevertheless cannot be indifferent to emotions. There exist sentiments in politics (cf. Duvignaud 1990 and Braud 1996), which can be staged and become spectacles,[1] but which may also give rise to legal rules, such as the obligation in French law to provide assistance to a person in danger. It is in this perspective that Hannah Arendt elaborated, in the second chapter of *On Revolution* (1963), the notion of "politics of pity", of which one development today is humanitarianism. The sentiments of compassion, indignation, anger, and revolt that can give rise to mass protests, even revolutions, certainly do not take us out of the realm of politics. Another example of this continuity between what we tend to consider separate domains is provided by the question of racism. This question, too, cannot be held to be foreign to political reflection and intervention. Racism, which is the most total and brutal rejection of the other as subject, effects a sensory devaluation. It is a perceptive, tactile, and undoubtedly more still olfactive rejection. The skin's color is unbearable, touching and smelling impossible because of repugnance. As Georg Simmel put it in his *Sociology of the Senses* (1997/1912), the social question is not only a moral one, it is a question of the sense of smell.

Political reflection and action, which in a democracy suppose a shared effort of discussion, critical confrontation, and refutation, must take this into consideration without, however, substituting the primacy of the emotional for the primacy of the rational. They are elaborated on the basis of the recognition of what Hannah Arendt calls "human plurality". These are the questions—how to make different sensibilities live together harmoniously? How to organize individuals' social relations within a shared history?—that confront the political.

Agreement and Gap

The sensible—which is reality—does not exist in itself, but in an act, which is a group act. The seeing-listening-tasting-touching-smelling of social life [*du vivre ensemble*] is inscribed in memory, that is to say shared duration, and not just a "public space" in which what are today called "social practices" are performed. It is therefore the question *what do we have in common? what do we share?* that must be reexamined through the life of emotions. This sharing of the sensible—outside of intense moments like wars, defeats, victories, commemorations and celebrations, about which there is anyway rarely unanimity—is not totalizable. It is not of the order of an integrated totality but rather is perceived through a certain tonality in which dissonances very readily arise. As Patrick Loraux puts it (in Mondzain, 2003: 70), "being together does not make one". This *together* of affect is unstable, precarious, problematic. It is prone to coming undone (in individualism) or on the contrary to being "perfected" (in the utopias of totalitarianism). Put differently, it is simultaneously threatened by dissemination, imminent separation, splintering, but also by fusion. The *feeling together* discussed here is located as far as can be from compliance, conformity to watchwords, that which no longer speaks except with a single voice, as in totalitarianism and sects, which leads to no longer listening and no longer looking but *believing together*.

The small little ties of the sensible are first improvised, ripen, and expand, but also sometimes grow old and disappear, in a logic that is not that of being but of the between and betweeness. While there is nothing unreasonable about them, they nevertheless resist submitting themselves to instrumental economico-political reason or the reason of the State. The latter only conceives of ties that are imposed or at best consented to (through pacts, treaties, contracts). Politics [*la politique*] as the struggle of parties for the exercise of power and the management of society—distinct from the political [*le politique*]—and aiming to make hold together, but also to favor certain interests, requires that individuals conform to its decisions. It is here that a politics of the sensible may disrupt the conformism of agreement. It consists, we shall see, in accepting the gap between each persons's respective sensibility and in particular of those who grew up in other cultures than our own, and in so doing, resisting the uniformization of tastes.

We do not perceive exactly the same things, the sensations we feel are not rigorously alike, we do not quite experience sentiments together and at the same moment. The realm of affects is the location and above all the time of misunderstanding, ambivalence, and quid pro quo. As Marie-José Mondzain (2003: 194) puts it: "seeing together does not mean all seeing the same thing like a Cyclopic eye".

There exist extremely diverse manners of seeing and listening together. They vary according to individual and collective histories and memories. They are also manners of conceiving and firstly of experiencing the political in the sensible. One becomes aware of this for example by being attentive to certain Afro-American musical forms. Blues, jazz, soul, rhythm and blues, rap and breakdance have resolutely political meanings. They are syncopated forms of music, made of rhythmic shocks, through which the shock of slavery continues to resonate. The past, far from being bottled up, is reactivated, but at the same time it is rich in potentialities. These deterritorialized forms of music that are constantly recreated in the flow of disasporic encounters are by no means music of reconciliation and even less so of forgetfulness, but rather of conflict—which does not however exclude dialogue. What is referred to as the antiphonic musical dialogue of afro music is profoundly democratic. It is made of calls and responses: of a veritable vocal and instrumental dialogue excluding any relationship of domination.

Cinema, Collaborator or Resistance Fighter?

The invention of cinema, an art of time and movement like music, and an art produced collectively and for a wide public, overturned knowledge, and above all our perception of the sensible. It allowed us to see and to hear—but to see and to hear differently every time—what we did not see and hear. But it did not merely show sensations, it metamorphosized them. It creates relations that are not just unexpected but previously unknown by bringing together images and sounds that were distant, and distancing images and sounds that were close together. Filmmaking—which does not concern only shooting and editing but also the reaction of the spectator, whom Jean Renoir spoke of as the one who "finishes the film"—does not merely reproduce and receive sensations. In entering into relations with one another, sensations—snippets of sound and image fragments—are mutually transformed. But each time in a different manner.

Cinema both models and modulates the sensible. It does not strictly speaking create fiction, but causes the reality of time's plasticity, reversibility, continuity or discontinuity, speed or slowness, to appear. It teaches us to think about time not in spatial terms, but the other way around. Trying to show the temporal character of the sensible—chromatic vibrations, the greater or lesser intensity of potentially overlapping sound flows, the impulses, frustrations, disappointments, small inflections and tiny curves of sentiments, the circulation of affects, the tension or easing of vital energy, the turbulence, oscillations and hesitations that precede the passage from one state to another, the ruptures of tonality, the hiatuses that make us roar or stutter—is in no way a question of abstract philosophy. It does not concern the human being in general, but what occurs between singular individuals and which is apt, as Hannah Arendt wrote, to "join" or "separate" them. It is a political question that stages social relations, relations of skin color, relations of gender and generation. But it is also an ethnographic and cinematographic question.

The reflection on the body interiorizing social and cultural models—in walking, gestures, ways to meet or avoid one another—but also seeking to escape roles that takes place in cinema is not played out through ideas, or even in images, and less still what are called "representations", but through camera shots. It is played out across shots that clarify or contradict one another, but above all within each shot, which can unite, through the depth of field process, masters and servants, for example in the hallway of the La Chesnay property at the end of *The Rules of the Game* by Jean Renoir. And each time, what is shown is determined by a choice. Thus, there is a contrast between the intensity of the moment (the supercharged bodies of Cassevetes' characters, that shift frenetically, in jerks, from embrace to brawl, paroxysm of excitement to depression, with only one thought in their minds, to exist at all costs in the present) and the duration of the long take in the cinema of Mizoguchi or Manoel de Oliveira, which is that of infinitely dilated time.

A large part of the political takes place through the manners in which we consider and deal with the sensible. There exists for example a cinema that has recourse to intimidation effects, aiming to pummel and exclude, so to speak, the spectator, so thoroughly is he stunned by sublime images (Spielberg, Luc Besson, Jean-Jacques Beneix, Jean-Jacques Arnaud, Alain Corneau). But there also exists a cinema that perturbs and questions sensibility and which is no longer that of the beautiful image (*Muriel* by Alain Resnais). Finally there is a multiple and profoundly democratic cinema of togetherness [*vivre ensemble*] in which the characters exist only in their relationships to others, are filmed together (Renoir, Rivette, Cassevetes, Lars von Trier, Trapero, Wang Bing), just the opposite of Antonioni's films in which the screen's field is progressively emptied so that there remains but a single character who in the end himself disappears.

The connections between cinema and the sensible (that is, the ways in which the body is affected by what it feels) no longer need to be demonstrated. What is prohibited in cinema (or in which case makes it no longer cinema but reportage, interview, or voyeurism, which quickly veers to obscenity) is direct access to the interiority of affective life. To film means to physically film sensations and emotions as they are felt (or simulated) in the bodies of actors. There exist cinematographic, which is to say aesthetic forms that are more physical and sensory than others. Jean Vigo, Maurice Pialat, John Cassevetes, Claire Denis, Bruno Dumont, Luc and Jean-Pierre Dardenne, João Cesar Monteiro (on whom I will now focus), are really filmmakers of the body. A single main character runs through most of Monteiro's films: he is called João de Deus and he is interpreted by the filmmaker himself. João de Deus is a bawdy character. Elegant, refined, but very uninhibited and obsessed with sex and in particular women's genitals, he combines a certain preciousness with truly scandalous triviality. *God's Comedy* (1995) is concerned entirely with the life of the senses, tastes, the pleasure of words, perfumes, flavors, odors, with a predilection however for that which is often referred to as the "low" and that which emanates: urine, excrement, and the body's most secret secretions. The filmmaker also concentrates his attention, in long fixed camera shots, on culinary pleasures. He films the making of sorbets, the cooking of sticklebacks, or (in close-up at a butcher shop) a block of liver, a lamb's head. All of the senses are mobilized in *God's Comedy*, in which João, a celestial clown, fool, and tramp, simultaneously grave and nonchalant, mystical and comical, poetic and erotic, ceaselessly tastes sensations, to the point of dizziness—but also fashions them, kneading them, molding them with his nostrils, ears, hands, mouth, and genitals. In this universe, immanent but haunted by a desire for absolutes and traversed by ghosts, the spiritual and the sensorial (and in particular the olfactive) are closely connected to one another, but also to the city of Lisbon. *God's Comedy*, which is a very indiscrete film, discretely expresses a certain Latinity. What João Cesar Monteiro obstinately defends is a particular *art de vivre*, threatened today by puritanical conformism, behavioral hygienism, and the uniformization of tastes.

This uniformization of tastes, and more precisely tastes in wine, is the subject of *Mondovino* (2004), directed by Jonathan Nossiter. *Mondovino* recounts the transformation of wine and the globalization of taste. It discusses traditional winemaking knowledge and *savoir-faire*, as well as the flavors connected to each vine variety. It shows that knowledge of wine requires extreme precision. As a Haitian interlocutor of Nossiter's says, wines are like mangoes: they change taste not only depending on the *terroir*, but according to the light they receive from the sun. The film, which begins in Brazil in the state of Pernambuco and ends in Argentina in the foothills of the Andes, takes us across three continents. It is not made of interviews but encounters with Brazilian, Argentinian, Bordeaux, Languedoc, Tuscan, Sicilian and Californian winemakers. In the course of his meticulous work, which lasted three years, Jonathan Nossiter[2] aims to patiently grasp the transformations currently underway in the production of great vintages. And seeking to do so as an ethnologist-oenologist (the director practiced the profession of sommelier), he takes time to listen (to the families of winemakers), to look, to smell, and of course to taste.

One of *Mondovino*'s characters, Hubert de Montville, a vineyard owner and winemaker in Bourgogne, gives the film its tone: "where there are vines, there is civilization, not barbarity". Except that the culture of the grape's always singular taste, tied to the love of terroir, is being transformed. The small winemakers of Argentina, Tuscany, Languedoc now face multinationals. Among these is the Californian empire of Mondovi, that reigns over wine, buying up European vineyards, particularly in Tuscany. This giant has shared economic interests with the Bordeaux consultant Michel Rolland and the critic Robert Parker, who grades wines from around the world on a scale of 1 to 100. And it is a Mondovi vintage that Parker grades a perfect 100. *Mondovino* is a film about the sensible, and more specifically, the gustatory sensibility that questions our sensibility and intelligence by scrutinizing processes of globalization and the manipulation of the sensible. It shows that wine is not simply a question of taste but of power and profit. The "rationalization" and the "optimization" of its production push in the direction of uniformization: producing standard tastes on all of the continents.

Nossiter's film is, in my opinion, one of the best contributions in recent years to the domain of the anthropology of the political. He poses the question of collaboration and resistance. But, doing so from a cosmopolitan perspective open to diversity, he in no way resolves the question in a protectionist identity-based [*identitaire*] way. To put things differently, he never falls into the trap that commonly consists of thinking of the local as against the global, when in fact they go together, and of entertaining the fiction of endogenous purity (the terroir, the territory) facing violence that can only be exogenous. Far from any Manicheanism, he does not oppose small old-fashioned French producers and the world's number one in wine, authentic and likeable artisans and horrible counterfeiters, the monopolized and the monopolies, the knowledges and savoir-faire of the hedonist Latin traditions and American acculturation. It is in no sense a film of indignation and denunciation that seeks to hunt down an enemy, but one of comprehension, in which we realize, as we draw nearer to the private realm of the Tuscan or Burgundy winemakers' families, but also to the expert oenologists (who are linked to a global market of wines listed on stock exchanges), that each one, like in Renoir's *The Rules of the Game*, has his reasons. Wine, like cinema, is work, worry, but also pleasure. The processes of homogenization currently underway with wine and cinema are so also with fruit, cheese, language, landscape, politics, perhaps even with anthropology too. This last point, which I mention but with a great deal of care, is not unknown to Jonathan Nossiter. The filmmaker, who splits his time between São Paulo and Paris, is currently making a film on French anthropologists in Brazil.

Filmed with a small digital camera, *Mondovino* is, like *God's Comedy* by Monteiro, an artisanal film, firmly opposed to Hollywood super-productions as to those made in France, Japan, and Brazil with *Tele Globo*. It is as tolerant a film as it is militant. It exhibits extreme respect for each person, who is not hastily interviewed in the manner of many journalists, but met at length the way ethnologists do.

Whereas *Salvador Allende* (2002) by Patricio Guzman, *Social Genocide* (2003) by Fernando Solanas, and especially *Fahrenheit 9/11* (2003) by Michael Moore (Palme d'Or at the 2004 Cannes Festival) adopt an exclusively militant approach that is explicatory and resolutory, in which the editing is totally subservient to demonstration and dissociates itself from ethnography while failing as cinema, *Mondovino* (like *Elephant* (2003) by Gus Van Sant) observes the world as it is rather than should be. And it is on the basis of the meticulous description of the state of the world today, entangled in relations of domination, in other words on the basis of this ethics of knowledge, that an attitude of critical vigilance, as well as an act of reasoned political resistance, are possible—and that a politics of the sensible can be sketched.

From the Anesthesia of the One to the Resistance of the Multiple

Critiquing the way the sensible has been commandeered by political power, the latter controlling, training, disciplining, correcting, orienting but also hierarchizing (particularly in the discrimination of smell) the former, was one of the major themes of philosophical but also cinematographic and more broadly artistic reflection in the 1960s. We encounter this equally in Michel Foucault as Jean-Luc Godard or Marguerite Duras. And the corollary of this critical work was the desire to liberate bodily and in particular sexual conduct, made captive in the name of imperatives of social organization.

The question of social relations of domination does not pose itself in the same terms today, at a time when the manipulation of the sensible is not solely an act of political power. What we are witnessing is a decline, or at least a certain withdrawal of the political, or more exactly its instrumentalization by the economic, to serve profit. What we call globalization leads to a leveling, a homogenization through the concentration of the production of merchandise, images, and sounds. It is the same programs, the same images, the same music—media of undifferentiated tastes—that are distributed the world over. In an environment (particularly an urban one) that is dirtied, polluted by an excess of carbon dioxide but also of images and sounds, the functionalization of the life of the affects tends to favor consumer behaviors from which small sensations are eradicated. The domination of economism (to the detriment of the political) creates exclusion for many, and saturation for all. Saturation in particular of noises and signage. The means for masking reality have become so potent that it is hard to fathom what will come next: societal forms in which, in the long term, there will be no solitude and silence. What tends to be eliminated, actually, is less outright silence as light murmur, rustling. It is less the night as the almost imperceptible luminosity of the minute gradations that are dawn and dusk.

The trampling of the subject in his intelligence and his affectivity and in particular the body-subject, more spoken than speaking, is therefore not less than before. The concern (particularly the "hygienist" one) of political power to legislate on all domains of activity by means of evaluations, expert assessments, appraisals has not at all let up. But we find ourselves increasingly confronted with a power that is much more diffuse, and all the more pernicious that it is anonymous, whereas we may elsewhere have the impression of being free. It has become extremely difficult today to perceive a situation that is not exactly one of outright repression, but of anesthesia and aesthetic poverty. An immense number of individuals are aesthetically conditioned: conditioned not to feel. They do not have access to any artistic experience and are deprived of all critical instruments.

A politics of the sensible consists of trying to go against the flow of a current leading to stupefaction and disgust: it implies, first, an act of resistance toward an exclusive and elitist conception of the sensible, that is to say of an art reserved for the minority. If there is a certain amount of *with* in this manner of envisaging a politics that would give back a proper place to the subject's sensibility, its receptivity, but also its capacity for attention and vigilance, there is also some *against*. It is *against* a single, dogmatic, and taken for granted way of looking and listening that a democratic political thinking may today take shape, that is to say a thinking which far from submitting the multiple to the One in an authoritarian manner, accepts the recognition of a desubstantialized multiplicity in each of us, not as a constituted value, but one in constant becoming.

Democratic division supposes recognition of disagreements (of cultural temporalities and economic interests) that a whole soothing, consensual discourse tends today to conceal in favor of resignation to worldwide uniformization. This may be the secret desire of a certain politics that would like to do away with history, which is made of conflicts and is not without negativity.

A politics of the sensible is a critical activity of a subject refusing submission to the One and conformity to the All, a conformity which leads to showing everything, saying everything, producing, as on television, blinding, unequivocal, overexposed images, saturated with meaning, dripping with truth, and deafening commentaries. The distinction proposed by Serge Daney between the *visual* and the *image* seems to me to be of extreme pertinence here. The visual is plenitude, vision that is immediate, total, transparent, absolute, and obscene, so to speak. In the visual, nothing is missing, like in the polished shots of Spielberg's *Raiders of the Lost Ark* (1981), which show the entire scene. In the image, on the other hand, which does not show everything, there is incompleteness and the unfinished.

Whereas the visual, which is the closure of vision, guarantees, in the massive and uniform insensibility of the ideology of the present and presence, the triumph of the One, in the image there is absence and there is other. Not difference—a designation that is too handy and which quickly transforms itself into a stigma—but singularity and gap, that is to say, in particular, duration. The image does not reveal itself immediately in a stunning perception, but may shrink from view. But, as Serge Daney (1991: 53) writes, "not only has the image become rare, but it has become a sort of obtuse resistance in a universe of sheer signposting".

Forcing oneself to think about the sensible and the political together is not without difficulty. One of the temptations of aesthetics, as a form of knowledge of the sensible, is to search for autonomous forms, independent of the conditions of social situations. As for the temptation of the political [le politique] (relative to politics [la politique]), it comes from its abstract and metaphysical, so to speak, character: to limit oneself to disembodied, external principles transcending the life of the subject. But the question of the political looms on the margins and in the gaps of speech, in particular, of speech organized into discourses. It begins in fact to be posed with the various manners we have of greeting one another, shaking hands (firmly and while kissing in Brazil, weakly in France), saying hello (inclining the head to various degrees in Japan and Korea, joining the hands in India), looking at one another, and speaking to one another. And indeed what matters is not so much what we say as the manner in which we say it, or silence it, in the expression of the face. These discreet acts, in encounters that are sometimes accidental and may often seem trifling, are not at all reducible to "transmitting information" or "exchanging messages". Semiology certainly excelled in that which consists of decoding or deciphering clues, but that realm of analysis, as relevant as it is, concerns only a very small part of social life. It leaves totally outside the field of knowledge the multiple intermediary states oscillating between the pleasure and the difficulty of living together.

The sensible, which is the real, is refractory to the One. It cannot but be experienced and invented each time in different ways. It exists only in the multiplicity of ways of speaking, singing, walking, dancing, that is in the mobility of languages and images, also in the aptitude we have to become other than what we were in encountering others. Without this possibility to critique the growing uniformization, without this right to sensible multiplicity, there is no democracy.

8

Sensible Thought: Thinking Through the Body-subject in Movement

He stood,—for I repeat it, to take the picture of him in at one view, with his body swayed, and somewhat bent forwards,—his right leg from under him, sustaining seven-eighths of his whole weight,—the foot of his left leg, the defect of which was no disadvantage to his attitude, advanced a little,—not laterally, nor forwards, but in a line betwixt them;—his knee bent, but that not violently . . .

LAURENCE STERNE

The rationalist knowledge on which we normally rely effects, as we have been seeing since the beginning of this book, a series of cascading separations in which sensibility is rejected into the realm of error and illusion, and is considered a major obstacle to knowledge, particularly scientific knowledge. The separation of the body-object from the reason-subject is, in this view, the result of an operation that constituted them as distinct, an operation that chained the sensible to the unclear and the particular, and decided autocratically that only the intelligible was capable of clarity and universality. Descartes characterized the body in terms of properties belonging to what he called the extended, that is of space. This can only give an account of a small part of human bodily experience, which involves deploying oneself not only in space but in time, that is in history and in language.

Spinoza Once Again

Giving an account of this experience without subordinating the body in its different states to what it is not, without sacrificing a critical approach to an apology for the emotions, or even what was once called physical culture, is a difficult enterprise, but one that is not at all impossible. And once again, it is possible to engage in it through recourse to Spinoza. For the author of *Ethics* (2002: 259), "mind and body are one and the same individual thing, conceived now under the attribute of Thought and now under the attribute of Extension".

Questioning not Descartes' method but the impossibility created by Cartesian dualism and mechanism (the soul incapable of feeling, the body incapable of thinking), Spinoza shows that what we call "body" is no more material than what we call "soul" is intellectual or spiritual. In so doing he lifts a major prohibition, the prohibition on sensual—perceptive, auditive, tactile, olfactive, gustatory—thinking. For him, thinking is by no means a "faculty" confined, as for Descartes, only to "understanding", and distinguished from "will". There exists no thinking in itself, but an always singular act that involves understanding, will and affectivity, which result from intensities of varying strength, modalities that are different each time, oscillating between joy and sadness. These inflexions of the will and of intelligence are not only "movements of the mind" but "affections of the body by which the body's power of activity is increased or diminished, assisted or checked" (2002: 278).

The notion of affection, constituted "solely by bodily movements", is at the heart of Spinoza's philosophy. It is with this word, *affectus*, that the *Political Treatise* begins, and it is the subject of the third part of the *Ethics*, which studies in minute detail all the possible transformations of the passions and the sentiments, from hatred to shame via desire, pride, anger, vengeance, fear, pity, repentance. What characterizes the life of affect (which Spinoza also calls desire or, as we have seen previously, *conatus*) is that it is inseparably both thinking and corporeality in action. It cannot be opposed to concept since it is part of the same energy, which does not however come without conflicts, without contradictions, or without oscillations:

So here I mean by the word "desire" any of man's endeavors, urges, appetites, and volitions, which vary with man's various states, and are not infrequently so opposed to one another that a man may be drawn in different directions and know not where to turn (2002: 311).

The perspective Spinoza opens up is extremely rich in implications, of which I would emphasize two. On the one hand, continuing to speak about the body without problematizing what we say when we speak about it, without asking ourselves in particular about the physicalist connotation coming from the model of the natural sciences, supposes, again and again, the existence of another sphere (an entity or principle), that we normally call mind, intelligence, conscience, reason. Under these conditions the body is but instrument, material, machine, organic material, object (and not subject) of pleasure but also object of illness (and not being sick). It is at best a means of "expression" (of thoughts and sentiments), and the misunderstanding that hangs over the sensible is far from being dissipated.

Granted, Spinoza does indeed use the words body and mind. But let us not forget that his language is the double language of an extremely prudent Marrano thinker who, condemned at once by the Synagogue and all the

Netherlands's Synods, preferred to forego publishing the *Ethics* during his lifetime. In following the path he began to blaze as practically the only person in his time period to think in such a way, it is necessary in my view to abandon the very idea that there might be something resembling a link, a relation, or even a process of interaction between the body and the mind conceived in the manner of preexisting elements, that is to say previously substantivized.

We have every reason to distrust the word *body*, just as we have every reason to distrust the terms *life* and *ethics*. Although I have not ceased to have recourse to them since the beginning of this book, they must constantly be questioned. The use of the terms *flesh* (which in the Epistles of Saint Paul always goes with the *body*, the *world*, and *sin*) in the various forms of Christianity and, more still, the notions of incarnation (also called the "mystery of incarnation") and *transubstantiation* (or the actual presence of the body and blood of Jesus Christ in the Eucharist) should also be questioned. What engendered so many debates of incredible theological complexity, quarrels and spilt blood in the presence of the body and blood of the Christ is the *hoc* (this) of *hoc est corpus meum* ("this is my body"). While that particular question takes us beyond my argument (and competencies), it nevertheless has the merit of reminding us that the fiction of a body that, in itself and for itself only, is incapable of grace (and therefore submitted to the ordeal of disgrace) echoes, in Platonism, the idea of the sensible being subordinated to the intelligible, and in classical philosophy, that of affect submitted to the order of concept.

Spinoza on the other hand is very far from any form of orthodoxy, whether religious or philosophical. For him, knowledge of the sensible, or more precisely through the sensible, is far from being concerned with private life alone. The same holds for him with respect to thinking, as it does for life in the city, or what we would today call citizenship. For him there isn't the sensible to one side and the social and the political to the other, but solidarity between them, what the previous chapter proposed to call a politics of the sensible.

This question of the political so preoccupied Spinoza that rather than finish the *Ethics*, he wrote and published the *Theological-Political Treatise*. But it is in the *Ethics* that he shows us that sensibility, which is corporeality at work in language, necessarily implies political reflection. Part IV of the *Ethics*, entitled "Of human bondage", has for its subtitle "The nature of the emotions".[1] It aims to comprehend how, when power becomes abuse of power, it submits the body to its demands for domination, imposing on it a relationship of repression or at least domestication. Tyrants attack beliefs by lashing out *physically* at that those who hold them. They persecute them, humiliate them, lock them up and sometimes even exterminate them. But subjugation can also come from an individual himself contributing to his own downfall.

That is the reason why, in Part V of the *Ethics*, entitled "Of human freedom", the philosopher considers that it is through knowledge of the passions and the affections that we may, individually and collectively, be "freed from external causes". It is therefore still the affections—affections that can be converted into reason—that are involved here, but the conditions under which they evolve are characterized by a tension between the paths of liberation and those of servitude, the latter being imposed by the cleric and the monarch, but which, as La Boétie was the first to envisage, may equally proceed through voluntary consent. This tension invites an eminently political reflection.

It may seem strange at this stage of the present work, which began with the question of thinking the body that speaks, walks, sings, and plays music in contemporary Brazilian society, to yet again refer to an 18th-century European philosopher. Yet, beyond the incontestably Marano component of this society, this rapprochement is not incongruous. "It is through Spinoza", Marilena Chaui says,

> that I was able to understand Brazil. This Catholic, and very religious, country was from the 16th to the 20th century the prototype of a Theologico-Political power, of which Spinoza provides the most powerful analysis. It is he who made me understand the invisible violence of power, the internalized violence that allows it to perpetuate itself. This violence, more powerful than any which is visible, is at work in racism, male chauvinism, in all the instances where we no longer see that the other exists.[2]

Detour via Tehran with Jafar Panahi

Rather than going from the political (and from its principles) toward the sensible, it is therefore necessary to begin with the sensible (and the aesthetic), which is not a value added to the political. To put things differently, the sensible cannot be considered an extension or an appendix of the conflicts (and sometimes combat) that run through or more precisely constitute society. This is given to us to see and hear by the Iranian filmmaker Jafar Panahi in *Crimson Gold* (2003).

Crimson Gold is what is called a thriller, plunging the spectator into Iran's not only inegalitarian but also totalitarian social organization. But knowledge of this form of political organization does not proceed from denunciation (of a repressive state). It is not imposed on us in an authoritarian manner as self-evident, or explained didactically; it is recounted to us through the story of two modest delivery men, Ali and Hussein, who live in Tehran's poor neighborhoods and make nightly pizza deliveries to inhabitants of rich neighborhoods.

To show the two characters' continually injured sensibility, Panahi, as in *The Circle* (2000), constructs his film on the basis of a circular movement of inexorably closing doors. In the long opening sequence, Hussein, a tough guy, carries out an armed robbery of a jewelry store off-screen, while his scrawny acolyte Ali, posted outside, paces up and down next to a motorcycle the two thieves plan to use for a fast getaway. Hussein roughs up the owner of the jewelry shop but then finds himself trapped by the security system's metal grille, and shoots a bullet into his own head.

The grille that closes and leads Hussein, deprived of any escape route, to commit suicide, in fact constitutes, chronologically, the dénouement of the story, which then starts by going back in time, that is by following the two poor wretches' wanderings on their scooters. They ceaselessly run up against doors that close in front of them. Hussein cannot take his pizzas into a posh building of a rich neighborhood because an armed Islamist militia is waiting in front of it to ambush partygoers. He can only confusedly perceive, through the curtains on the windows, the muffled sounds of their dancing. This is how impossible it is for the two worlds to meet. In the following sequence—since *Crimson Gold* advances shot by shot, in a pattern of increasing separation between the spaces of rich and poor—flanked by Ali, Hussein, with the money from a handbag found by chance, would like to buy a wedding ring for his fiancée. But our two accomplices are invited, through a half-opened shop door, to kindly get lost. It is only in the following sequence, once Hussein is dressed up in a bourgeois suit and tie, that he will be let in. In the film's very last scene, Hussein shows up at the door of the apartment of an ultra-rich but depressed daddy's boy. The door hesitantly opens, first a crack then, for the first time on this Tehran night that will be Hussein's last, completely. The (wimpy) young man, who has just been dumped by a woman, even goes as far as to invite the corpulent Hussein in to share a pizza with him. However, primarily preoccupied with calling the woman, he then forgets about Hussein who, increasingly alone, explores the flashy house's different rooms. To a backdrop of lounge music, he wanders around, stopping in an exercise room, continuing his stroll down a crimson-colored hallway that leads to a turquoise pool into which he lets himself fall. Hussein remains emotionless in *Crimson Gold*. He takes everything in unflinchingly. Panahi's art consists of making us physically experience the minute nuances of rising revolt in this body without a future. The social injustice, disdain and repeated humiliations suffered by the character inscribe themselves into the topography of the city of Tehran. And the imposing mass of Hussein's body does not weigh heavily against Iranian society's power of exclusion and enclosure.

Aside: Splitting Wood

Having established the irreality of an incorporeal reason consisting of pure knowledge shielded from all suspicion and all relation to the question of power, we can continue our advance. It will be an advance made "by leaps and gambols", in Montaigne's expression, an advance along a "difficult road" as Spinoza writes in the final lines of the *Ethics*. A somewhat torturous advance that becomes, as we will see, more and more curved in the two chapters that follow the present one.

Contrary to things that normally advance in straight lines (Jean-Luc Godard: "the only things that advance in a straight line are ogres and tanks"), the body's conduct is often clumsy. The body that advances by running, overcoming all obstacles by striding over them or, on the contrary, the body that slows its pace, that strolls, saunters ramblingly with its hands in its pockets, are different modalities of the living body. But this body can also stumble, blunder, stray, take one step forward and two steps back as it hesitates, wavers, feels its way through what it will do, not sure where it stands. It may also misstep, slip, trip, lose its balance, stagger, keel over, vacillate, and fall before standing up straight again.

The body has none of a robot's "perfection". It is far from always mastering what it aims to accomplish. For example chopping wood when one is inexperienced with an ax. The ax never falls in the same place twice. It doesn't cleave through in a single hit, but gets jammed. It is by first getting it unstuck then lifting it above one's head, which is more complex than it seems, that we once again try to split this log that resists us.

Montaigne

Montaigne (1533–1592) in his *Essays* was one of the first in Renaissance Europe to take a genuine interest in the study of the fluctuations of the sensible without any value judgment concerning "authenticity" or "inauthenticity". Far from opposing activities supposed to be important (devoting oneself to the life of the mind) to those that are supposed not to be because they are linked to the body; far from distinguishing noble and trivial sectors of existence, which leads to repudiating a part of the self as foreign to us, Montaigne is interested in and speaks of everything: politics, cooking, medicine, sport and in particular horse riding, dance, singing, music, home economics, manners of sleeping and eating. With him, humans are not only reason but imagination, memory, and above all desire. There is no aspect of human experience, up to and including the culture of others, that cannot be regarded as legitimate.

Contrary to Saint Augustine in the *Confessions*, the author of the *Essays* does not at all shy away from speaking openly about the body, beginning with his own. He describes himself in Book II as "a little below middle stature", of gathered corpulence and rather slow in his movements. He tells us that to feel good he needs nights of eight to nine hours' sleep, and that it sometimes even happens for him to return to bed and fall back asleep after having gotten up. The reader also learns that he does not possess his father's physical agility, that he especially hates walking because "I get splashed with mud up to the waist", that on the other hand he cannot think at all when seated on a chair, though things go much better when he mounts a horse, at which he considers himself fairly able.

What Montaigne wishes to tell us is in some senses this: no, it is not a sin to be tired, to be afraid, to fear death, to be morose or cheerful, to prefer one dish over another, to drink a glass of wine. Far from destroying morals, Montaigne on the contrary makes them possible. Finally, and above all, the observations he proposes to make concerning the instability of the senses, the transformation, the plurality of the self: "I do not portray his being; I portray his passage" (1958: 235), "our life, like the harmony of the world, is composed of contrarieties" (1958: 374). Or again: "an honest man is a confused man".

If "temperamental and varied" man is ceaselessly different from himself and by no means equivalence and closure, it is because the entire world is in movement, change, instability, variation. Montaigne cites Lucretius: "For time does transform the nature of the entire world—all things must shift from one condition to another, and nothing continues the way it is. All things move from where they are, and nature alters everything, forcing it to change to something else" (Lucretius 2010: §1170). The self cannot be thought, and above all felt, except in the temporal dimension, which destabilizes everything. It is itself flux, movement, metamorphosis: "there is no constant existence, neither of the objects' being nor our own; both we, and our judgments, and all mortal things, are evermore incessantly running and rolling; and consequently nothing certain can be established from the one to the other, both the judging and the judged being in a continual motion and mutation" (Montaigne 1948: 455).

The body and the mind, the concrete and the abstract, the other and the self, far from being separated, interpenetrate one another, are interlaced, intermingled, without mixing and merging into one, however. "Our life, like the harmony of the world, is composed of contrary things—of diverse tones, sweet and harsh, sharp and flat, sprightly and solemn: the musician who should only affect some of these, what would he be able to do? he must know how to make use of them all, and to mix them" (Montaigne 2009: 774). Since the past insinuates itself surreptitiously into the present, like the other in the same and the same in the other, to know under such conditions is to recognize that there is something of the other in the self, of the self in the other, of the past in the present, of the present in the past; it is to study (in the details of their details) gaps, variations, transformations of the singular in order to arrive at the universal.

Montaigne, a Marano thinker like Spinoza but, long before Spinoza, one of the very first authors to have begun thinking about the body for its own sake, as a nonseparate domain, is in the same breath the precursor of what was to become anthropology: a mixed genre that cannot be content with differentialist and identity-based languages of fixity, stabilization, and separation—precisely of the body and the mind, but also of the past and the present, the self and the other. The *Essays* present us with a challenge that is at once epistemological, semantic, and linguistic. If indeed, never ceasing to transform itself, the real is mobile, paradoxical and contradictory, it requires temporality in the text, in particular words that cannot turn inward toward preestablished meanings. As Montaigne says, "what generate thoughts are the details of life and the movement of writing. It is not ideas that, from their throne, are responsible for the accidents of the text".

Corporeality, Vocality and Gestuality

With Montaigne—and before him with Rabelais—we realize the extent to which the body is at work in language. The body—that is to say things like cries, laughter, sighs, in short the physical character of not only processes of enunciation, but also modalities of intonation—brings into play and stages both the vocality and the gestuality of the subject. Since the life of language, which cannot be considered, as in official linguistics, as an incorporeal mental activity (cf. Martinet 1963: 11–13), ceaselessly evolves in the whole subject.

This life of language is a corporeal activity. It is an activity related more to language than to linguistics in the technical sense of term, literature being the full exercise of language which, in its singularity, can no more be reduced to a sum of words than to the abstract and generalizing character of concept. There in effect exists a solidarity (more than a relationship) between the body and literature. And inversely, whereas the body and literature are closely imbricated, there exists an incompatibility between literature and abstraction: they are mutually exclusive. All of literature indeed speaks only of the always singular physical and sensible (and not abstract) character of our experience. Thus, almost all novels tell a story (which might be of a journey, or an amorous encounter, but most often both at once) in which the subject is the body in movement. Literature's uniqueness is to make it possible to free language (from social conventions) and more precisely to free the body from its engagement in language. Rabelais, Montaigne, Swift, Artaud, Bataille, Miller, but also Kafka, Proust, Clarice Lispector speak to us only of that: of the body's singularity and multiple metamorphoses.

This return to the reality of body-language [*corps-langage*] as a subject—and no longer a means, tool, device, instrument, expression, representation—lends yet more weight to a critique made since the beginning of this work, concerning the semiotic reduction brought about when we fail to be attentive to the totality of *langage* and above all else when we consider only *langue, langue* alone, that is to say a totality constituted of distinctive units: signs.

Today it is not in the terms of a system of discontinuous signs, assembled, disassembled, reassembled in space, but in the discontinuity of the rhythm of that which forms, deforms and transforms itself that a thinking of language [*une pensée du langage*] encounters the experience of the body, an experience not of "meaning" in itself, but of the sensible. Beginning to approach a question from the angle of signs, cutting everything in two (mind and body, form and substance . . .) or putting everything end to end is itself a bad sign. This attitude and habit bode ill for what comes next.

Constructing a critical theory of knowledge [*connaissance*] (and not a knowledge [*savoir*]) of the body as an always singular subject of history and of life (that of the senses and of language) leads to abandoning the at times sinister, at times grotesque binary logic of signs. To put it differently, thinking anthropologically about the body consists today not in inverting (in an adulatory celebration of the body), but in overturning this sterile play of oppositions. To cease, with Spinoza, opposing concept and affect and to work, with Gilles Deleuze, at constructing concepts that are at once affects and percepts, and I would add, for my own part, decepts. It is to abandon essentialist or culturalist models, but also structuralist ones, which have the effect of spatializing thought and fixing the body in frames.

The life of the body cannot be limited to a route (and even less so a predefined route) consisting of motor movement from one point to another. Recourse to the mobility of a certain number of verbs capable of carrying the sentence (drawing near and pulling away rather than "the" near and "the" far) certainly constitutes linguistic and epistemological progress relative to the sedentary spatial determinations of depth (the soul, the mind, consciousness) and surface (the skin), high (seat of the brain) and low. But it is also possible to move differently than in the metaphor of climbing (for example to Carmel as in Theresa of Avila or toward generality of concept as in Aristotle) and descending (toward affect or to Hell as in Dante's *Divine Comedy*). We may also, as when following the thread of Lewis Carroll's narrative in *Alice in Wonderland*, slide laterally from right to left, left to right, turn, bifurcate, jump, zigzag. Finally, and especially, we cannot give an account of corporeality in all its states by limiting it in a mechanistic fashion to mobility and motricity. The discourse of "place", "emplacement", of "location", and even of "movement" are spatial markers incapable of giving an account of all the body's transformations. The body is not only prone to walking or standing still. It grows, loses vigor, but also falls ill, shrinks, withers, bends, becomes stooped, and reddens when it becomes angry or is ashamed, trembles and grows pale when it is afraid.

Epilogue in the Form of Seven Propositions: Toward a Modal Anthropology

What I propose to call *modal anthropology*, radically different from structural anthropology, is an approach that allows for apprehending *modes* of life, action and knowledge, *manners* of being, and more precisely still, *modulations* of behaviors, including the seemingly most trifling, not only in their relationship to space, but in the dimension of time, or, rather, of duration. Whereas structural logic is a combinatory logic of composition or assemblage, presupposing discontinuity of invariable signs capable of arranging and rearranging themselves in a finite ensemble, a modal approach is much more attentive to rhythmic processes of transition and transformation. It is less interested in the nature of the relations of elements to the whole than in the question of tonality and intensity, that is of degrees oscillating between fast and slow, the body in movement and the body at rest, contraction and relaxation.

A structural approach to the sensible accounts for but a very small part of life. It considers it from the angle of space (systems of relationships of opposition or correspondence between classes, genres, and living species), only with difficulty from the angle of time (which is in that case divided between childhood, adolescence, adulthood, old age, or spring, summer, autumn, winter), and never in the texture of duration (in the Latin sense of *duratio* which is not equivalent to *tempus*). Whereas time can be "constituted", "organized", "arranged", like *langue*, into discontinuous elements, duration, like the life of *langage*, advances, comes back, speaks but also contradicts, in short, evolves through movements that are continuous and discontinuous.

The singularity of a living being, which cannot be separated from its relationship, under circumstances that are always changing, to an environment, cannot be broken down into the sum of its parts (which would be anatomism) or of its functions (physiologism). Nor, where human beings are concerned, can it be any more reducible to a given culture (culturalism), or even to formal relations maintained with a totality in which it is situated (structuralism). This singularity is not only structural but modal and historic. It concerns not states (at a given moment of a delineated "system"), even less substantialities, but rather intensities: not of being (even in its kinetic sense of the Spanish and Portuguese verb *estar*), but manners of being. Put differently, a human being's singularity is the manners he has of being affected—in Spinoza's sense—and of reacting to what affects him over a duration, which is the opposite of eternity. A modal anthropology, which is therefore an anthropology of modes, modifications and modulations, implies a mode of knowledge capable of accounting for the ductile and flexible character of sensible experience.

The modal is everything that has been rejected by the order of logos (be it Platonic, Christian, Cartesian), which culminates in denotative logic, a univocal, uniform, unilateral, monological, monocultural, monolingual logic the major concern of which is to define, to put legends beneath images, for example, and to subject us to this injunction: "listen", "look".

Denotative thought of course has major advantages. It is the thinking of "clear and distinct ideas". But it is a form of thought that is reductive and oblivious (to the irregularities of existence). It is above all an imprecise form of thought since it eliminates modal variations and inflexions in favor of an explanatory power and metalinguistic authority the equivalent of which in cinema is the omnipotent and omnipresent narrator's voice. In denotative logic relations are only indicative and synoptic ("ID documents"). The indicative indicates what is. It knows only one temporal mode: the present indicative.

This form of thought, which indicates, signals, fixes, immobilizes, never suggesting or evoking, is refractory to time and history. It causes contradictions, fluctuations, shadows, and penumbra to disappear. It is a very pretentious form of thinking, inflexibly Western-centric, that systematically favors being over non-being, the said over the unsaid, and reduces the sensible to nomination and assignment.

The modal[1] consists of a suspension of denotation. It allows for envisioning the relationship, or more precisely passage, to the past, and for understanding that reality has within it virtuality. A modal anthropology brings out the variations and fluctuations of our sensory but also intellectual behaviors. It tears us away from the speculative domain of metaphysics and restores the various forms of action and conjugation: the indicative, the optative, the conditional, the gerundive.

To consider social existence as a modal existence requires examining the paradigms in which anthropology was constituted. Marcel Mauss (1960: 368), in my opinion, perceived this horizon of knowledge—he even speaks of a sort of "revelation"—when, hospitalized in New York, he paid special attention to the way the American nurses moved. Back in Paris, he also observed these "American ways of walking", propagated through cinema, among young French people. More broadly, "it is necessary", he believed, "to study all of the modes of disciplining bodily movements, imitation, and especially those fundamental ways that can be called lifestyle, *modus, tonus*, 'matter', 'manners', 'way'" (1960: 375).

The divergence of paradigms frequently discussed in the present book are due to differences in approach that may in fact coexist in a single author. For example Aristotle: he can be considered the founder of European categorizing and classificatory thinking. But he also insists (in his treatise *De Anima*) on the *potential* (not just categorizable) character of the real, which cannot be reduced to actuality because of its susceptibility to that which does not yet exist but nevertheless does, as he puts it, exist in "potentiality". Finally, as an even more unfaithful disciple of Plato, he gives great attention in the *Poetics*, to the plasticity of the *logos*, to modal flexions of verbs, that is to say to time, as well as to the inflexions of adverbs.

A second example is Claude Lévi-Strauss. Nothing is more categorizing than the approach of structural anthropology. There is nothing more rebellious to the modulations of experience than this method, concerned above all with understanding the fluctuations of sensibility on the basis of the immutable order of intelligibility. And yet the founder of French structuralism never ceased insisting he was a follower of Jean-Jacques Rousseau (cf. Chapter 5, note 8), and much more so the Rousseau of the *Confessions* and *Reveries of the Solitary Walker* than of the *Social Contract*.

Many of the authors discussed above can help to now introduce or reintroduce some life, temporality, movement, and multiplicity into thought and to move outside what Roland Barthes (2002, vol. III: 30) calls "the great mythical opposition between the lived (the living) and the intelligible". But it is not a matter of *returning* to the pre-Socratics (against Plato), to Spinoza (against orthodox Cartesianism), to Freud (against the therapeutic pragmatism that is currently flourishing). Heraclitus and Democritus relative to Plato, Spinoza and Rousseau relative to the positivism of the 19th century, Freud relative to the contemporary behavioral therapies were not behind, but ahead.

The present work has sketched the confrontation between different modes of knowledge, some of which, we saw, are irreconcilable. I believe that in the construction of an anthropology of the sensible, what is necessary is more to revitalize the antitheses than to find syntheses or, worse still, to accept compromises that would do away with the question of the ethical and the political, as well as the negativity that befits the act of thinking.

It is on the basis of lines of fracture—outlined below in the form of seven propositions—that we can move toward another horizon of knowledge than the one to which we are still often accustomed.

Proposition 1: The Illusions of the Principle of Arythmicity

One of the models, which remains dominant in social sciences today, operates on the basis of a static approach that acts as a fixer. It is an approach into which the flow of life and thought (cognitive but also affective) enters uncomfortably. Having learned to favor invariance over movement, regarded as an accident or an alteration that perturbs the stability of a "system", and having grown accustomed to thinking about social reality in terms of presence and, correlatively, representation, we have great difficulty reintegrating sensible experience of time into our way of knowing.

It is however a very simple experiment, that anyone can do. This book you hold in your hands at the moment, or that is sitting just next to you on the table, you can only perceive three of its sides at once. It in fact has six sides, but those six sides cannot be seen in the simultaneity of space, only in succession, that is to say, in time. That is why the spectator of Robert Bresson's *A Man Escaped* (1956), like Lieutenant Fontaine himself, does not have a complete perception of the cell in which he is locked. It is impossible for him to see it "in its entirety". The spectator and hero have even less knowledge of the Montluc prison's overall configuration, which would aid the escape.

We do not have knowledge *at once* of a place *in its entirety*. We have but a partial perception of it: bits of the courtyard, corners of the cell, pieces of walls, in sum fragments of space that Bresson describes as "duration movement" blocks. The filmmaker's work is more precise even than that. What he films is a precise point on the cell door, never the door in its entirety, a corner of the mattress, a corner of the cell window located far above head height and which allows only a very narrow field of vision: silhouettes that appear fleetingly then disappear. The firing squad's courtyard, like the women's building, are out of view, but we nevertheless hear (very muffled) sounds emanating from them. Auditory details and inflections of sound such as these (the tramway's distant clinking, the sound of guards' footsteps and their keys jingling) allow the filmmaker to deepen the images' spatiality through sound's temporality. Since the prisoner perceives what surrounds him only through echoes, resonances, and rumors, he must guess, by listening, at *what is hidden from him*.

If "in a Bresson film, it is more a matter of hiding than showing" as François Truffaut remarked, it is because in perception there is absence, loss (of what has disappeared into the imperceptible or the inaudible) as well as non-simultaneity. This cinema of parceling and dividing comes not only from an aesthetic choice that leads to employing certain techniques, but also from a critique and an ethics of knowledge. It underscores, in a way that had not—with the exception of Dreyer[2]—been done before, the falsifying character of an omniscient vision that supposes the existence of a prior totality that precedes the fragments. What is shown sensorially, and not theoretically, in each of Bresson's films, is the concrete impossibility of a totalizing vision, and correlatively, the intellectual fraud of any compact and coherent, unifying construct of the perception and explanation of the "world". Those are dishonest, deceptive manipulations of the real, which, for its part, is never given whole, in its complete dimensions, but can only be approached with a partial and parcellary vision.

"To not show all the sides of things", wrote Robert Bresson (1977: 104), specifying that "there is only one point in space from which a thing, at a certain time, can be looked at". Bresson's films allow us to awaken. They allow us to understand that the logic of pure conjunction (the catch-all *and* of fusion, the *and* as the *at once* and *at the same time* of a ready-made history) is not only an illusion, but a lie. They surrender the *and* of simultaneity for the *and then* of successiveness, thus introducing progression (often imperceptible) into perception, and therefore into knowledge. Directing *Pickpocket*, in 1959, Bresson turned cinema upside down. The film recounts how one *becomes* a pickpocket, through trial and error experimentation with successive bodily positions, ways of brushing up against, learning under the cover of the impassiveness of people's gaze. Progressively, Michel perfects his technique: he is *in the process* of becoming a pickpocket.

One of the merits of cinema is that it allows us to abandon what is not merely an illusion, but a lie: to the extent that rationalization (in the Freudian sense of the term) carries out a totalization of experience, it not only has the effect of spatializing, but of solidifying thought, which begins with the perception we have of the real. This spatialization and solidification, accompanied by an optical conception of the social, retains from vision only states, permanancies, freeze-frames of images—it completely lacks the temporal and historic dimensions of our sensory experience—constructing fixed poles between which the subject may move, but not transform itself. To move refers to a topological frame: that of place, placement (in particularly "voluntary"), location. Whereas to transform brings into play that which occurs, arises, becomes.

This process of dehistoricizing the subject's experience (both social and individual) begins with words. It postulates that there are a preexisting high and low, an inside and an outside in and of themselves, a near and a far. In fact, in the perception of something that, not alternatively but successively, can appear and disappear, all that can be shown is descending, entering, stopping, going back, drawing near, pulling away. This experience of oscillation is at the heart of the aesthetics of Diderot (2007), who, in *Le salon de 1763*, wrote of a Chardin painting: "Come closer and everything becomes blurry, flattens out, disappears; move back and everything is recreated, reproduces itself". This is what creates surprise and malaise from the earliest pages of Kafka's *The Castle*. For the surveyor K., the progressive perspectives on the castle, first "in the distance", then "as he came closer", do not allow themselves to be aggregated into a homogeneous totality. They are, on the contrary, points of view that contradict one another as he advances at a walking tempo (in both senses). The "near" and the "far" transform themselves to the point of inversion, but not irrevocably:

> Altogether the castle, as seen in the distance, lived up to K'.s expectations. . . . If you hadn't known it was a castle you might have taken it for a small town. . . . But as he came closer he thought the castle disappointing; after all, it was only a poor kind of collection of cottages assembled into a little town (2009: 11).

Adopting this perspective, which is one of mobility, we would cease speaking of a finished, completed, final "work", full stop, to speak instead of craftsmanship in the process of being outlined, of taking form, but which, as soon as it is accomplished, can be modified or added to—the way the

Postman Cheval constructed his Palace—but may also deteriorate or even disappear. What counts, as Humboldt underscored as early as the 18th century, is not *ergon* (accomplished work), but *energeia* (energy in motion). Not "social facts" but social acts, the social in the making and capable of being unmade.

By thinking, speaking and writing in terms of *doing* rather than *being*, of processes rather than states, we begin to gain access to the real, which has none of the stability with which it is often credited. That is the second proposition starting to take shape, which will now be examined.

Proposition 2: To No Longer Fear the Real[3]

A misunderstanding hangs over the notions of the real and reality. What the social sciences in their hardest versions call real is either the factual, or the idealized. The factual: a cat is a cat, an asparagus is an asparagus and, despite Magritte, a pipe is a pipe. We restrict ourselves to what we have just heard and above all what we can see: facts and facts alone, raw, compact, complete facts untroubled by temporality. By keeping just to what is (or appears), we engage in an auditory and above all visual determination of things, we tend to reduce the visible to mere optical presence as though what we see and hear could never appear in mere outline form, be temporarily absent, decline, disappear, or be in the process of dissolving before our very eyes like in Wang Bing's *West of the Tracks* (2004). As though there was no absence or off-screen [*hors-champ*], which designates, as discussed previously, everything in cinema that has not yet entered or has just left the rectangle of the screen, which is not or is no longer present, yet is not for that reason nonexistent.

The idealized, on this view, always comes after the factual. It is the "upper floors" of the building. The metalanguages that dominate their object from above, at times very high above, and might be referred to as "perched branch discourses". Discourses *on* (life, death . . .), discourses *of* and not *in* (an experience that is singular but can be shared). The tendency of "intelligibility" (even the intelligibility of the sensible), of "idea" or of "meaning" is to construct by means of abstraction, to the detriment of sounds and images, which can be either forgotten or absorbed into a higher order. What risks being sacrificed in idealized thinking—a thinking that aims for coherence and cohesion and which leads to closure of speech—is everything that resists determination in the exclusive order of concept: the flow of sensations, events that perturb the linear order of causality.

Idealized thinking constructed on a factual basis, regarded as having the traits of symmetry (in the realm of perceptions) or harmony (in the realm of sound), is made up of "constancies" (Durkheim), of regularities (what Pierre Bourdieu calls *habitus*) or periodicities: regulators of structure. Everything that presents itself as inadequate, irregular, odd, impure, hybrid and more specifically *métis* in the precise meaning given to that term in an earlier work

(Laplantine and Nouss 2001), that is to say the better part of our experience, not only sensorial but also intellectual, is eliminated.

Having primarily retained contours and contrasts, which are not facts but effects of language as it stabilizes discontinuous states, having excluded the body, sensations, the subject, the author-actor caught in the rhythm of singular stories and life histories, a whole part of the social sciences had succeeded in furnishing us with a model of the real that is a skeleton, a framework, an outline. This perspective leaves very little room for gradations, nuances (translation of the Greek term *diaphora* which means gap, difference), details, which are quickly characterized as "superfluous", even "useless".

The form of thought that describes itself as rationalist or formalist never took much interest in such details. It paid them almost no attention, considering that it was better to deal with anything other than these inessentials that hampered access to the truth. However, this inessentiality of sensations, which cannot exist "in general", and are constantly transforming themselves, is the real, and not its illusory abstraction or stabilization.

Whereas the proposition "the tree is green" is linked only to attribution (the definitional fastening of an attribute), in the reality of perception we are much more attentive to the fact that the tree is not green, but has turned green, or that the young girl who is affected in some way is not red but has gone red because she is blushing. To say turn green, or turn red is to recognize that colors are in movement and the real is in constant vibration. Whereas green is but a temporary attribution, it is the greening of the tree, its color but insofar as it is not unchangeable, the ephemeral moment during which green is in the process of transforming itself to yellow, that matters. Thus, Ruskin properly perceived the gerundive character of the real in saying that "when grass is lighted strongly by the sun in certain directions, it is turned from green into a peculiar and somewhat dusty-looking yellow" (1971/1856: 27).

It is a lie, an illusion, a form of stupidity as Flaubert put it, to think that the grass is green, always green, and of the same green, regardless of the day, regardless of the time. It is to this false precision, to this lack of rigor, that knowledge's violent insistence on sameness can lead, as though there existed only the absolutely green or the totally blue or the definitively red, for example, when it is necessary to speak of the becoming-purple of the color blue. Cézanne showed that there could exist thousands of blues, and Beckett describes the suit of the character Murphy in this way: "His suit was not green, but æruginous". *Æruginous*, that is to say between black tending toward gray, greenish, and whitish.

From the moment we feign to have gained access, by bleaching out and soundproofing, to the universe of thought and ideas, the body and the sensible are regarded as secondary. Not exactly inexistent, but constituted in a separate domain. What is experienced is of little interest. Nor is language since this idealized conception of the individual and society considers there to be mainly, even exclusively, thought, and that it is "expressed" in a form that only comes afterward, and in a very accessory way.

The language of themes, theses and ideas is one of pure thought free of all physical constraint and exempt from any desire. It is that of a sterile logicism that creates binaries, which are characterized not only by simplification, but falsify by putting an end to temporality. This idealist—that is to say derealizing—conception of reason (in the singular, considered to be a rising up, an elevation, a conversion that allows for accessing a higher intelligibility) begins with Socrates and Platonic philosophy. In its ascetic and incorporeal ideal, it is loath to consider the reality of "a life which is also a thought, and of a language which is also a body" (Deleuze 1990: 129). It is this conception that leads to the schizoid character of the disaffected concept that no longer manages to feel the slightest desire and, correlatively, the fictitiousness of an affect that is not also thought.

But reality is such that it does not allow itself to be brought back to the choice of this binarism that Henri Meschonnic (2002: 231) described as a "dialogue of the dead". How could reality not be living, and for human beings—but also animals—lived? There is no real without temporality, without movement, without flows leading to what is to become and to transform itself, that is to say also to undo itself and one day disappear. It is the moving and ephemeral character of existence that is real, just as much, it is true, as defensive reactions aimed at protecting oneself from it. To put things differently, there is something in reality that troubles and destabilizes, that we are wary of, something that hurts, that imposes suffering, humiliates, and sometimes even leads to giving up. Freud realized very well that reality is strange and uncanny (*unheimlich*), and Lacan even went as far as to say that it is "unacceptable". It could well be that a certain use of reason— a reassuring, tranquilizing, sedentary and sedative one, self-satisfied and believing that it is possible to inhabit "meaning" like an owner or co-owner— is none other than a frightened attempt to ward off dread.

Finally, I will but evoke here a certain "realism" in art that, bringing about this time not only a simplification of the real but its eradication, agrees all too well with fascism, which indeed claims it as its own. Fascism, that hatred of others that begins with hatred of a part of oneself, and more broadly totalitarianism, consists of a purification of the complexity of the real. It attacks the conflictual and irreconcilable character of the individual and the social. It does not allow for the tension of difference, which it aims to exterminate through policing, for the sake of the fiction of agreement. As Raoul Audi puts it (2003: 122) in his book on Romain Gary, fascism "rejects the real by *really* destroying it".

This destruction begins with *langage*, or rather with its reduction to *langue*—Barthes speaks of the "*langue*'s fascism". Since what opposes the real is the idea of an already constituted totality and unity of seeing and speaking that passes itself off for reality, reality cannot be given in an immediate (that is to say, without mediations) and simultaneous manner. It only arises in the movement of successiveness, but also in reversion and irruption.

Finally, the real, which appears but is also prone to disappearing, is never only transparency, but rather obstruction and transparency, as Jean

Starobinski (1988) shows in his book on Jean-Jacques Rousseau. It is not something we might have at our disposal, that we might "grasp". It is not substance, but event. It is not being, but way of being, while unreality comes in particular from the dirty tricks language plays on us through attributes, substantives, adjectives that are no longer pulled along by verbs.

Proposition 3: Language as Question[4]

The misunderstanding that hangs over the notion of reality comes in large part from a confusion between *langue* and *langage*. In a language [*langue*] there are only signs and laws: an ensemble of words, as well as a syntax, defining their rules and usages. This primacy given to the discontinuity of sign implies a representational conception of *langue*: words are but signs of things (*signa rerum*). What is postulated is the old Latin rhetoric that separates *res* and *verba*: on the one hand, things, on the other, words. On the one hand content (which may be called, depending on the era or disciplinary approach, *substance*, *referent*, or *meaning*) and on the other the form given to this raw material, truth (*veritas*) being, like in medieval metaphysics, the *adaequatio rei et intellectus*.

This opposition of *content* (the "thing in itself", the "essence", the "world", "meaning") and *form*, which in itself has no meaning and is but a vehicle used to transport ideas, remains the uncriticized assumption of the sort of thinking that describes itself as "rationalist", but which is in fact quite unreasonable. It most often only discusses *langue* (a lexicon and a syntax, those "traditional divisions" that were questioned by Saussure), and not *langage*. It almost never speaks of literature, which is, as mentioned previously, the full use of language. It is absolutely refractory to a theory of language. It is impossible to find such a theory for example in Descartes, any more than in Durkheim.

This indifference to *langage* (reduced to the lexical and the grammatical) bears heavy consequences, not only in the realm of knowledge, but also of ethics and the political, which, from the perspective I adopt, cannot be considered "separate fields". It is language in all its states that concerns us, and not its reduction to a system of signs. It is in the *manners* of speaking and writing (manners that are quickly gotten rid of by rejecting as part of a, once again, separate sphere of "style") that much of experience and reflective scrutiny are at play.

Thought does not take place independently of language [*langage*] nor even *through* language (regarded as but a means serving an end), but *in* language, which is breathing, intonation, voice, that is to say the active body. It is not separable from the movement in which it takes shape and is organized: *langage* and not *langue*, which is but an ensemble of signs that aim to designate a preexisting meaning. There is something energetic and vital in *langage* that does not allow itself to be reduced to "messages" to be "decoded", "information" to "communicate" nor even meanings to be "interpreted".

This liveliness of language becomes almost numbed, paralyzed, anemic when it is analyzed according to the mere *logic of enunciations*, which attributes the greatest importance to lexicography (where a word is but a sign cut out of a continuum) and much less to *processes of enunciation* as they take place: the dynamics of the sentence in all its states, in which the subject (which is not pure mind but the entire body engaged in language) is, in turn, the person who improvises its pronunciation, listens, interrupts it in conversation, writes it and contradicts it upon reflection, in sum, transforms it. To put things differently—though it is not at all a question of things here—language is not an object but a subject. It is not matter but manner, that is to say the rhythm of thought in its cognitive and affective dimensions at once. Thus, it is necessary to give up asking the perpetual *language question*, as though it were a realm among others, in order to ask instead about *language as a question*, affecting not only knowledge but ethics and the political, which cannot be considered separate from knowledge.

Proposition 4: Words That Don't Reify the Subject

A reifying conception of language [*langage*] cannot but affect the manner in which we conceive of the subject, and more precisely the sensibility of the subject in society. Put differently, language considered as an instrument contributes to instrumentalizing the subject and the social. There exists still today a dominant positivism that never let go of the pragmatism of signs. This positivism-as-excuse (an excuse, based on "science", of rupture between objective knowledge, the life of the emotions, the ethical, and the political) tends to confuse the visible and the optical, hearing and the acoustic, rhythm and meter, wrong and unfortunate, destiny and destination (or "plan"), the reader or the spectator and the "public", love and sexuality, experience and being able to pass a formal test.

Today, everything, or almost, has become information (unequivocal), image (rather than simulacrum of images) and almost nothing is imaginary any more. Everything, or almost, is recycling, reproduction, representation, reality show, exhibition, and almost nothing is creation. Practically everything is required to reveal itself from the first glance or the first lap of speech, and almost nothing anymore is a relation requiring attentiveness, effort, elaboration over time.

This ideology is none other than the technocratic and utilitarian ideology of our era. It is the ideology of the economistic and productivist rolling mill of total integration, which in fact creates indifference and exclusion. It progressively invades the realm of culture (with "cultural products"), which becomes increasingly commercial every day. The social sciences themselves are far from being spared by the process, if we judge by certain banking expressions used to describe the subject's life in society. We say that he or she "functions" as though speaking about a machine. It is also a matter of conflict "management", "managing" emotions, "human resources", "symbolic goods", and even "symbolic capital".

These expressions, which insinuate themselves in a practically imperceptible manner, into many of our discourses and behaviors, are without a doubt gaining more ground every day. We must be extremely vigilant toward this world of rationalization which presents itself as calmly mechanical, in which everything appears to work out, and where we end up accommodating everything. For my own part, I am not resigned to arbitrary power, authoritarianism, of the center, of capitals and of capital taking shape in society and language. Words and more still sentences are not interchangeable, indifferent (without difference). It is not possible to give an account of different realities, of the "diverse" in the sense of Victor Segalen, with identical and stereotyped words. Yet it seems to me today that many words are worn out, sick. They hang about, moribund, blocking thought, numbing it. We must resist the technocratic and utilitarian use of language, which we often pay less attention to than the price of oil. That is one of the objects of this book, which aims to be a place and above all a time of nonmercantile reflection. A reflection taking us not into the technicalized *agreement of the language* of "expertise" or "evaluation", but rather into the *gap of language* that exists relative to the latter, in order to be more precise at a time when part of the social sciences is often lax when it comes to dealing with things that are nuanced and do not easily lend themselves to head-on resolution: the little events of daily life that give rise to emotions, make us change color, alter our breathing.

The dominant discourses, Barthes (2002 vol. III: 30) already noted in 1968, are "armed" discourses. They are the result of a "war machine" that is against the sensible, "as though, by an automatic exclusion, what lives cannot signify—and vice versa". From the viewpoint of statements that can be described as "major", which progress by means of generalization, looking down upon their "object" from above, the minute gradations of the sensible are held to be subaltern relative to "meaning", which, for its part, is regarded as indispensable, important, the only thing worthy of consideration *et cetera*, there is no sense in revisiting this, it is the nature of things. On the one hand, a deep content onto which we cling. On the other, a form that is only surface and finery. And in putting into this form we use the first words we happen upon, words that are most often imprecise, very crude notions and evoke in only an approximate manner what we seek to "communicate". We are an era, Mallarmé already thought in his time, that acts "indelicately". Confronted with the body engaged in language, which is not an object, means, utensil, tool box, receptacle and transmitter of "information", budget, or bank account, but the at once physical, emotional, and cognitive activity of a subject, everything takes place as though there was an abdication of reflection. This abdication is linked to the indifference to language that accompanies the simplification of the real.

Proposition 5: Language for Saying What Exceeds It

Language and the body, I believe I have shown throughout these pages, are therefore not outside one another. The body is implicated in language and in particular in orality, which is first and foremost vocality. Speaking is a physical act, it is an activity of the body. The body precedes language but it is quickly socialized into the language that we constitute and which constitutes us. What we call socialization is a process of passage into language, which does not however do away with our much more archaic experiences. Nevertheless, the body and language may separate from, exclude, even combat one another. There exist, in particular, situations where the body prevails over language, which becomes inadequate, insufficient, inopportune, even obscene. How can we speak of the Holocaust? How can we speak suffering or pain that go as far as destroying language, which may at the same time have contributed to causing them?[5] How can we speak of the the most intense pleasures, particularly those of love?

Sensible experience, which is tactile, gustatory, olfactive, perceptive (images), and auditory (the three families of sounds: voices, noises, and music), cannot be reduced to formal linguistics, nor even to language [*le langagier*]. What we might call the linguistic paradigm gives an account of only a minute part of the sensible. It does not manage even to approach that which is nonpropositional, nonpredicative, noncategorical in experiences such as the rhythms of dance, acts of love, modulations of voice, astonishment, surprise, enthusiasm, love at first sight. These are behaviors that are most often unconscious and involuntary, that psychoanalysis has studied through processes of transfer and counter-transfer, and which maintain great closeness to the animality within us. These behaviors (intuition, instinct, having a "nose" for things), which are not for that reason less cultural, are not language-based. They are indissociably nonverbal forms of experience and modes of knowledge. In premonition, presage (of a danger), discovery (including scientific ones), there is of course thought, but it is a form of thought that is not organized discursively, a thinking that is for example iconic and acoustic.

The experience of cinema, which is made up of associations among snippets of images and fragments of sounds, and which is primarily a matter of permanently transforming sensations, and secondarily one of discourse, allows for a final clarification of this point. If cinema is capable of touching us, but also of making us more intelligent, it is more on the basis of nonconscious and nonverbal knowledge than through remarks exchanged in dialogues. These may in fact be almost nonexistent, like in *Chocolat* (1988) or *Beau Travail* (2000) by Claire Denis, Bruno Dumont's *Humanité* (1999), Jia Zang-Keès *Platform* (2000), or *In Vanda's Room* by Pedro Costa. Dialogue may even be completely absent, like in *Il dono* (2003) by Michelangelo Framartino, an extremely restrained film in its fragmented sequences and meticulously constructed soundtrack, just as there was no dialog at the time of silent films.

Cinema is by no means a language, except precisely through abuse of language. What counts in a film is the emotional and sometimes (but not necessarily) dramatic tension. Hitchcock even went as far as to consider that during the silent period, the greatest filmmakers had "achieved a manner of perfection". "The advent of sound, in a certain sense, endangered this perfection".

What is said in cinema (in dialogues or replies) is certainly an important element, but it must not be so to the detriment of the sensations generated by the images and the nonverbal sounds. Here we're touching on what would be an overdialogued film as well as a mode of understanding that would give its attention exclusively to the script, which is the object of a "reading". A film is not a book. Unlike a script, it cannot be "read". It is made to be seen and heard. By the same token, it does not "say" something; just as it is difficult to "recount" it. One of the both sensory and critical roles of cinema is precisely to make visible and audible what we did not see or hear. On the other hand, that which is on the level of intention (to be expressed), of thesis (to be defended), of message (to be delivered), in sum the order of ideas, discourse, writing, text does not concern cinematographic art. Nor photographic art either.

What prevents us from seeing today is the semantic padding of both visual and auditory denotation. Denotative logic does not speak what can be seen or heard. It dictates, in an authoritarian manner, what must be seen and what we must believe. But when an image is made explicit by deafening commentaries, when it is over-underlined and inundated with speech, we no longer see it. In fact we no longer see anything, and we no longer understand anything. It is thus harder and harder, as Serge Daney had already noted, to find postcards that are just images. If on a view of Rio de Janeiro I find written in enormous letters the word *Rio de Janeiro*, I no longer see Rio. This postcard has ceased to be an image, in other words something which permits the work of the imagination.

One of the demands of cinematographic art is to resist the hegemony of the text-as-king and the preeminence of speech. That's the reason why a film with actors can be without words, whereas it is impossible to imagine it without facial expressions. In short, the mode of knowledge invented by cinema consists of unlearning a form of thought that prioritizes the discursive. This knowledge is a form of concrete thinking (that shows us the transformations of the face of this or that singular man or woman and never "man" or "woman" in general) that points toward something infinitely more physical and perhaps more primitive than supposed "cinematographic language" or so-called "body language".

The body therefore cannot be considered, and as a result treated, as a linguistic structure. The body in motion of the *ginga* movement, the gestures and expressions of the *malandro* who walks zig-zaggingly through the streets of Rio de Janeiro cannot be broken down into statements, nor can they be completely analyzable in terms of processes of enunciation. There is something nonlinguistic and not even language-based in bodily conduct and the images of the body as it is possible to show, edit and work upon them in cinema.

One of the specificities of these images is that they are indeed thought, but not discourse. Except for this: If in the sensible there is but a single term, affect—which encompasses the sensation of being alive and the attempt to give an account of it in language—it is a nonexclusive but nevertheless very promising way of understanding what we live.

One of Wittgenstein's great originalities lies in the reversal of the final proposition of the *Tractatus* ("What we cannot speak about we must pass over in silence") in another proposition, which would continue to stir all of his later reflection: "what cannot be said can be shown". Two films may help us in articulating the conflictual relations between the unsaid of the sensations, the attempt that consists of showing them, and the necessity of continuing to speak about them. These are *The Stranger* (1946) by Orson Welles and *Shoah* (1985) by Claude Lanzmann. *The Stranger* is the first fiction to *show* images of the extermination camps. These images (four very short sequences filmed by the English at Bergen-Belsen) are only glimpsed by the film's viewer. What is seen, on the other hand, are the faces of the people to whom the footage is shown, lit up by the reflected light of the screen. *The Stranger* begins a process that would arrive at its maturation only much later with *Shoah*. Claude Lanzmann never has recourse to images of camps that could serve as evidence. What he films are traces that he reorganizes into a narrative based on landscapes, faces, but also witnesses' accounts. It is with these accounts (inseparable from faces and landscapes) that Wittgenstein's proposition reverses itself a second time: "What cannot be shown, must be said".

This third proposition, eminently anthropological, is also resolutely psychoanalytic. A person suffering from hysteria is not able to speak. He shows with his facial expression what he cannot, does not want, or does not know how to say (the unconscious). Psychoanalysis' great innovation was to no longer photograph the hysteric person's body in trance, nor even to speak about him, but to seek to make him speak. Put differently, from this standpoint the question of images (images in themselves, images of others, photographic and cinematographic images) cannot be understood in images, only through speech.

If there exists a gap between what is difficult to say in the lived experience of emotions and sensations and the comments provoked by this experience (comments that often have a tendency to become long-winded), then we cannot do without language. It is in the distance introduced by language that the subject (that is to say, in particular, conflict) is apt to constitute itself as a subject of reflection involved in a story.

Proposition 6: Against the Sirens of Irrationality, a Resolutely Critical Form of Thinking

The fact that the sensible has been, and still is, considered to be a residue that can be brought back into intelligible order does not therefore inevitably lead to a trade-off between reflection and sensation, and having to return to mythologies of the ineffable, the unsayable, of the mystery of life and the cherished secret. Giving sensations back their full place does not condemn to silence, but rather pushes toward recognition of a gap, a stimulating tension between perceptual, auditive, tactile, olfactive, gustatory activity, and its elaboration through the acts of a speaking subject. The crisis (crisis, tiredness, worn-out-ness) of formalist paradigms (semiology, structuralism...), in their inability to provide an account either of desire, pleasure, or pain, has opened the way for an irrationalism with only very limited critical potential.

Here we find ourselves in the presence of a counter-model (capable of taking the form, as was the case in the 1970s and 1980s, of a counter-culture) that aims to reassert the value of life's movement, wandering, flow, swaying, endless fluctuation. This irrationalist counter-model favors osmosis in its perception of a world without seams, without borders, without limits. It claims, alongside a certain strand of phenomenology and film theory (the ontology of André Bazin), an immediate relationship to the real. It counters discontinuous thinking (Cartesian, Kantian, Durkheimian) with an often reactive apologetics of generalized continuity between human beings, nature, and culture.

What I am taking aim at here is not the resolutely playful character of manga comics, or the methods of "free association", which is the means through which processes of transfer and counter-transfer occur during psychoanalytic treatment, nor, in a very different register, the pleasure of feeling the oscillation of water in a bath or on a boat, any more than the posture of the body that, in Amazonia and the Nordeste of Brazil, relaxes by swaying laterally in a *rede* (hammock). What is being questioned are not those very diversified experiences, but a certain contemporary fascination provoked by movement for movement's sake, what Peter Sloterdijk (2003: 23) calls a "kinetic utopia".

There is something in the attraction to pure mobility (keeping oneself "informed", hour after hour, of what is going on in the world, staying glued to the news, fashion, becoming an over-achiever, constantly changing profession, partner, running, rushing forward at the accelerated pace of technological innovation) that is nihilistic. The generalized obsession with movement, "moving toward more movement" (Sloterdijk) may lead to a regression, to the intra-uterine becoming all powerful, to a return to the unquestioned "patent truths" of the nonverbal, in sum to a position "prior" to language (or "beyond" language as with Saint John of the Cross). By insisting too much on the irreducibility of that which transforms itself in images, sounds, smells, tastes, and tactile exchanges, we risk not subjecting the sensible to critical examination.

A certain number of approaches that describe themselves as "holistic", guided by the search for a "higher" intelligibility, and aimed at abolishing all distance (and in particular the critical distance that allows for the mediation of concept over the immediateness of affect), are carrying out an

"Asianization" of thought, but which is often only a Westernizing desire for an imagined Orient. For instance some people go searching along the banks of the Ganges, carried back toward a prelapsarian state, where there would be no separation, and in particular no separation between languages. The sometimes nonsensical but almost always ahistorical desire to reintegrate the cosmic into individual experience, which can go as far as the fantasy of a "cosmic body" endowed with transcendental status, is not a reassertion of the body's value, but as always just pure mind.

It is in large part the anthropocentrism and the logocentrism of a certain rationalism that provoke the distorted reaction of its negation. This pendulum movement between Scylla and Charybdis may also be observed in an entirely different context, in a genuine horizon of critical thought this time, where no transcendence is called to the rescue. Two of its formulations are to be found in the rival positions that were, at a certain moment in their thinking, those of Claude Lévi-Strauss and Roland Barthes. Lévi-Strauss: "the worst form of order is better than disorder"; Barthes: "I prefer incoherence to order that misrepresents".

We are oriented, at the end of this book, no more toward rehabilitation of the life of affect than toward reduction to the logocentric and Eurocentric logic of concept, but rather toward a thinking of concept-affect solidarity, which is a conflictual solidarity, that is to say toward reciprocal involvement of the life of the senses and the subject, of history and of language in its relationship to that which is not strictly speaking language-based. This involvement is not a resolution, and even less so a fusion, but tension.

An example of this tension is given to us in the double language (requiring a double reading) of Spinoza's *Ethics*. The propositions and demonstrations (all extremely concise), advance in a rectilinear fashion. They interlink methodically according to the order of arguments without much concern for specific cases. The commentaries (which take more time to linger) unfold, for their part, in a curvilinear fashion. They are willingly impulsive and breathe life back into what may have seemed arid and impersonal about the strict explanatory logic. Another example of this gap (in particular between different rhythms and intensities) is suggested in Kurosawa's *Rashomon* (1950), of which the subject is the variation of perspectives. The film is organized around an alternation between *action* (which takes place in a dense forest that is nevertheless penetrated by rays of sunlight) and *reflection* (which takes place beneath the gate of the ancient temple of Kyoto while rain pours down without relent).

It is this tension which is conspicuously absent from the return of the repressed through which it is believed today that the value of the body and the emotions can be reasserted, against models of fixity, through a celebration of fluctuation and generalized turbulence. This attitude is illusory: it nourishes, in a confused rhetoric for which there are no more conflicts, and therefore no more history, the illusion of moving to a point "outside" (reason, history) in order to taste an immediate spring freshness, in a simple relationship to the "world" and to nature, into which we might melt. There is every reason to be wary of this simplicity and this simplification of the real (which is also a confrontation capable of causing ruptures), just as there is every reason to be wary toward spontaneity, which is often habit and conformism. It is necessary, finally, to be very vigilant toward the denunciation of what some have called the "tyranny of logos", which may easily lead us to obscurantism and fascism.

What we need in order to think about the sensible is therefore not an infra-language that would aim, by going beyond limits and borders (even if they have been rigidified), to reconcile us to ourselves, but rather even greater demands for rigor and precision, which cannot do without language for articulation and mediation. And it is one of these mediations—the aesthetic—that I wish to reexamine a final time.

Proposition 7: The Necessary Mediation of the Aesthetic

Modern and contemporary aesthetic reflection, insofar as it was elaborated beginning particularly with Baudelaire and rests on an experience that is no longer that of the work and the beautiful, of the "work of art" and the "fine arts", and even less so the "masterpiece", but rather that of the sensible, is in my view extremely fertile. To begin with, it reexamines the idea that art has a purity and and radicality capable of bringing about an absolute transformation of society and leading us to "another life". It no longer consists in an idealistic conception that runs from romanticism to the avant-garde surrealists via Artaud, and which made "art" into an anti-rationalist counter-model, of going beyond reason, but rather of contributing to thought, by showing its contradictions. It is not dispositive, but aporetic and questioning. No critical reflection on the relationship between the social and the subject (that is to say of the body engaged in language, but also in the sharing of a nondiscursive sensibility, as is the case in music, cinema, or dance) can do without this mediation.

The second advantage of an aesthetic reflection is to reintroduce that which is at play in the oppositions, or at least the distinctions of Westernizing classificatory and category thinking. These distinctions do not manage to give an account of the presence of the nonartistic in artistic creation (since Andy Warhol in particular), nor of the impossibility of speaking of art "in general", the notion of art itself as a separate realm of activity being perfectly foreign to non-European societies. An anthropological aesthetic leads to freeing oneself of a certain number of oppositions, and in particular from the sterile dichotomy of a rationalocentrism without morals and a moralizing humanism. It allows us to no longer oppose "science", born of disillusionment and leading to a certain submission, and "art" regarded as seduction, delight, relaxation, entertainment ("to enjoy oneself is to agree", Adorno wrote), forgetting oneself and others. Reflecting on the sensible, or rather *in* the sensible, and more precisely still in the infinitely problematic relations between what we hold to be sensible and what we hold to be intelligible, leads us to think about the ethical and the aesthetic together, as Wittgenstein invites us to do in a proposition from the *Tractatus* that has often seemed obscure: "ethics and aesthetics are one" (Proposition 6.421). It leads us to think them together, but not in any which way. Not the aesthetic based on the ethical, which can only lead to the moralization of artistic creation, but the opposite: "the birth of the ethical on the basis of the aesthetic" as Romain Gary wrote (1978: 312).

Aesthetic experience, which is connected to the possibility of multiplying and diversifying ourselves, while at the same time recognizing this multiplicity and diversity among others who are not replicas of ourselves, is a way of going through life. It introduces fiction, that is to say vitality—the capacity to lead other possible lives—but also a potential for resolutely critical negativity toward the social and language. It simultaneously questions, on the one hand, the univocality of *concept* (reconsidered in light of it also necessarily being affect and percept) as well as its definitional and totalizing character, and on the other the transparence of *sign*, aimed at perfect accordance between words and things, and finally the *symbol*'s tendency toward concordance.

Fiction opens up possibilities. It is on the order of the virtual and the multiple. It opposes the factual but not the real, except of course if we consider that the latter is completely absorbed into the now. The novel, which has often been described as "the art of the lie", along with cinema, which constantly poses the question of the relationship between seeing and believing, are a few of the possible explorations that create the alterity without which there is no ethical recognition. Meanwhile, when lying is impossible or prohibited, in narcissistic self-satisfaction and transparency to oneself, it leads to a refusal of or indifference toward both an aesthetics and an ethics, in particular an ethics of knowledge.

It is, as we have seen previously, language in all its states that matters the most, along with that which may overflow into the experience of walking (*ginga*), of dancing (*capoeira*) or in the perception of always new links between images and sounds (cinema)—and not the monovalent character of signs. And it is the *manner* in which, individually or collectively, we move away from the latter in scholarly or artistic experience, as well as daily life with its minute variations of sensibility, that teaches us the most about the possibilities of the subject. The primacy conferred upon signs has led to regarding artistic creation and aesthetic experience as an aside, an error, a distraction. It has relegated, on the basis of an instrumental conception of the subject, language, sounds, and images, this form of creation and of experience, to the adjunct and separate realm of decoration, ornamentation, and frills described as "style". It is this language gap, or even this gap relative to language in its act of perceptive and auditory reorganization, it is this infidelity as a gap of thinking itself, that must be asserted. Infidelity, once uncoupled from its religious connotation and its reference to adultery, is a demand, a springboard, an impetus to think. It is for example the infidelity of Maimonides, of Spinoza, or of Freud toward Judaism that allowed those authors to free themselves from repeating the same things in submission to the authority of the father and to become creators. It is the infidelity of Mario de Andrade and the modernist artists of São Paulo (on the basis of which were formed Brazilian anthropology and sociology) to Lusitanian culture that contributed to the birth of a wholly original society: Brazil. To be unfaithful to oneself is to provide oneself with the conditions under which it is possible to recognize that which is strange within us.

Aesthetics today are opposed to a universe in which we no longer feel the rhythm of variation, an anesthetized universe, that is to say without suffering but without pleasure either, without desire, in which all is equal, indifferent, deprived of sensibility. Aesthetic and ethical experience—aesth*ethics*—is capable of introducing multiplicity into the subject and in the manner in which we envisage not only knowledge and research, but also action. On the basis of the becoming-multiple (in the Greek sense of *métabolè*) of *langage* and not only of plurality and change (*kinésis*) in *langue*, the relationships to the ethical and the political are no longer the same. The becoming-multiple of the ethical-aesthetic thwarts necessary relationships of meaning that are relationships of force. Aesthetic experience, in the Greek sense of *aisthésis*, questions submission to this policing of the real. It is insubordinate relative to this fundamentalist conception of a uniformized, normalized and controlled real. It frustrates simplifications by introducing perplexity and discordance into thought. It undoes symbolic completeness and brings forth what Michel de Certeau and Giorgio Agamben called the diabolic.

Reestablished within the horizon of sensible experience—sensible but also reflexive, since there is thinking in the sensible—"art", "music", "literature", but also "reason", "science", which tended to be hypostatized, even fetishized, in any case confined to separate genres, can no longer be said in the singular. They are not made of a single block, they have declinations, conjugations, transformations.

Supplement: Sensing Tokyo

I lived for three months in Tokyo where I was a professor at Chuo University. The approach that I adopt to try to give an account of that city in *Tokyo, ville flottante*[1] consists of impregnating myself with it. It involves letting sensations come and ripen, and not intervening (too much). In Tokyo I don't seek to have complete control over the situation. It is not me who looks at the city, but the city that looks at me, surprising me with its ambiance, which is not at all stressful or oppressive the way Paris can be, but enveloping. I allow myself to be carried and steered, so to speak, by the matrix-like character of the Japanese capital, where one is constantly guided, remote-controlled, kept, helped, thanked (*aligatō gozaimasu*) by means of gestures but above all aurally and visually. Daily behaviors, in the metro, on the bus, in the streets, in stores and restaurants, are policed and disciplined. But progressively I realize that behind one Japan lies another. The initial images of the urban scene (security, serenity, beauty, and ritual of harmony) are completed and sometimes even contradicted by other images showing the dissolution of social ties, defection and the uncoupling of conventions from the norms of tradition.

This is how Tokyo appears to me: soothing and unsettling. Unsettling not just because of the risk of earthquakes but because outside the railway stations that are shopping malls and leisure centers as well, there is, strictly speaking, no center. It is an decentered and eccentric city in which the actual and the virtual become blurred. Tokyo seems to me to foreshadow what we are experiencing or might be brought to experience: a hybrid, *métis*, mutant humanity, the greatest magnification of which is visible in the trendy neighborhood of Harajaku.

The perspective I choose, or rather, which imposes itself on me is above all a perception, the perception that Tokyo is an iconic city. This iconic-ness manifests itself in the signs, vertical as in China, but rather than red and yellow, they are black and white like in the art of *shodō* (calligraphy). Shop signs, advertising billboards, road signs all blend four writing styles of which it is the kanji (i.e. the Chinese characters) that attract my attention.

The particularity of kanji is to be an iconic, not phonetic, form of writing. Access to meaning takes place not through sounds but images. The kanji characters are animate. They are part of a universe of animism. They do not signal, but suggest (gestures, postures of the body, elements of nature). It is not an arbitrary writing like our own (which is alphabetic and rests on the arbitrariness of sign), but a figurative form of writing. Through the kanji, the city-dweller is constantly connected to nature.

In Japanese cities, like Chinese ones, we move through a universe of drawing and painting. We cannot distinguish iconicity from discursivity since they proceed from the same graphic activity. It is the graphic character not just of the Japanese city but of the society itself that makes the latter what Aby Warburg called, in a completely different context, a society of "visual tradition".

Tokyo's visual richness is not only in advertising (the neon signs and lights of the city) but also in food. In Japan, the preparation of a meal and the meal itself involves smells, tastes, and also colors. I am struck by the colorfulness of the ready-made *Bentō* meal platters, as well as the presentation of the dishes in the front windows of Japanese restaurants: the red of peppers, the black of olives, the white of rice and tofu, the green of seaweed. These dishes, made of plastic, are simulacra, like the Tokyo Tower, a simulacrum of the Eiffel Tower, like the Statue of Liberty near the island of Obaida, a simulacrum of the one in New York.

Tokyo has no concern for what Marx called "capitalism's representation costs". It is an encumbered city. Not by the density of its population or its traffic jams, which never reach the extremes of Paris or São Paulo, but by everything that is, in Europe, integrated into the inside of houses or buildings (piping, electrical installations, the cages of staircases) and which finds itself pushed outside and thus exposed to sight. Tokyo is encumbered by propane tanks, pylons, telephone poles, antennas, cables, electric and telephone wires which, because of the risk of earthquakes, are not buried. It is thus a visually encumbered city but one which, paradoxically, does not seem overpopulated, and rarely agitated, in a hurry, stressed.

Another salient trait of Tokyo is its cubism. Through its forms and volumes, making up a heterogeneous assemblage, Tokyo is a cubic city. It is made up of cubes that interlock with other cubes, or which are simply cubes set upon other cubes. The architectural forms may be square, but also round, oval. We perceive, in the absence of symmetry, a curious geometry: broken or undulating lines, an ensemble of cubes, cones, cylinders, diamond shapes, rectangles, isosceles triangles, right triangles, which invite revisiting and re-reading Paul Klee and Kandinsky in light of Tokyo, or *vice versa*.

What is visible is the surface, which in Tokyo favors glass and steel and still sometimes even wood over stone. The steel surfaces are polished, decorated, colored. The aluminum plating oscillates between tones of metallic gray, greenish-gray, whitish-gray, Granny Smith green.

Tokyo is a metallic city made up of surfaces that reverberate on other surfaces, layouts that are often curved, translucent panels, large bay windows (which, in the daylight, become mirrors). These surfaces, of great simplicity, are aimed at achieving the greatest possible illumination: the interior must have the greatest possible luminosity. The lighting of the architectural volumes evolves in step with the gradation of the colors of the day and night. Thus, the chic Hermès, Vuitton, Prada, Cartier buildings in the neighborhoods of Harajuku and Ginza shift from light grey to bluish, from bluish to light green, and from light green to dark green.

What surprises me greatly is that economic and technological development, and in particular electronics, computers, and robotics, with respect to which Tokyo is one of the most advanced places on earth, has not led at all to a mechanical and materialistic civilization. Far from destroying traditional culture, it reinvigorates it without giving rise to a dilemma.

This is a society, and above all a city, that is consumerist to the extreme. But this society of hyperconsumption built itself (and in many respects continues to evolve) within a culture of mediation. Put differently, the capitalist pleasure of consumption (of clothing, food, alcohol—*sake* of course, but especially beer) is tempered and softened by an entirely different sensibility: a pessimistic sensibility that comes in particular from Buddhism. Expenditure (in the mercantile sense, in the material sense as in Georges Bataille) is indeed a value, but by no means an absolute one.

The same is true of the new, the novel, of fashion. They are plainly values, but they are not absolute values. What distinguishes Japanese society from European and American societies is a conception of time that is as far from the (conservative) idea of an immutable order of things as from the (Messianico-revolutionary) idea of progression and revolution. The relationship to time has a cyclical and rhythmic character. It is made up of continuous flow, renewal, passing away and creation.

In this resolutely seasonal conception or rather perception of time, reality appears to be swaying, undulating, sinuous, serpentine. Thus, in a universe in perpetual fluctuation, the human being is predisposed to consider that existence is of an illusory, ephemeral, inconstant character. What the Japanese language designates as *mujō* (the sensation of the impermanence of all that exists) is not incompatible with the great energy given off by the country's capital. The city is more eclectic, but also more electric and electronic (in particular in the neighborhood of Akihabara) than New York or Montreal, in which there still remains something of old Europe, built with the permanence of the civilization of stone.

Tokyo is a cinematographic city par excellence. Constantly playing off its visual resources, it is photogenic, telegenic, cinegenic. But it is above all kinetic, chaotic, and dispersed. Made of a multitude of entangled and frequently superimposed frames, it was not conceived of on the basis of a grid. Nor has the past left any trace. The term city seems inadequate to designate Tokyo, which is why the architect Livio Sacchi has proposed to call it a "post-city" (Sacchi 2005).

The dispersal here is so great that unity, coherence, logic (Western and even Chinese) are not easily applicable. Tokyo is an improbable city, making a classic ethnography an uncertain project. On the other hand, by favoring a culture of form (and not ideas), of percept (and not concept), of the concrete (and not abstraction) and of transformation (and not petrification), it is more compatible with cinema.

An anthropology of the sensible formed through contact with Japanese society cannot be constructed independently of a reflection (and above all perception) in terms of surface, and not structure. The surface harmonizes with the Japanese culture of *tatémaé*, in other words of façade and facial expression, which always seems to tend toward acquiescence. *Tatémaé* is intended for the outside, for you, for me, whereas *honné*, which can be translated as interiority, is reserved for those who situate themselves within a group to which one belongs.

The logic on the basis of which Japanese sociality is organized proceeds from a principle of demarcation: the distinctions designated by the terms *uchi* and *soto*, as well as *wa* and *yō. Uchi*, the inside, the interior, the family, the school, the company and by extension the Japanese nation. *Soto*, the outside, the exterior, the foreign, others, up to and including other Japanese, those who went abroad long ago and who, returning to Japan, are no longer considered to be (entirely) Japanese. *Wa* signifies that which is (or has become) Japanese, and *yō* what comes from the West. Thus, *wafuku* designates Japanese clothing and *yōfuku* Western clothing; *washitsu* Japanese furniture and *yōshitsu* Western furniture; *hōgaku* Japanese music and *yōgaku* Western music; *washoku*, Japanese cuisine and *yōhoku* Western cuisine; *wagashi* Japanese sweets and *yōgashi* Western ones. This goes on the same all the way down to paper, which can be *washi* (Japanese) or *yōshi* (Western).

We are, nevertheless, by no means in the presence of an opposition between what is made at home and what comes from the outside, and even less a choice between Japan and "the West". In a society that is the result of the encounter with other cultures, each in turn accepted, absorbed, transformed, the terms of the confrontation are ones of alternation between a traditional Japan and a modern, even virtual, Japan. Thus the *yō* tends to become *wa*, as in the case of the techno music, rock, pop, and even tango produced in Japan.

To put things differently, *uchi* and *soto, wa* and *yō* have the misleading appearances of outright structural oppositions, but I realized in the course of my stay in Tokyo that they can be considered, according to the situations and circumstances (*tsugo*, a critical notion in Japanese culture) to be modal flexions of behavior.

What progressively attracts my attention is not a logic of alternative (the being Japanese or being Western dilemma), but rather a rhythmic of alternation. Students who took my classes at Tokyo's University of Chuo, I would say they where sometimes rock, sometimes zen. And young women sometimes wear miniskirts—much more mini than elsewhere—and sometimes a kimono of fine silk with gold embroidery, as for Coming of Age Day, which takes place on the second Monday of January.

What surprised me is less the rigidity of codes than the flexibility and plasticity of behaviors, which consist of shifting from sobriety during the day to inebriety at night, from meditation to ostentation and exaggeration. This is a society that is at least as theatrical as Brazilian society, a society that loves masks and make-up, but not for that reason idle chit-chat, and which is little inclined toward behavioral hysterics (like in Brazil, and more still Korea).

Whereas the term *métissage* imposed itself to designate Brazilian society, it is not the right one for Japan. However, there nevertheless exists a properly *métis* variation of this country. It has four writing styles (*kanji, hiragana, katanga,* and "Roman" writing), two closely imbricated religions (Shintoism and Buddhism), and infinitely diverse "paths" (*dō*) which are at once forms of knowledge and of aesthetics, of which none has the pretension of being the only or true one.

One of the goals of anthropology is to contribute to no longer confining societies and cultures in stereotypes. Japan as I observe it and attempt to immerse myself in through Tokyo is not only solar in the manner of its flag. It can be lunar and lunatic. It is not only puritanical. It can be libertine. It is a country that manifests a very pronounced preoccupation with death, and an extreme avidness for life, a heightened sense of duty and discipline, and a *gourmand*'s search for pleasure.

F.L., 26 May 2012

NOTES

The Extended Sensorium: Introduction to the Sensory and Social Thought of François Laplantine

1 Laplantine went on to obtain a second doctorate, in anthropology, also from the Sorbonne, in 1982, making him a philosopher anthropologist, as it were.

2 All translations of passages from works other than the main text are my own.

3 Castaing-Taylor is the Director of the Sensory Ethnography Lab at Harvard University, which is dedicated to experimental ethnographic sound and film production. Grimshaw, Pink and McDougall are all prominent theorists and practitioners of visual anthropology. Visual anthropology and sensory anthropology are both offshoots of the sensory turn in the humanities and social sciences (on which more below).

4 The word "sensible" has only a limited semantic range in English, as in the expression "sensible shoes" or the command "Be sensible!" In French, by contrast, it connotes "everything pertaining to the senses" (Sankey and Cowley 2008: x), or in Laplantine's terms, it is a "word for designating the body in all its states and multiple metamorphoses" (p. 84). The sensible thus stands for whatever affects the body; this would include silence as well as sound, and the invisible alongside the visible (see further the Translator's Preface).

5 For Laplantine, a *terrain* is not a site, "not a space, but a human relation" (in Lévy 2002: 39), and it engages *all* of the anthropologist's faculties—"Anthropology is a mode of knowledge which implicates the totality of the senses and the intellect" (in Bragard 2007: 14), and not only the intellect and the senses but the emotions too, for Laplantine "never accepted the idea that, to arrive at objectivity, it is necessary to neutralize affectivity" (in Lévy 2002: 24).

6 Laplantine's work also invites comparison with that of two other key figures of contemporary continental philosophy, Jacques Rancière and Gilles Deleuze. Rancière is another proponent of a "politics of the sensible" (see Panagia 2009) while Deleuze was another advocate for the epistemology of cinema and image-based thinking.

7 Laplantine's love of language is apparent in the way he revels in drawing out the hidden meanings and implications of a range of keywords, such as "multiple" and "sensible" in Chapters 2 and 5 of this book. As for literature, he treats it as a "way of knowing" (the same way he treats cinema) but not, as one might expect, as a "reflection" of society. Rather, literature "attacks, contradicts, transforms the social" (in Lévy 2002: 53), according to Laplantine, which is

precisely what makes it such a powerful and valuable source of insights. Laplantine also speaks of "the liveliness of literature" and, above all, of its "solidarity with the body". This definition effectively recasts literature as an extension of perception (see further Hertel 2014). Even writing, which we ordinarily think of as having to do with representation (e.g. Clifford and Marcus 1986), is a physical activity for Laplantine—and a source of pleasure: "I like to write by hand. There is something carnal about the contact between pen and paper . . . It is an experience of tactile pleasure that I hold dear. The creation—or the putting in crisis—of meaning [through the activity of writing] unfolds for me in a rhythmic movement which unites the eyes, the hand, cigarettes, pens—never ballpoint pens—and sheets of differently colored paper" (in Lévy 2002: 12).

8   Other targets at which Laplantine takes aim include: the discontinuity of the sign, the ideology of the present and presence, representation, identity, the stabilized subject and totality—all of which constitute so many manifestations of categorical thinking (i.e. mainstream Western thought). Modal thinking, by contrast, proceeds "little by little," foregrounding the past and future in the present, modulation, alterity, the multiple subject, tonality, and energy (in place of structure). Commenting on the opposition between these two modes of knowledge in Chapter 9, Laplantine writes (refreshingly): "I believe that in the construction of an anthropology of the sensible what is necessary is more to revitalize the antitheses than to find syntheses, or, worse still, to accept compromises that would do away with the question of the ethical and the political, as well as the negativity that befits the act of thinking" (p. 107).

9   One of the objectives of the Sensory Studies series is to expand the forum of sensory studies internationally through translations, such as this one, that multiply the voices in circulation by overcoming language barriers (here that of French). It is instructive to compare the different genealogies of the various branches of sensory studies—such as sensory anthropology—in different national traditions. For example, in Chapter 6 of this book, Laplantine distinguishes modal anthropology from structural anthropology (which he regards as tainted with "logicism") and hails Roger Bastide and Georges Bataille as precursors (while sidelining Lévi-Strauss). The English counterpart of modal anthropology, sensory anthropology, took shape in part as a reaction to the excesses of textual anthropology (while embracing structural anthropology, if somewhat ambivalently) and counts a different array of anthropologists among its precursors, such as Rhoda Métraux and Edmund Carpenter (for a fuller genealogy see Howes 2003: Chapters 1 and 2).

Chapter 1   The Brazilian Art of the *Ginga*: Walking, Dancing, Singing

1   Translator's note: Because "spectacular" also simply has the meaning of "in the nature of a spectacle or show", and not necessarily dazzling, dramatic, or eye-catching, Pradier's Ethnoscenology can also, more mundanely, be thought of as concerning "organized human performing practices".

2 Translator's note: "*système D*" refers to figuring things out on one's own, finding a solution to an adverse or unexpected situation, or muddling through. The letter D comes from the reflexive verbs *se débrouiller* and *se démerder*. *Débrouiller* means to untangle oneself or make clear that which is complex, obscure or confused. *Démerder* is to remove *merde*, or in this case to remove oneself from *merde* (shit). Both words (*se débrouiller* and *se démerder*) also refer to finding the kinds of solutions that *système D* is capable of providing.

3 Ritualization and scripting of techniques of the body do not, as such, mean pre-planning that leaves no room for play and improvisation. We see this clearly in John Cassevetes' *A Woman Under the Influence* (1974) and in *À nos amours* (1983) by Maurice Pialat, two films that are very close to one another. In a certain number of scenes, the actors surrender themselves to a body under great tension. They release very strong discharges of energy that the script could not have provided for.

4 Paola Berenstein Jacques, *Estética da ginga*, Casa de Plavra, 2000.

Chapter 2   The Choreographic Model

1 Translator's note: the etymology in this section is based on the French word for "fold", *pli*, also used in the original of Deleuze's 1993 work, *The Fold*. French originals are given where the English term has a distinct etymology; where the etymology is shared, only the English term is given.

2 Translator's note: the French term "simple" has the dual meaning of that which is singular and that which is simple. Since no English term seems to quite capture those dual meanings, I have preferred to use the English term "simple" despite the fact that it may sound slightly off to a native English speaker's ear.

3 Chantraine, *Dictionnaire étymologique de la langue grecque*, p. 1269.

Chapter 3   Pains and Pleasures of the Binary: The Dichotomy of Meaning and the Sensible

1 No cause to defend as a novelist, since as an individual and a citizen of the United States, he struggled against racial segregation.

2 Translator's note: the French term used, *idiot* or idiotic, is intended in the English meaning of "private, personal, individual, associated with the now obsolete term 'idiotical'". In order to make that clear, subsequent uses of the word *idiot* in this section are rendered as idiotical.

3 F.L. Gwynn and J.L. Blotner (eds), *Faulkner in the University*, Charlottesville/London: University of Virginia Press, 1995, p. 1.

4 Interview with Marilena Chaui, *Le Monde*, 14 July 2003, p. 10.

5 This word, *cadrage*, appeared for the first time in 1923, the year of publication of *The Prisoner*, one year after Proust's death.

Chapter 4   The Semantic Obsession

1 On this notion, I permit myself to refer to pages 161 to 172 (On the concept of decept: minor deception) of my book *De tout petits liens*, Les mille et une nuits, 2003.

2 I proposed a critique of the notion of representation in my book *Je, nous et les autres*, Paris, Éditions Le Pommier, pp. 85–134.

3 Translator's note: in this section the expression *hors-champ* is rendered as "off-screen". François Laplantine contrasts the *hors-champ* with the *champ*, a word more easily translated (as "field"). Since in English the contrast field/ off-screen would not resonate the way (on-) screen/off-screen does, that translation has been preferred. Readers should however be aware that *champ/ hors-champ* invoke a wider range of meanings.

4 Translator's note: in the juridical and legislative sense, the French expression *huis clos* is in fact translatable into English with the—very apposite, given François Laplantine's discussion—expression *in camera*.

Chapter 5   The Sensible, the Social, Category and Energy

1 Translator's note: several of the French meanings of the word *sensible* discussed in this section are not part of the constellation of meanings associated with that word in English and cannot easily be captured by a single term. The nearest English approximation of these varies: the terms sensitive and perceptible have been used in several instances where the original text employs French *sensible*.

2 Translator's note: the *banlieues*—suburbs, in a direct translation—refer to the housing projects on the edges of French cities in which poor social classes, particular of immigrant backgrounds, predominantly reside. In an interesting spatial inversion, the nearest English approximation is perhaps youth of the "inner-city".

3 Contrary to many pre-Socratics, Parmenides made permanence a model; this would become, in the fourth century BC, the ideal of eternity of the statues of Phidias in the Parthenon.

4 "[Y]ou will not misapprehend me if you interpret the journey upwards to be the ascent of the soul into the intellectual world", Plato, *The Republic*, Book VII, translated by Benjamin Jowett.

5 This book is a resolutely pioneering work, published for the first time in 1872. It calls for being read with the 1934 article by Mauss on "Techniques of the Body", *Economy and Society* 2(1): 70–88.

6 Translator's note: the word *temps* simultaneously means "times" and "tenses"; translation into English forces a choice between the two meanings.

7 Political tyranny, superstition, obedience to the religious dogmas of the Synagogue or the Church.

8 As Lévi-Strauss wrote (1976: 34) about Rousseau: "this ethnology that did not yet exist, he had, a full century before it appeared, conceived of it, desired it,

and foreshadowed it, placing it alongside the already constituted natural and human sciences from the outset".

9 This criticism of the hypocrisy of civilization and in particular of art and good manners is the object of what has been called the first *Discourse* of Rousseau, published in 1750: *Discourse on the Sciences and Arts*, Collected Writings of Rosseau, Book 2, Dartmouth: Dartmouth College Press, 1992.

10 Energy is a notion that Rousseau uses very frequently, but in an acception that is not rigorously vitalist.

11 Freud published *Studies on Hysteria* in 1895, the year of the invention of cinema by the Lumière brothers, then *The Interpretation of Dreams* in 1899.

12 Recall Lévi-Strauss's now famous sentence (1976: 19). Expressing himself in terms almost identical to those of Freud concerning psychoanalysis, he considers that anthropology entertains a "secret dream": "It belongs to human sciences, as is clearly enough proclaimed by its name. But if it is resigned to being in a purgatory next to the social sciences, it is because it has not yet lost hope of awakening, in the hour of the Last Judgment, among the natural sciences."

13 The gerundive forms are the verbal forms designating an action that is in the process of taking place (whereas in Latin, they designate an action that must be done). They are much more used in English than in French. For example: "trying to say", which comes up like a *leitmotiv* in Benjy's long monologue in *The Sound and The Fury*. Or the title of the Lars von Trier film, *Breaking the Waves*.

Chapter 6   Two Precursors to an Anthropology of the Sensible: Roger Bastide and Georges Bataille

1 Idealist and rationalist in the precise sense of the term, since behind Durkheim is Kant, just as behind Lévi-Strauss is Leibniz, that is to say Cartesianism.

2 Translator's note: in French, the word *bête* (as a noun, animal; but as an adjective, stupid, idiotic, silly, foolish) as well as two of its derivatives used by the author, *bêtement* (stupidly, foolishly, idiotically) and *abêtissement* (to become stupid), have meanings not normally associated with the lexical set of either "beast" or "animal" in English.

3 Translator's note: Although "the accursed share" is used here to maintain parallelism with the English translation of Bataille's work *La part maudite*, a phrase like "the excluded/rejected/despised/hated part" would better fit Laplantine's meaning.

4 Recall that Roger Bastide (1898–1974) taught at the University of São Paulo between 1938 (when he took over the position Lévi-Strauss had occupied) and 1954 (when he returned to France to be named, five years later, Professor of Sociology at the Sorbonne). He is the author of a considerable *œuvre* (30 monographs and approximately 1300 articles).

5 Lévi-Strauss carried out his earliest fieldwork in Brazil at the same time as Bastide. The former devoted himself to the study of very small tribes—the Bororo and the Nambikwara—of the Mato Grosso, isolated from urban centers. The latter studied what he called the "interpenetrations of civilization" in the immense city of São Paulo.

6 It is in the three works *Sociologie et psychanalyse* [*Sociology and Psychoanalysis*], *The sociology of Mental Disorder* and *Le rêve la transe et la folie* [*Dream, Trance, and Madness*] that Bastide's greatest contribution to ethnopsychiatry, which he preferred to call social psychiatry, can be found. One can hardly imagine two personalities more different than Bastide and Devereux. But they were united by a profound affinity, not just intellectual but affective. I remember the immense grief of George Devereux when I informed him of Roger Bastide's death.

7 George Gurvitch (1897–1965), Professor of Sociology at the Sorbonne from 1948 onward, is among other things the author of *La vocation actuelle de la sociologie* [*The Present Calling of Sociology*] (Paris: PUF, 1950). Close professional ties united Gurvitch and Bastide. In 1947 Gurvitch joined Bastide at the University of São Paulo, where he taught for one year. He supervised Bastide's two doctoral theses (*The African Religions of Brazil* and *The Candomblé of Bahia*), defended in 1957, and entrusted him with drafting three chapters of the *Traité de sociologie* he edited.

8 The schema is neither a concept nor an affect, but an intermediary between understanding and sensibility. It is through it that the work of relating form and substance, the intelligible and the sensible, takes place.

9 In Candomblé, the *Ogan* does not play a priestly role, but rather one of protecting the *terreiro* to which he belongs. This role requires a brief initiation lasting, at the period when Roger Bastide was initiated in February 1944, three days and three nights. Another particularity of the *Ogan* is that he cannot be possessed by an *Orixa* ("Ruler of the head").

10 A medievalist by training, Georges Bataille (1897–1962) was successively librarian of the Department of Coins and Medals of the Bibliothèque Nationale, and conservator of the Municipal Library of Orléans. Composed over the course of a very tumultuous career, his *œuvre* is strictly unclassifiable. What can be considered its anthropological part is profoundly inspired by Marcel Mauss and is elaborated in constant dialog with Michel Leiris and Alfred Métraux.

11 Translator's note: a play on words, meaning both (literally) "Bataille's horse" and "warhorse".

12 Translator's note: the title of this incomplete and untranslated work is a play on Thomas Aquinas's *Summa Theologica*.

13 Translator's note: Bataille of course means "battle".

14 Translator's note: The *Section française de l'Internationale ouvrière* (SFIO) or French Section of the Workers' International was a political party; the *Mouvement contre le racisme et pour l'amitié entre les peuples* (MRAP) or Movement Against Racism and for Friendship Between Peoples is a non-governmental association.

Chapter 7   Living Together, Feeling Together: Toward a Politics of the Sensible

1 Recalling of course the ritualities of Nazi or Stalinesque Fascist regimes. But the movement to abolish slavery in the United States in the 1820s, the struggle

for civil rights in the 1960s, or presidential elections in Brazil could also be mentioned.

2 Jonathan Nossiter, who is 43 years old, is the author of two fiction films: *Sunday* (1997) and *Signs and Wonders* (2000). *Mondovino* (2003), which came out in France in November 2004 in a version that was 175 minutes long, was even longer in the first version shown at the Cannes Festival in May 2004.

Chapter 8 Sensible Thought: Thinking Through the Body-subject in Movement

1 Translator's note: this is the translation given by Samuel Shirley in the 2002 edition of Spinoza's complete works. However, the French translation of the subtitle (in the original: *seu de affectum viribus*) to which Laplantine refers, "*des forces des affections*", has a rather different meaning, given its emphasis on force/power (rather than nature) and affection/affect (rather than emotion).

2 Interview with Marilena Chaui, *Le Monde*, 14 July 2003, p. 10.

Epilogue

1 A term which was first used in music for scales, then in grammar with the verbal modes.

2 In *Jeanne d'Arc* the whole of the space where the trial takes place is never shown.

3 Each time we use the terms *real* and *reality* we must never lose sight of the fact that there cannot be a "reality in and of itself", but several, and in perpetual transformation. What can be known are only *aspects* of the real (which we might also call the gradual, the processual, the occurrent), which can only be apprehended from a certain perspective. These aspects are formed, like in cinema, of fragments (of perception) and of moments (of hearing).

4 This third proposition owes a great deal to Henry Meschonnic's theory of language as well as the work of Émile Benveniste. However, rather than repeating what the author of *Critique du rhythme* wrote, I propose to think *with* Meschonnic and spare the reader a string of "Meschonnic says that", "Meschonnic believes that . . .", "according to Meschonnic", etc.

5 Cf. Victor Klemperer (1996), *Lingua Tertii Imperii: Langue du Troisième Reich*, Paris: Albin Michel; Judith Butler (1997), *Excitable Speech: A Politics of the Performative*, London: Routledge.

Supplement

1 François Laplantine (2010) *Tokyo, ville flottante. Scène urbaine, mises en scènes*, Paris, Stock, 2010.

BIBLIOGRAPHIES

Introduction to Laplantine

Bragard, Romain. 2007. "Entretien avec François Laplantine", *Cultures et Sociétes* 2(2): 13–24.

Bull, Michael and Back, Les. (eds) 1993. *The Auditory Culture Reader*. Oxford: Berg.

Bull, Michael, Gilroy, Paul, Howes, David and Kahn, Douglas. 2006. "Introducing sensory studies", *The Senses and Society* 1(1): 4–7.

Castaing-Taylor, Lucien. (ed.) 1994. *Visualizing Theory*. Berkeley, CA: University of California Press.

Clark, Andy. 2008. *Supersizing the Mind: Embodiment, Action, and Cognitive Extension*. Oxford and New York: Oxford University Press.

Clark, Andy, and Chalmers, David J. 1998. "The extended mind", *Analysis* 58: 7–19.

Classen, Constance. 1993. *Worlds of Sense: Exploring the Senses in History and Across Cultures*. London: Routledge.

Classen, Constance. (1997) "Foundations for an anthropology of the senses", *International Social Science Journal* 153: 401–12.

Classen, Constance. 2000. "The senses" in Peter Stearns (ed.) *Encyclopedia of European Social History*. New York: Charles Scribner's and Sons.

Classen, Constance. (ed.) 2005. *The Book of Touch*. Oxford: Berg.

Classen, Constance. 2012. *The Deepest Sense: A Cultural History of Touch*. Champaign, IL: University of Illinois Press.

Classen, Constance, Howes, David and Synnott, Anthony. 1994. *Aroma: The Cultural History of Smell*. London: Routledge.

Clifford, James and Marcus, George. (eds) 1986. *Writing Culture: The Politics and Poetics of Ethnography*. Berkeley, CA: University of California Press.

Daniels, Inge. 2010. *The Japanese House: Material Culture in the Modern Home*. Oxford: Berg.

Drobnick, Jim (ed.) 2006. *The Smell Culture Reader*. Oxford: Berg.

Evans, J. and Hall, S. (eds) 1999. *Visual Culture: The Reader*. London: Sage.

Grimshaw, Anna. 2001. *The Ethnographer's Eye: Ways of Seeing in Modern Anthropology*. Cambridge: Cambridge University Press.

Hertel, Ralf. 2014. "The senses in literature: from the modernist shock of sensation to postcolonial and virtual voices", in David Howes (ed.), *A Cultural History of the Senses in the Modern Age, 1920–2000*. London and New York: Bloomsbury.

Hesse, Herman. 1968. *Narcissus and Goldmund*, trans. Ursule Molinaro. New York: Farrar, Straus and Giroux.

Heywood, I. and Sandywell, B. (eds) 2012. *The Handbook of Visual Culture*. Oxford: Berg.

Howes, David. 1990. "Les techniques des sens", *Anthropologie et Sociétés* 14(2): 99–115.

Howes, David. (ed.) 1991. *The Varieties of Sensory Experience: A Sourcebook in the Anthropology of the Senses*. Toronto: University of Toronto Press.

Howes, David. 2003. *Sensual Relations: Engaging the Senses in Culture and Social Theory*. Ann Arbor, MI: University of Michigan Press.

Howes, David. 2008. "Screening the senses", in Rob van Ginkel and Alex Strating (eds.), *Wildness and Sensation: Anthropology of Sinister and Sensuous Realms*. Apeldoorn, Netherlands: Het Spinhuis.

Howes, David. 2011. "Hearing scents, tasting sights: toward a cross-cultural, multimodal theory of aesthetics", in Francesca Bacci and David Melcher (eds), *Art and the Senses*. Oxford: Oxford University Press.

Howes, David and Classen, Constance. 2014. *Ways of Sensing: Understanding the Senses in Society*. London: Routledge.

Howes, David and Pink, Sarah. 2010. "The future of sensory anthropology/the anthropology of the senses", *Social Anthropology* 18(3): 331–40.

Ingold, Tim. 2011. *Being Alive: Essays on Movement, Knowledge and Description*. London: Routledge.

Korsmeyer, Carolyn (ed.) 2005. *The Taste Culture Reader: Experiencing Food and Drink*. Oxford: Berg.

Laplantine, François. (ed.). 1985. *Un voyant dans la ville: étude anthropologique d'un cabinet de consultation d'un voyant contemporain: Georges de Bellerive*. Paris: Payot.

Laplantine, François. 1994. *Transatlantique: entre Europe et Amériques latines*. Paris: Payot.

Laplantine, François. 2005. *Le social et le sensible: introduction à une anthropologie modale*. Paris: Téraèdre.

Laplantine, François. 2010. *Tokyo, ville flottante: scènes urbaines, mises en scène*. Paris: Stock.

Laplantine, François and Nouss, Alexis. 1997. *Le métissage: un exposé pour comprendre, un essai pour réfléchir*. Paris: Flammarion.

Lévy, Joseph J. 2002. *Entretiens avec François Laplantine: anthropologies latérales*. Montréal: Liber.

Lévy, Joseph J. 2013. "Saisir le vif: esquisse d'une anthropologie du sensible chez François Laplantine", in Mohammed Seffahi (ed.), *Autor du François Laplantine. D'une rive à l'autre*. Paris: Éditions des archives contemporaines.

Lock, Margaret and Farquhar, Judith. (eds) 2007. *Beyond the Body Proper: Reading the Anthropology of Material Life*. Durham, NC: Duke University Press.

McDougall, David. 2005. *The Corporeal Image: Film, Ethnography and the Senses*. Princeton, NJ: Princeton University Press.

Macpherson, Fiona 2010. *The Senses: Classic and Contemporary Philosophical Perspectives*. Oxford: Oxford University Press.

Mauss, Marcel. 1966. "Techniques of the body", in Margaret Lock and Judith Farquhar (eds), *Beyond the Body Proper: Reading the Anthropology of Material Life*. Durham, NC: Duke University Press.

Panagia, Davide. 2009. *The Political Life of Sensation*. Durham, NC: Duke University Press.

Paterson, Mark 2009. "Haptic geographies: ethnography, haptic knowledges and sensuous dispositions", *Progress in Human Geography* 33(6): 766–88.

Pinch, Trevor and Bijsterveld, Karin 2012. "New keys to the world of sound", in T. Pinch and K. Bijsterveld (eds), *The Oxford Handbook of Sound Studies*. Oxford: Oxford University Press.

Pink, Sarah. 2006. *The Future of Visual Anthropology: Engaging the Senses*. London: Routledge.

Rée, Jonathan. 1999. *I See a Voice: A Philosophical History of Language, Deafness and the Senses*. London: Flamingo.

Rodaway, Paul. 1994. *Sensuous Geographies: Body, Sense, and Place*. London: Routledge.

Saillant, Francine. 2013. "Vers le regard *oblique*. Contribution à une lecture de l'anthropologie de François Laplantine", in Mohammed Seffahi (ed.), *Autor du François Laplantine. D'une rive à l'autre*. Paris: Éditions des archives contemporaines.

Sankey, Margaret and Cowley, Peter. 2008. "Sense and sensibility: translating the bodily experience", in Michel Serres, *The Five Senses: A Philosophy of Mingled Bodies*, trans. Margaret Sankey and Peter Cowley. London: Continuum.

Serres, Michel. *The Five Senses: A Philosophy of Mingled Bodies*, trans. Margaret Sankey and Peter Cowley. London: Continuum.

Smith, Mark M. 2007. *Sensing the Past: Seeing, Hearing, Smelling, Tasting and Touching in History*. Berkeley, CA: University of California Press.

Synnott, Anthony. 1993. *The Body Social*. London: Routledge.

Vannini, D., Waskul, D. and Gottschalk, S. 2012. *The Senses in Self, Society and Culture: A Sociology of the Senses*. London: Routledge.

Wittgenstein, Ludwig. 2004. *Tractatus Logico Philosophicus*. London: Routledge.

The Life of the Senses

Adorno, T. 2001. *Dialectique négative*. Paris: Payot.

Andrade, M. 1988. *Macunaima*. London: Quartet Books.

Arendt, H. 1963. *On Revolution*. New York: The Viking Press.

Audi, R. 2003. *L'Europe et ses fantasmes*. Paris: Léo Scheer.

Bachelard, G. 1968/1940. *The Philosophy of No: A Philosophy of the New Scientific Mind*, trans. G. C. Waterston. New York: Viking Books.

Balandier, G. 1955. *Sociologie des Brazzavilles noires*. Paris: Armand Colin.

Barba, E. 2004. *The Paper Canoe. A Guide to Theatre Anthropology*. London: Routledge.

Barthes, R. 1989/1984. *The Rustle of Language*, trans. Richard Howard. Berkeley, CA: University of California Press.

Barthes, R. 2002. *Œuvres complètes*. Paris: Gallimard.

Barthes, R. 2008. *The Neutral: Lecture Course at the College De France (1977–1978)*. New York: Columbia University Press.

Bastide, R. 1950. *Sociologie et psychanalyse*. Paris: PUF.

Bastide, R. 1972. *The Sociology of Mental Disorder*. London: Routledge.

Bastide, R. 1995. *Images du nordeste mystique en noir et blanc*. Paris: Actes Sud.

Bastide, R. 2003a. *Le prochain et le lointain*. Paris: L'Harmattan.

Bastide, R. 2003b. *Le rêve, la transe et la folie*. Paris: Seuil (Points).

Bataille, G. 1928/1977. *Story of the Eye*. New York: Urizen Books.

Bataille, G. 1945. *Sur Nietzsche*. Paris: Gallimard.

Bataille, G. 1955. *Lascaux ou la naissance de l'art*. Geneva: Slatkine.

Bataille, G. 1976. *Œuvres complètes*. Paris: Gallimard.

Bataille, G. 1977. *La part maudite*. Paris: Minuit.

Bataille, G. 1992/1973. *Theory of Religion*. New York: Zone Books.

Bazin, A. 1954. "Hitchcock contre Hitchcock", *Cahiers du cinéma* 7(39): 25–36.

Benveniste, E. 1971. *Problems in General Linguistics*. Miami. FL: University of Miami Press.

Bergson, H. 1889/2001. *Time and Free Will: An Essay on the Immediate Data of Consciousness*. New York: Dover Publications.

Bergson, H. 1944/1907. *Creative Evolution*. New York: Random House.

Bergson, H. 1991. *Matter and Memory*, trans. N.M. Paul and W.S. Palmer. New York: Zone Books.

Bhabha, H. 1994. *The Location of Culture*. Routledge: New York.

Bonitzer, P. 1999. *Le champ aveugle, essai sur le réalisme au cinéma*. Paris: Petite bibliothèque des Cahiers du cinéma.

Braud, P. 1996. *L'émotion en politique*. Paris: Presses de l'IEP.

Bresson, R. 1977. *Notes sur le cinématographe*. Paris: Gallimard.

Butler, J. 1997, *Excitable Speech: A Politics of the Performative*. London: Routledge.

Canetti, E. 2005. *Notes from Hampstead*. New York: Farrar, Straus and Giroux.

Chantraine, P. 1968. *Dictionnaire étymologique de la langue grecque*. Paris: Editions Klincksieck.

Daney, S. 1991. "Montage Oblige", *Cahiers du cinéma* no. 442, reprinted in *Devant la recrudescence des volds de sacs à main*. Lyon: Éd. Alia, pp. 187–196.

Darwin, C. 1890/2009. *The Expression of the Emotions in Man and Animals*. Cambridge: Cambridge University Press.

Deleuze, G. 1990. *The Logic of Sense*. New York: Columbia University Press.

Deleuze, G. 1993. *The Fold*. London: The Athlone Press.

Deleuze, G. and Parnet, C. 1977. *Dialogues*. New York: Columbia University Press.

Derrida, J. 2000. *Of Hospitality*. Stanford, CA: Stanford University Press.

Devereux, G. 1951. *Reality and Dream: Psychotherapy of a Plains Indian*. New York: International University Press.

Devereux, G. 1970. *Essais d'ethnopsychiatrie générale*. Paris: Gallimard.

Devereux, G. 1994. *De l'angoisse à la méthode dans les sciences du comportement*. Paris: Aubier.

Diderot, D. 2007. *Essais sur la peinture. Salons de 1759, 1761, 1763*, edited by Gita May. Paris: Hermann.

Dilthey, W. 1991. *Wilhelm Dilthey: Selected Works, Volume I: Introduction to the Human Sciences*, edited by Rudolf A. Makkreel and Frithjof Rodi. Princeton, NJ: Princeton University Press.

Dupont, F. 2002. "Rome ou l'altérité incluse", in *L'Étranger dans la mondialité*, Special issue of *Rue Descartes* no. 37(2002/3): 41–54.

Duvignaud, J. 1990. *La genèse des passions dans la vie sociale*. Paris: PUF.

Faulkner, W. 1995/1929. *The Sound and the Fury*. London: Vintage.

Freud, S. 1953. *Beyond the Pleasure Principle*. London: Penguin.

Gary, R. 1978. *Europe*. Paris: Gallimard (Folio).

Grotowski, J. 2002/1968. *Towards a Poor Theatre*. London: Routledge.

Gurvitch, G. 1950. *La vocation actuelle de la sociologie*. Paris: PUF.

Gwynn, F.L. and Blotner, J.L. (eds) 1995. *Faulkner in the University*. Charlottesville, VA and London: University of Virginia Press.

Jacques, P. B. 2000. *Estética da ginga*. Rio de Janeiro: Casa de Plavra.

Jullien, F. 2009. *The Great Image Has no Form, or on the Non-Object of Painting*. Chicago, IL: University of Chicago Press.

Kafka, F. 2009. *The Castle*. New York: Oxford Classics.

Kafka, F. 1972. *The Diaries of Franz Kafka, 1910–23*, trans. J. Kresh and M. Greenberg. London: Penguin Books.

Klemperer, V. 1996. *Lingua Tertii Imperii: Langue du Troisième Reich*, Paris: Albin Michel.

Kuhn, T. 1962. *The Structure of Scientific Revolutions*. Chicago, IL: University of Chicago Press.

Laplantine, F. and A. Nouss 2001. *Métissages, d'Arcimboldo à Zombi*. Paris: Pauvert.

Leenhardt, M. 1979. *Do Kamo: Person and Myth in the Melanesian World*. Chicago, IL: University of Chicago Press.

Levi, P. 2000. *Conversations et entretiens*. Paris: 10/18.

Lévi-Strauss, C. 1976. *Structural Anthropology, Vol. II*. New York: Basic Books.

Linton, R. 1956. *Culture and Mental Disorders*. Springfield: C.C. Thomas.

Lucretius. 2010. *On the Nature of Things*, trans. Ian Johnston. Arlington, VA: Richer Resources Publications.

Martinet, A. 1963. *Éléments de linguistique générale*. Paris: Armand Colin.

Mauss, M. 1960. *Sociologie et anthropologie*. Paris: PUF.

Mauss, M. 1973. "Techniques of the body", *Economy and Society* 2(1): 70–88.

Mauss, M. 2009. *Manual of Ethnography*. London: Berghahn Books.

Meschonnic, H. 1985. *Les états de la poétique*. Paris: PUF.

Meschonnic, H. 2002. *Spinoza : poème de la pensée*. Paris: Maisonneuve and Larose.

Mondzain, M.-J. 2003. *Voir ensemble. Autour de Jean-François Desanti*. Paris: Gallimard.

Montaigne, M de. 1947. *The Complete Works of Michel de Montaigne*, trans. D.M. Frame. Stanford, CA: Stanford University Press. Original: Book II, Essay XIII.

Montaigne, M. de. 1958. *Essay*, trans. J.M. Cohen. Harmondsworth: Penguin Books.

Montaigne, M. de. 2009. *The Complete Essays of Michel de Montaigne*, trans. C. Cotton. Digireads.com publishing. Original: Book III, Chapter XIII.

Musil, R. 1967. *The Man Without Qualities*, trans. Eithne Wilkins and Ernst Kaiser. London: Secker and Warburg.

Plato, *The Republic*, Book VII, translated by Benjamin Jowett. New York: Vintage, 1991.

Pradier, J.-M. 1996. "Ethnoscénologie: la profondeur des émergences", *Internationale de l'imaginaire*, nouvelle série, no. 5, Paris: Actes Sud, Babel.

Proust, M. 1954. *À la recherche du temps perdu*. Paris: Gallimard.

Proust, M. (1992), *In Seach of Time Lost. Vol. I Swann's Way*, trans. C.K. Scott Moncrieff and Terence Kilmartin revised by D.J. Enright. New York: The Modern Library.

Rousseau, J.-J. 1992. *Discourse on the Sciences and Arts, Collected Writings of Rosseau, Book 2*. Dartmouth: Dartmouth College Press.

Rousseau, J.-J. 1983. *Les rêveries du promeneur solitaire*. Paris: Livre de Poche.

Rousseau, J.-J. 2011. *Reveries of the Solitary Walker*. Oxford: Oxford University Press.

Ruskin, J. 1971/1856. *The Elements of Drawing*. New York: Dover.

Sacchi, L. 2005. *Tokyo: City and Architecture*. New York: Random House.

Saussure, F. de 2001. *Cours de linguistique générale*. Payot: Paris.

Schutz, A. 1999. *Le chercheur et le quotidien*. Paris: Méridiens-Kluncksieck.

Simmel, G. 1997/1912. *Simmel on Culture: Selected Writing*. London: Sage.
Simmel, G. 2009. *Inquiries into the Construction of Social Forms*. Leiden: Brill.
Sloterdijk, P. 2003. *La mobilisation infinie*. Paris: Seuil (Points).
Spinoza, B. 1996. *Traité politique*. Paris: Garnier-Flammarion.
Spinoza, B. 2001. *Ethics*. London: Wordsworth Classics.
Spinoza, B. 2002. *Complete Works*. Indianapolis, IN: Hackett Publishing Company.
Starobinski, J. 1988. *Jean-Jacques Rousseau: Transparency and Obstruction*. Chicago, IL: University of Chicago Press.
Veyne, P. 1988. *Did the Greeks Believe in Their Myths? An Essay on the Constitutive Imagination*, trans. Paula Wissing. Chicago, IL: University of Chicago Press.
Warburg, A. 2003. *Le rituel du serpent*. Paris: Macula.
Wittgenstein, L. 1981. *Tractatus Logico-Philosophicus*, trans. C.K. Ogden. London: Routledge & Kegan Paul.

The Works of François Laplantine

L'ethnopsychiatrie. Paris: Éditions Universitaires, 1973.
Les trois voix de l'imaginaire: le messianisme, la possession et l'utopie, étude ethnopsychiatrique. Paris: Éditions Universitaires, 1974.
Les 50 mots-clés de l'anthropologie. Toulouse: Privat, 1974.
La culture du psy ou l'Effondrement des mythes. Toulouse: Privat, 1975.
Le philosophe et la violence. Paris: Presses Universitaires de France, 1976.
La médecine populaire des campagnes françaises aujourd'hui. Paris: J.-P. Delarge, 1976.
Maladies mentales et thérapies traditionnelles en Afrique noire. Paris: J.-P. Delarge, 1978.
Un voyant dans la ville: étude anthropologique d'un cabinet de consultation d'un voyant contemporain: Georges de Bellerive (ed.). Paris: Payot, 1985.
Anthropologie de la maladie: étude ethnologique des systèmes de représentations étiologiques et thérapeutiques dans la société occidentale contemporaine. Paris: Payot, 1986.
L'ethnopsychiatrie. Paris: Presses Universitaires de France, 1988.
L'anthropologie. Paris: Seghers, 1987.
Les médecines parallèles (with Paul-Louis Rabeyron). Paris: Presses Universitaires de France, 1987.
La table, le livre et les esprits: naissance, évolution et actualité du mouvement social spirite entre France et Brésil (with Marion Aubrée). Paris: Jean-Claude Lattès, 1990.
Um olhar frances sober São Paulo (with Claude Olivienstein), trans. Maria Carneiro da Cunha. São Paulo: Brasiliense, 1993.
Transatlantique: entre Europe et Amériques latines. Paris: Payot, 1994.
O que é o imaginario? (with Liana Trindade) São Paulo: Brasiliense, 1996.
La description ethnographique. Paris: Nathan, 1996, 2005.
Le métissage: un exposé pour comprendre, un essai pour réfléchir (with Alexis Nouss). Paris: Flammarion, 1997.
Je, nous et les autres. Paris: le Pommier, 1999.

Métissages: de Arcimboldo à Zombi (with Alexis Nouss). Paris: Jean-Jacques Pauvert, 2001.

De tout petits liens. Paris: Mille et une nuits, 2003.

Le social et le sensible: introduction à une anthropologie modale. Paris: Téraèdre, 2005.

Ethnopsychiatrie psychanalytique. Paris: Beauchesne, 2007.

Leçons de cinéma pour notre époque: politique du sensible. Paris: Téraèdre 2007.

Le sujet: essai d'anthropologie politique. Paris: Téraèdre, 2007.

Tokyo, ville flottante: scènes urbaines, mises en scène. Paris: Stock, 2010.

Quand le moi devient autre. Paris: CNRS, 2012.

Une autre Chine: gens de Pékin, observateurs et passeurs des temps. Paris: De L'incidence 2012.

L'energie discrete des lucioles: anthropologie et images. Louvain-la-Naeuve: Academia 2014.

INDEX